S60 Programming
A Tutorial Guide

S60 Programming
A Tutorial Guide

Paul Coulton, Reuben Edwards

With
Helen Clemson

Reviewed by
**Alex Wilbur, Alastair Milne, Filippo Finelli,
Graeme Duncan, Iain Campbell, Kal Patel,
Matthew O'Donnell, Phil Northam, Phil Spencer,
Richard Harrison, Ricky Junday, Stuart Fisher,
Tom Janssens, Twm Davies**

Head of Symbian Press
Freddie Gjertsen

Managing Editor
Satu McNabb

John Wiley & Sons, Ltd

Other Wiley Editorial Offices

John Wiley & Sons Inc., 111 River Street, Hoboken, NJ 07030, USA

Jossey-Bass, 989 Market Street, San Francisco, CA 94103-1741, USA

Wiley-VCH Verlag GmbH, Boschstr. 12, D-69469 Weinheim, Germany

John Wiley & Sons Australia Ltd, 42 McDougall Street, Milton, Queensland 4064, Australia

John Wiley & Sons (Asia) Pte Ltd, 2 Clementi Loop #02-01, Jin Xing Distripark, Singapore 129809

John Wiley & Sons Canada Ltd, 6045 Freemont Blvd, Mississauga, Ontario, L5R 4J3, Canada

Wiley also publishes its books in a variety of electronic formats. Some content that appears
in print may not be available in electronic books.

Library of Congress Cataloging-in-Publication Data

Coulton, Paul.
  S60 programming : a tutorial guide / Paul Coulton, Reuben Edwards, with Helen Clemson.
     p. cm.
  Includes bibliographical references and index.
  ISBN 978-0-470-02765-3 (pbk. : alk. paper)
1. Computer software – Development. 2.   Wireless communication systems – Programming.
3. Mobile communication systems. 4. Symbian OS (Computer file)   I. Edwards, Reuben.
II. Clemson, Helen. III. Title.
  QA76.76.D47C675 2007
  005.1 – dc22

                                                                        2006102086

British Library Cataloguing in Publication Data

A catalogue record for this book is available from the British Library

ISBN 978-0-470-02765-3

Typeset in 10/12pt Optima by Laserwords Private Limited, Chennai, India
Printed and bound in Great Britain by TJ International, Padstow, Cornwall
This book is printed on acid-free paper responsibly manufactured from sustainable forestry
in which at least two trees are planted for each one used for paper production.

Contents

About this Book

S60 is the world's leading, feature-rich, smartphone software and it is based on Symbian OS, the market-leading operating system for smartphones. S60 includes an easy-to-use and intuitive award-winning user interface. With over 100 million mobile phones using Symbian OS, this book will give you the potential to develop applications on a global scale. Created for the academic and professional programmer and based around a series of exercises, this book has a unique approach to developing for Symbian OS.

As well as being essential for students learning about Symbian OS, this book is also an invaluable aid to academic and professional programmers who want to learn about Symbian and quickly attain a level of competence allowing them to develop their own applications for the commercial market. This book focuses on developing an application using Symbian C++ and is fully up to date for the latest version of the operating system (Symbian OS v9), with sample code that runs on Symbian OS v9 smartphones and advice on the impact of platform security on application development.

S60 Programming: A tutorial guide aims to help readers to develop commercial quality applications and to provide a route to market. It does so in a fun and innovative way.

Why this Book?

S60 Programming: A tutorial guide is based on our experiences in developing and teaching an academic course on Symbian software development. The book is based around a series of exercises for a Symbian Game Design module that forms part of the MSc in Mobile Game Design and M-Commerce Systems. When designing the exercises, we were very conscious of the steep learning curve experienced by many programmers (including ourselves) when getting started with Symbian, and that the majority of text books, although useful for programmers with some knowledge of Symbian, provided a set of unrelated and often incomplete examples, rather than taking programmers through a process of creating an increasingly complex application.

This book develops a programmer's understanding by providing a series of examples based on the same application. It leads a programmer through the rigors of developing Symbian applications capable of being launched in the commercial market. The exercises take the reader from the initial development of a console game engine to a two-player blackjack game based on a graphical user interface (GUI) operating over a Bluetooth connection between two mobile phones.

Another aspect that we feel is worthy of inclusion in this book is an introduction to the operation and environment of mobile-phone systems and the devices which operate in that environment. We believe that understanding these systems, and particularly that the mobile environment is much less predictable than a wired system, aids the application development process. Successful applications will be those that cope with all eventualities. Programming mobile-phone applications also requires an understanding of the resource constraints of mobile phones which, again, affects the development process.

Who is it For?

This book comes from our experience in developing and teaching an academic course. However, we believe it will prove an invaluable aid to academic and professional programmers alike. Indeed, developing commercial quality applications and providing a route to market is one of the underlying aims of the course from which the majority of this work is taken. The only assumption this book makes is that you have experience in C++ (an essential for all budding Symbian developers) and that you are keen to get started developing applications for Symbian smartphones.

About the Authors

Paul Coulton and Reuben Edwards are internationally renowned researchers and developers of innovative mobile-phone systems and applications. Their work has been recognized within both academia and industry. Paul was selected by Nokia as one of the top 50 developers of mobile-phone applications in the world, chosen from a community of two million to become an inaugural Forum Nokia Champion. Pioneering academics for Symbian education, Paul and Reuben are part of the Nokia Symbian Educators Group. They run the only MSc in Mobile Games Design and M-Commerce Systems in the world and have formed a company that specializes in Mobile Applications Development.

Helen Clemson is a mobile-phone programmer, now working with Mobica, who has extensive experience of Symbian OS, both in research and development. Helen has contributed to many of the most innovative projects developed by Reuben and Paul and provides practical training for the Mobile Games Design and M-Commerce Systems MSc.

Acknowledgements

The authors wish to express their sincere thanks to those friends and colleagues at Lancaster University, Symbian, Nokia and Wiley for their invaluable contribution in bringing this project to fruition.

Symbian Press Acknowledgements

Symbian Press wishes to thank the authors Reuben, Paul and Helen for their enthusiasm and hard work with this book and Richard Harrison for his support and expert advice on all matters Symbian, S60 and anything between.

Glossary of Terms

3GPP	3rd Generation Partnership Project
ACS	Authenticated content signing
AI	Artificial intelligence
AMPS	American mobile phone standard
API	Application program interface
BREW	Binary runtime environment for wireless
CDMA	Code-division multiple access
CPU	Central processing unit
DAB	Digital audio broadcasting
D-AMPS	Digital American mobile phone standard
DEA	Data element alternative
DECT	Digital European cordless telephone
DES	Data element sequence
DNS	Domain name system
DRM	Digital rights management
DSP	Digital signal processor
DVB	Digital video broadcasting
EDGE	Enhanced data rates for GSM evolution
ETSI	European Telecommunications Standards Institute
FDD	Frequency-division duplex
FDMA	Frequency-division multiple access
GGSN	Gateway GPRS support node

GPRS	General Packet Radio Service
GSM	Global System for Mobile Communication
GUI	Graphical user interface
HTTP	Hypertext Transfer Protocol
IDE	Integrated development environment
ITU	International Telecommunications Union
JPEG	Joint Photographic Experts Group
MBM	Multibitmap (graphics format specific to Symbian OS)
MIDP	Mobile-information-device profile
MMS	Multimedia-messaging system
OMA	Open Mobile Alliance
OS	Operating system
OTA	Over the air
PCS	Personal communications system
PDA	Personal digital assistant
PHS	Personal handyphone system
QoS	Quality of service
RNC	Radio network controller
SDK	Software development kit
SDP	Service-discovery protocol
SGSN	Serving GPRS support node
SIS	Symbian Installation System (a software installation file specific to Symbian OS)
SMS	Short message service
TACS	Total-access communications system
TDD	Time-division duplex
TDMA	Time-division multiple access
UI	User interface
UID	Unique identifier
WAP	Wireless Application Protocol
WCDMA	Wideband code-division multiple access
WLAN	Wireless local area network
XML	Extensible Markup Language

1

Introduction to Mobile-Phone Systems

Our background in mobile-phone systems has led us to the conclusion that an understanding of such systems helps developers to exploit to the full opportunities for their applications. This chapter will give an overview of such systems.

1.1 Wireless Technologies

Before starting, we must consider the fact that although a wide variety of wireless technologies exist, not all of these are suitable for use by someone who is moving around. Many wireless systems are wrongly described as mobile (and not just by the general public). We must therefore ask the question: what defines a system as mobile? The International Telecommunications Union (ITU) and the European Telecommunications Standards Institute (ETSI) have a very specific definition: 'The term mobile can be distinguished as applying to those systems designed to support terminals that are in motion when being used.'

This definition precludes such systems as the Wireless Local Area Network (WLAN) technology 80211.b which is not, at present, capable of supporting 'terminals' in motion; it is classed as a portable, or nomadic, system, despite Intel's publicity for its Centrino technology. At present, the only systems that can claim to be truly mobile are the mobile telecommunications networks, irrespective of whether they are using first, second or third generation (1G, 2G or 3G) technology.

As we will see in this chapter, not only does the fact that a mobile phone can be used when in motion affect the definition of the system of which it forms a part but also the degree of motion greatly affects data transfer rates available for a given application. The specification for 3G systems, for instance, incorporates a steadily decreasing data-rate capability (expressed in bits per second (bps)) as the speed at which the mobile phone is traveling increases:

- A phone moving at 0 km/hr can achieve data rates of up to 2 Mbps.

- A phone moving at 3 km/hr, data rates up to 384 Kbps.

- A phone moving at 30 km/hr, data rates up to 144 Kbps.

- A phone moving at 150 km/hr, data rates up to 64 Kbps.

1.2   Cellular Systems

Modern mobile-phone systems are cellular systems, and mobile phones are referred to as cellular phones in some parts of the world. A cellular system divides geographic regions into cells. A cell is the area of coverage within which a transceiver provides a wireless link to mobile phones. Each cell is assigned a unique identification number which identifies its geographical location. Cellular systems were developed in response to the limited availability of radio spectrum. Because only a finite part of the radio spectrum is allocated to mobile-phone systems, only a finite number of users can be supported. To overcome this limitation, cellular systems effectively re-use the available frequency spectrum from one cell to another and so accommodate many more users than would otherwise be possible over the required area of coverage.

The concept of frequency re-use, as employed by a cellular network, introduces the possibility of interference between cells that use the same portion of the frequency spectrum. Mobile-phone networks minimize this possibility by implementing re-use patterns (see Figure 1.1, which shows a re-use factor of seven). Cell sizes and re-use patterns are varied to accommodate the fact that there are more users in some areas than in others. For example, the system may have smaller patterns in urban areas with a large number of potential users and larger patterns in rural areas with smaller numbers of users. For simplicity, cells are often depicted as hexagons but in reality they are often very irregular formations that are dependent on the terrain which in turn affects propagation (see Section 1.6).

As a mobile-phone user moves from one cell to another, the process of maintaining the connection is known as *handover*. The mobile-phone

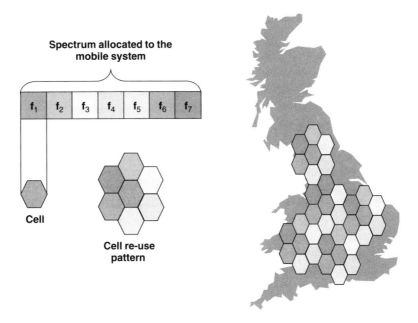

Figure 1.1 Spectrum re-use in a cellular system

system monitors the quality of the signal between a given mobile phone and a cell controller or base station against the quality of the signal that would be available if the mobile phone were connected to a base station in an adjacent cell. If the quality of the connection falls below a pre-determined threshold, the connection is handed over to the new cell. This handover process results in a momentary loss of connection. This loss was not a problem for voice-orientated first and second generation mobile-phone systems. The 3G mobile-phone system is primarily data-orientated and a system that allows a loss in connection could result in the failure of transfer of large data blocks. For real-time systems, this problem has been solved in intra-system handover (between cells of the same system, for example from 3G cell to 3G cell) using a 'make before break methodology'. It remains an issue for inter-system handover (between cells of different systems, for example a 2G cell to a 3G cell); streaming services, such as video calls, cannot be transferred in this situation.

The portion of the frequency spectrum allocated to a cell must be further divided, both to support multiple users within a cell (the multiple-access method) and to separate the connections to and from each mobile phone (the duplex method). In other words, we must keep separate the calls from different users in the cell and, within each call, we must separate the user's voice from that of the person they are talking to. In Section 1.4, we discuss multiple-access methods, which follow the changes in mobile-phone-system generations, but first we consider the basic components of mobile-phone systems.

1.3   Elements of a Mobile-Phone System

Figure 1.2 shows the basic components of a mobile-phone system and their purpose. The base station (the antenna and associated electronics that control a cell) provides a wireless connection to mobile phones in a given cell and consists of a transceiver and its associated transmitting equipment. Transceivers can be omni-directional (able to transmit in all directions around the transceiver) or sectored (directed at a specific area). Sectored transceivers are able to provide targeted coverage to areas where there are likely to be considerable numbers of users, for example, a football stadium. Providing good coverage represents a considerable monetary investment by the mobile-phone-system operator and is a means by which one operator can differentiate their service from that of a competitor. The base-station controller manages a number of cells and is responsible for handover between cells. The operational center is where the mobile-phone-system operator manages the network. It is responsible, amongst other things, for authentication, billing, maintaining information on the current location of its active users, and providing the interface between other mobile networks and the wired telephone network.

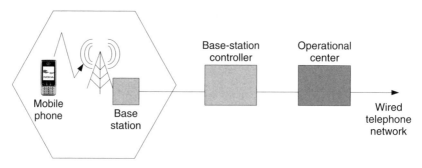

Figure 1.2   Components of a mobile-phone system

When a user makes a call, a channel is established with the base station, which relays the information to the control center. The control center directs the call to its required location. If the call is to another mobile phone, the control center passes the call to the control center and base station of the cell where the other mobile phone resides. The question often asked is, 'how does the system know where that mobile phone is located?' When a user switches on their mobile phone, it registers its location using the identification number of the cell that it is currently in; this information is stored within a database in the operational center. This mechanism allows a mobile phone to be located and connected to calls wherever it may be within a network.

1.4 Keeping Users' Calls Separate

For the majority of data communications, there is a requirement for several users to simultaneously share a common channel. This channel could be a high-speed optical-fiber link between two countries or the frequency spectrum in a mobile telephone system. For this sharing to occur, we require an access protocol that defines when or how the sharing is to take place. This sharing process is referred to as *multiplexing* in wired communication systems and *multiple access* in wireless communications. Three classes of multiple access are particularly relevant to mobile-phone systems; they assign individual users different frequency or time slots, or identify individual users by different codes, as shown in Figure 1.3.

Frequency-division multiple access (FDMA) splits the available spectrum into smaller portions, each of which is then allocated to an individual user. FDMA was used in many of the first-generation (1G) analog mobile phone systems and extended a technique used to transmit multiple calls down a single wire of a telephone network. FDMA is particularly susceptible to frequency-selective fading (a phenomenon that is discussed in Section 1.5), which is why it has been superseded by other techniques.

Time-division multiple access (TDMA) allows a single user to occupy all of the available bandwidth, but only for an allotted period of time. TDMA has improved immunity to frequency-selective fading and was

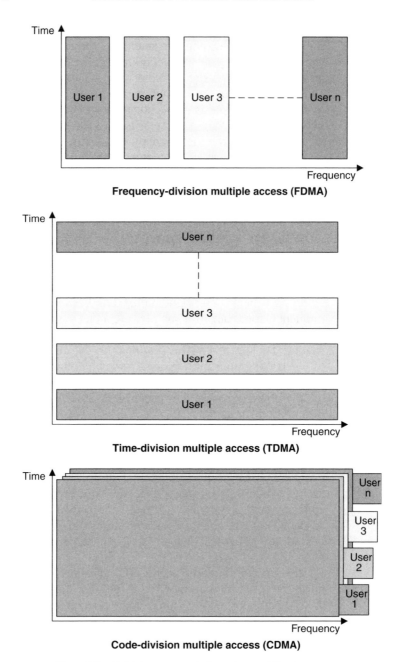

Figure 1.3   Multiple-access techniques in a mobile-phone system

chosen for some of the second-generation (2G) mobile-phone systems, most notably Global System for Mobile (GSM) communications.

Code-division multiple access (CDMA) allows users to share the time and frequency domains simultaneously by allocating each user a unique identification code. This code means that the system is able to separate one call from the other even if two calls are transmitted at the same time. CDMA is the main technique chosen for third-generation (3G) mobile-phone systems as it allows a higher data rate for each user.

Having separated the individual users within a cell, we must also separate the outgoing and incoming traffic (the *uplink* and *downlink*) to each user (for example, for a voice call we separate what the user hears from what the user says). 3G systems use frequency-division duplex (FDD) in which separate frequency bands are used for the uplink and downlink. An alternative is to use time-division duplex (TDD), in which the uplink and downlink transmit on the same frequency but share the resources in time. It is worth noting that TDD is being considered for use in indoor environments, such as museums and shopping centers.

1.5 Multipath Propagation

The mobile channel is one of the most challenging environments in which communications systems must operate. This is predominantly due to the fact that mobile phones operate in the microwave frequency range, where the resulting wavelength is in the range of centimeters. This means that any object of that size or greater can obstruct or reflect the signal. Reflections from objects can result in multiple copies of the same signal arriving at a location via different paths. These copies are combined in the channel to form the overall received signal. The lengths of these paths are likely to be different, causing some reflections to be delayed in arriving and resulting in positive or negative additions of the overall received signal – in other words, the signal gets either stronger or weaker because of the reflections. A simple way to view this effect is to consider the signal as a binary sequence of −1 and +1. When the reflections occur, sometimes two values add together to enhance the signal, giving a result of −2 or +2; in other cases, +1 will be added to −1 to give a resultant of 0 (see Figure 1.4). This effect is known as multipath propagation and it can be observed by the user as a change in the signal strength display on their mobile phone as they change position. Negative additions are usually referred to as fades.

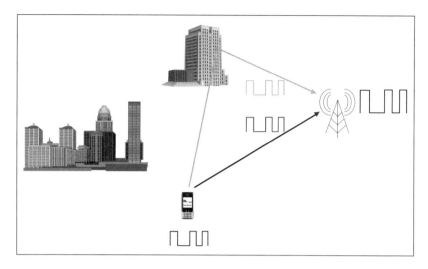

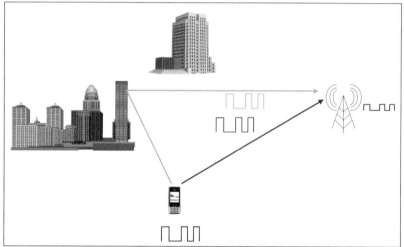

Figure 1.4   The effect of multipath propagation

Obviously, the faster the speed at which the mobile phone is moving, the greater the change in the quality of the signal. This is one of the reasons that data rates are inversely proportional to the speed at which a mobile phone is moving. However, the positive aspect of multipath propagation is that it enables us to receive a signal on a mobile phone within the heart of a crowded city.

Multipath propagation is frequency-dependent (generally referred to as frequency-selective). Different frequencies experience different effects from path lengths and some frequencies are negatively affected, while others are positively affected for a mobile in exactly the same position – which means two mobile users can experience different system performance even if standing in the same spot. This brings us back to the point we made earlier about FDMA. As users are assigned a small portion of the frequency, they may be completely within a fade area. Using TDMA, which operates over the entire bandwidth, only a small part of the user's signal would be in fade and the problem can be overcome by the application of error-correcting codes.

1.6 2G Mobile-Phone Systems

The evolution of mobile-phone systems from 1G to 2G is principally viewed as a move from the original analog systems of the late 1970s and early 1980s, in which the transmitted signals consisted of modulated versions of the original speech, to the digital systems of the 1990s, where the speech was converted to a series of ones and zeros by passing the voice signal through a transformation process. There was a plethora of analog standards around the world, amongst them the American Mobile Phone Standard (AMPS) in the USA and the Total Access Communications System (TACS) in the UK, all of which suffered from a number of limitations. The number of users was limited because analog signals cannot be compressed; security was virtually non-existent as analog signals cannot be encrypted and anyone with a cheap scanner could listen in on the phone calls; and error-correction techniques could not be applied as an analog signal has an infinite number of possible levels which cannot be predicted – all of which resulted in higher power requirements from the mobile phone.

In Europe, there were nine different analog standards and no facility for mobile-phone users to 'roam' around the continent. Europeans therefore saw the need to adopt a single standard for the entire continent and took the rather brave decision to abandon their original 1G provision for an entirely new system. National phone operators, manufacturers, and regulators came together to produce the standard known as GSM. In the USA, where there was no problem of competing standards, a legacy system was chosen. Digital AMPS (D-AMPS) mobile phones could switch between digital and analog operation. In the 1990s, another 2G system appeared in the USA, based on CDMA technology; it is now known as cdmaOne. This system proved important in the provision of 3G systems (see Section 1.8).

Network operators started thinking about possible 3G systems around the same time the Internet expansion started and this very much shaped the vision of 3G systems as principally orientated towards data rather than voice. The problem with sending data over 2G systems came from the fact that they used circuit switching to make connections between locations. In a circuit-switched system, the connection between the source and the destination is maintained throughout the duration of a call. This technique is very effective for voice calls where the transmission is fairly constant throughout the call but for data sessions, such as web browsing, where there are large periods of inactivity, it is extremely wasteful of capacity because the connection cannot be utilized by other users. Packet switching, on the other hand, splits data into small packets which can be routed down any available path. This maximizes system utilization, allowing multiple connections to transmit packets simultaneously across the system, as opposed to a single connection blocking the system to other connections (see Figure 1.5).

The first stage of the evolution to 3G systems was the introduction of packet data into the existing 2G network via the General Packet Radio Service (GPRS). This extension of the 2G service, but without the rapid data transfer rates associated with 3G systems, has been called 2.5G systems.

1.7   GPRS Systems

GPRS is an essential part of the migration of GSM services to 3G systems and allows the user to have a constant connection to the Internet.

We have already discussed the need for packet data in Section 1.6. The ability to stay connected is also a requirement that comes from the intermittent nature of the activity of data traffic. In circuit-switched systems, users have to connect to the data service and are charged for as long as they stay connected, regardless of whether they fully utilize the link or not. This leads to a situation where users must go through the long connection and verification procedure every time they wish to access data. In packet-switched data systems, where capacity is allocated as and when it is required, consumers are only charged by the amount of data they transmit and receive. This means the system can allow users

Packet-switching system

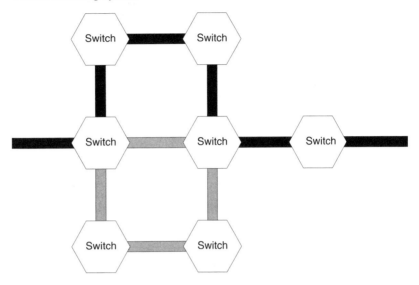

Circuit-switching system

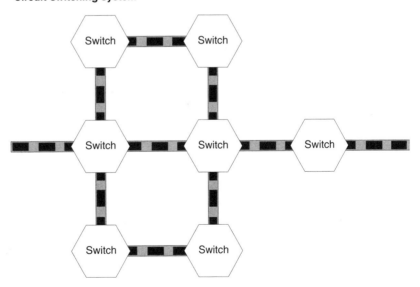

Figure 1.5   Circuit-switching and packet-switching systems

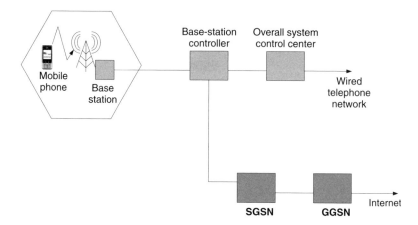

Figure 1.6   Introduction of GPRS into GSM systems

to remain logged into the network as long as their mobile phone is switched on.

Comparing Figure 1.6 with Figure 1.2, we can see the addition of two new hardware elements to the existing GSM system. The Serving GPRS Support Node (SGSN) controls the routing of packet data within the mobile network and the Gateway GPRS Support Node (GGSN) connects the mobile network to the general Internet infrastructure. Packet data is therefore added to the existing GSM structure and is separated from voice traffic at the base-station controller, which has a new hardware element, the packet data control unit, for this purpose. All other changes are achieved through software, making GPRS a very cost-effective upgrade because no physical changes were required at the base stations.

Fitting packet data within the GMS structure means that its performance is limited, and the data rates achieved in practice are relatively modest. Voice traffic has priority and data services are provided when spare capacity is available. Furthermore, data rates are generally asymmetric in provision (users tend to receive more data than they transmit) so the uplink can deliver much lower rates than the downlink. Typical values would be in the range of 10 Kbps in the uplink and 40 Kbps in the downlink, depending on phone capabilities. Note that there are no end-to-end delay guarantees for GPRS and latency (that is, the time taken for data to be received from when it was transmitted) could be in seconds.

Application developers wishing to take advantage of GPRS services must carefully consider whether their application will provide effective services when operating in this environment.

1.8   3G Mobile-Phone Systems

While the vision for 2G systems was very much concerned with increasing capacity in terms of the number of users it was able to support, 3G technology was more concerned with increasing the available data rates to those users. Initially, the 3G system was envisaged as a global system. To achieve this, it was proposed to use the 2 GHz frequency band. However, Figure 1.7 shows that there were a number of problems in this band, particularly in the USA, which had already allocated a significant proportion of it for the Personal Communications System (PCS). PCS is the same operational standard as GSM, but operates at higher frequencies (1800 and 1900), hence the need for a tri-band phone when traveling in the USA. Europe and Japan had also allocated part of this band for cordless telephone systems, the Digital European Cordless Telephone (DECT) standard and the Personal Handyphone System (PHS), although these were easily overcome by limiting the allocation of licenses. This meant that any standard using the 2 GHz band was unavailable to the USA and the result was that multiple 3G standards were developed under the auspices of the 3rd Generation Partnership Project (3GPP).

Europe and Japan opted for wideband CDMA (W-CDMA) using frequency-division duplex (FDD) in the two paired bands of the spectrum.

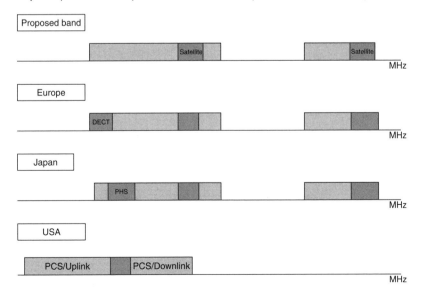

Figure 1.7   Allocation of 3G frequencies

The USA opted for an extension to cdmaOne, which uses multiple bands from this system to produce the so-called multi-carrier CDMA or CDMA2000. Another W-CDMA system is available in the unpaired band of the allocated spectrum. It uses time-division duplex (TDD) and is envisaged for providing 3G services in an indoor environment. Although not truly a 3G system, there is a further extension to GPRS called the enhanced data rates for GSM evolution (EDGE), which modifies the wireless link between a mobile phone and the base station of the GSM/GPRS system to further improve data rates. This standard is also developed by 3GPP.

In Section 1.7, we described GPRS as a stepping stone from 2G to 3G systems. Figure 1.8 shows how W-CDMA is incorporated into the infrastructure shown in Figure 1.6 to provide 3G services.

The two new hardware elements introduced are W-CDMA base stations and the radio-network controller (RNC), which provides much of the same functionality as the base-station controller but with improved handover for data streaming services and provision for the allocation of Quality of Service (QoS). 3G technology can therefore be introduced into the existing system in a controlled manner with the urban areas being serviced first. Indeed it is questionable whether network operators will consider it cost-effective to introduce 3G services into rural areas for some time. This means that network operators must supply dual mode mobile phones (capable of operating in both 2G and 3G modes). This

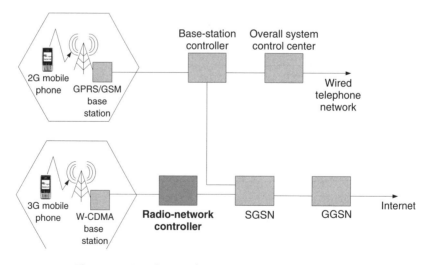

Figure 1.8   Introduction of W-CDMA into GSM/GPRS systems

also has implications for applications developers if their application is to allow operation over the complete coverage area.

Potential data rates are dependent on a range of factors, such as the number of users in a cell, the noise levels in the cell and the speed of the mobile phone. In previous generations of mobile networks, everyone was effectively provided with the same level of service irrespective of how much they paid. The data-centric orientation of 3G systems allows for the collective effect of service performance to determine the degree of satisfaction of the end-user of the service. Different data services require different levels of support from the system, for example, a video call transmits more data than a voice call and that data must be transmitted at regular intervals to ensure the video appears smooth, whereas web browsing requires intermittent data transfer when the user selects a new page or link.

When connected to a 3G network, a user is assigned a profile which includes essential parameters of the mobile phone's application to describe its required level of QoS, such as traffic classes, target transfer delay, reliability, guaranteed bit rate and priority. QoS for 3G systems is categorized into four traffic classes as shown in Table 1.1, where the

Table 1.1 QoS classes for 3G systems

Traffic Class	Characteristics	Typical Applications
Conversational (real time)	Low end-to-end delay Preserves time relation between packets	Voice, highly intensive games
Streaming (real time)	Preserves time relation between packets	Streaming media
Interactive (non-real time)	Request response pattern Preserves data integrity	Web browsing
Background (non-real time)	Best effort Non-time-critical data Preserves data integrity	Background synchronization, downloads, etc.

main distinguishing factor between these classes is the sensitivity to delay of the expected traffic.

The QoS profiles offered to users are tariff-dependent and represent another variable that can affect the likely take-up of a developer's application.

1.9   IP Multimedia Subsystem

The IP multimedia subsystem (IMS) aims to merge the two successful paradigms of the Internet and cellular systems. IMS is an architecture that defines how IP networks should handle voice and data sessions by replacing circuit-switched telecommunications. It is a service-oriented architecture and employs a distributed component model for the applications running on top of it. This means that it aims to separate the services from the underlying networks that carry them. It originated from 3GPP as a means of allowing 3G mobile-phone-system operators migrating from GSM to deliver more effective data services. Since then it has been adopted by other standards organizations for both wired and wireless networks. With Session Initiation Protocol (SIP) as the backbone of the system it is gaining widespread backing from service providers, mobile-phone vendors, application developers and infrastructure vendors.

The architecture of IMS consists of three layers: the transport layer, the control layer and the application layer. Since IMS can separate the services from the underlying carrier, a GPRS-enabled mobile phone can connect to IMS equally as well as a PC connected via a Digital Subscriber Line (DSL). More importantly in a mobile environment, where a user has the ability to roam, the access-independence of IMS does not only allow both the physical roaming of the user, but also provides the ability for the device to roam between various connection methods. For example, WiFi-enabled mobile phones could switch seamlessly between GPRS and WiFi and users could even switch from using their mobile phone to a PC within the same session and as the same user. Both of these features ensure that the upper layers of the communication system are saved from large amounts of data traffic; in other words, only essential information is passed to the application and all other data is maintained at the physical interface.

In simple terms, IMS can be regarded as turning current mobile-phone systems – with their mixture of circuit- and packet-switched systems – into fully packetized IP networks including all voice traffic. This means that developers will have greater resources with which to work: IMS is a platform for creating and delivering a wide range of services. Note that it is only responsible for connection, state management, QoS and mobility while the actual data transfer takes place directly between devices.

When IMS infrastructure is available for commercial applications in a few years' time, applications will be greatly enhanced and may take advantage of SIP, the signaling protocol for IMS, to synchronize, for instance, with a game server so that a multiplayer game can ensure that all players are experiencing the same game action at the same time. Further, a SIP message initiated by the server can send out requests to all mobile clients to take certain actions or wake up from running as a background process and bring updates to the display. This is beneficial for applications in which users are often interrupted.

When all user information is available, IMS can be added to an application without major overheads. The ability to detect the presence of a user can initiate better community features, encouraging users, for instance, to compete against their friends in a particular multiplayer game.

IMS has exciting new services and functions and is a step towards utilizing even more of the potential of mobile-phone systems and services.

1.10   Mobile-Phone Hardware

In the previous sections we focused on the constraints imposed by mobile-phone systems and the environment in which they operate. In this section, we will focus on the resource constraints of mobile phones.

The applications that we will teach you to develop in this book will be designed for mobile phones based on Symbian OS and the S60 user interface. Symbian OS is an open operating system derived from technology initially developed by Psion Software, but subsequently licensed and developed by an affiliation of major mobile-phone manufacturers (more information on Symbian OS and its history can be found at **www.symbian.com**). Symbian OS supports a range of user interfaces and development languages; in this book we will focus on S60 and the native programming language of Symbian OS, C++.

The S60 user interface was originally designed for one-handed use and, as a result, S60 phones normally offer a standard ITU-T keypad, two soft keys, buttons for starting and ending phone calls (these are not available to application developers), and a directional keypad. There are, however, exceptions to this and Nokia in particular have come up with a number of non-standard key layouts which could cause problems to the unwary developer. Having limited key options available has a direct bearing on the user interface (UI) design and applications must be developed accordingly. Another limitation to UI design is the small screen size, which means that developers must get their ideas across in a very small area. At present, most S60 phones have screens that are 176×208 pixels with 12-bit color resolution, though this is not actually defined within the S60 specification, and future devices may well deviate from it.

The hardware architecture of the S60 mobile phone is currently based around fixed-point digital signal processors (DSP) rather than the more generic floating-point microprocessors commonly found in PCs. This is because mobile phones must principally carry out the algorithmic data manipulation associated with both audio and video coding and are portable devices that must conserve power. Typical processor speeds are in the order of 100 MHz, which both conserves power and prevents the excessive heat generation associated with the high clock speeds of a typical PC processor. Processor speed is a limiting factor for sophisticated graphics applications, particularly those using three-dimensional graphics, and applications of this type will generally drain the phone battery very quickly. While Symbian OS does allow the use of floating-point arithmetic within an application, developers should be aware that it is much less efficient in terms of application speed and power usage than using fixed-point arithmetic.

The memory of S60 mobile phones is generally limited to a few megabytes for applications and about a megabyte of heap memory (the memory available for applications to use while in operation). However, if you are intending to deliver your applications over the air (OTA), you should check the size allowed by operators; on average, it is currently only in the region of 64 KB.

The aim of this book is to give developers an overview of the operation of mobile-phone systems and devices in order to allow them to create novel applications that exploit these systems. Mobile-phone systems are still undergoing rapid technological change and thus we strongly urge developers to keep themselves updated with regard to future trends and directions or they will severely limit their options.

2

Introduction to Symbian OS

Introduction

To facilitate application development, phone manufacturers and network operators are now producing environments where an application is no longer developed for a particular brand or model of a mobile phone. This is partially because we are now seeing the wide-scale deployment of mobile phones equipped with standard operating system (OS) software. The two principal systems in use are Symbian OS and Binary Runtime Environment of Wireless (BREW), although Symbian OS has a larger installed base. Previously, we were only able to develop cross-platform applications using a cut-down version of the Java 2 Platform, Micro Edition (Java ME). Both Symbian and BREW maintain support for Java ME. Whilst the potential of the mobile-phone-application market has been acknowledged, the debate still rages as to which environment is the most advantageous and is likely to dominate the market. Many developer forums are still locked into this debate, which has led to reluctance on the part of software developers, currently using Java, to embrace either Symbian OS or BREW. This is a pity as both systems can complement Java ME in that both provide Mobile Information Device Profile (MIDP) 2.0 to run over the top of the operating system, or offer facilities and opportunities beyond those provided by Java ME.

Much of our aim for this book is to provide a way for potential developers to get started with Symbian OS. It is an attempt to improve on 'the steep learning curve' that seems to be a phrase often associated with development on Symbian OS. It will allow developers to realize the enormous potential that Symbian OS offers.

This chapter provides an introduction to Symbian OS, starting with the background of the company and the development of the operating system. We then explain the different user interfaces available for Symbian OS, which facilitate the production of software on mobile phones with very different screen layouts and input mechanisms. We then delve into the operating system itself by identifying the very specific coding idioms used in Symbian OS, which are part of the process of producing very efficient and reliable mobile software. The final section of this chapter is concerned with the tools available to would-be developers. It is fair to say that many people who have been programming on Symbian OS for a number of years have found the performance of the tools highly variable. It is, however, good to see that this situation is resolving itself.

2.1   The Development of Symbian OS

Symbian Limited was founded by a group of major shareholders, originally Psion, Nokia and Ericsson in July 1998, with Motorola joining later that year, Matsushita in 1999 and Siemens in 2002. Motorola sold its stake in the company to Psion and Nokia in September 2003, although it continues to produce phones based on Symbian OS. Psion's stake was then bought in pro-rata shares by Nokia, Panasonic, Siemens AG and Sony Ericsson in July 2004.

Symbian OS had its beginnings in the old Psion EPOC software, and the early versions of the operating system that shipped with phones in 1999 still carried that name. (More information on the history and evolution of Symbian OS is available in *The Symbian OS Architecture Sourcebook* by Ben Morris.) Mobile phones based on Symbian OS v6.0 were 'open', meaning that users of the phones were able to install their own software. Symbian OS v6.0 appeared in 2001 and shipped on the Nokia 9210 Communicator. Symbian OS continued to evolve with improved API functionality and market-leading features, with the next big change occurring in early 2005 when Symbian OS v9.0 was announced. This version was designed to be more secure and deliver major cost savings to manufacturers – partly through new, standard tooling, which necessarily meant that it would not support software compiled for earlier releases.

The major advantage of Symbian OS is that, unlike some of its competitors, it was specifically designed for mobile phones that have relatively limited resources and that may run for months or years without ever being switched off. There is a strong emphasis on conserving memory in programming idioms specific to Symbian OS, such as descriptors and the cleanup stack. Together with other techniques, these keep memory usage low and memory leaks rare. There are similar techniques for conserving disk space. Furthermore, all Symbian OS programming is event-based, and the CPU is powered down when applications are not directly dealing with an event. This is achieved with the aid of a programming idiom called active objects. Correct use of these techniques helps ensure longer battery life.

2.2 Symbian OS User Interfaces

The different user interfaces available for Symbian OS are designed to allow manufacturers to produce a range of phones in different styles, addressing many different market segments. They essentially fall into three categories: S60 (formerly known as Series 60), Series 80, and UIQ. There was a fourth category, Series 90, but this has now been amalgamated into S60.

S60 consists of a suite of libraries and standard applications and is intended to provide fully-featured modern mobile phones with large color screens, which are most often referred to as smartphones. S60 is most often associated with Nokia, which is by far the largest manufacturer of these mobile phones, although S60 is also licensed to other major mobile-phone manufacturers such as BenQ–Siemens, Samsung and Panasonic. S60 is most often associated with the standard ITU keyboard layout for one-handed entry, although recent versions also offer support for stylus entry.

S60 supports applications developed in Java ME, native Symbian C++, Python and FlashLite. The most important feature of S60 phones from an application developer's perspective is that they allow new applications to be installed after purchase.

The screen size is generally 176×208 pixels, however this is not defined in the specification. Some S60 devices have other screen sizes; for example, Nokia N90 has a resolution of 352×288 pixels.

Series 80 is primarily designed to target the more business-orientated user with a device that accesses, views and manipulates data using a large screen and a full keyboard. Currently only Nokia produces Series 80 devices with screen resolutions of $640 \times (200–240)$ pixels and a folding case that reveals the full keyboard, as shown in Figure 2.1.

Figure 2.1   Example phones with different Symbian OS user interfaces

UIQ-based phones feature a stylus-based graphical user interface and also employ touch screens with a resolution of (208–240) × 320 pixels and 12- or 16-bit colors. Mobile phones offering UIQ have been produced by Sony Ericsson, Motorola and BenQ–Siemens. An interesting point to note is that UIQ 3.0 will bring in a normal keypad interface.

A selection of mobile phones based on Symbian OS is shown in Figure 2.1.

2.3   Coding Idioms

Naming Conventions

Symbian OS has its own naming convention for classes, variables and functions. The idea of using prefixes is similar to Hungarian notation, with different letters being used. Naming conventions are used to improve readability, as they allow the programmer to determine the nature of an item without looking at its implementation. As a general rule of thumb, the name should be meaningful and neither overly abbreviated nor too long. As programmers we need to find a happy medium.

Capitalization

The first letter of a class or function name should be capitalized. If a number of words make up the name of a class, the start of each word should be capitalized:

```
class TMyClass;
```

Function parameters and variable names should start with a lower-case letter:

```
TMyClass myObject;
```

Prefixes

Non-static member variables are prefixed with the letter 'i', referring to an instance of a class:

```
TInt iCount;
```

Function parameters are prefixed with the letter 'a', which stands for argument:

```
void MyFunction(TInt aParameter);
```

Automatic variables do not require a prefix.

```
for (TInt x = 0; x < 5; x++)
```

A constant is a value that does not change throughout the lifetime of a program. To prevent this value being changed, it is defined as a constant, using const or #define. Constants are prefixed with the letter 'K'.

```
#define KMaxItemLength 32
```

An enumerated type is a list of constants that refer to integer values. This allows the programmer to compare, for example, states of a game such as playing, paused or finished. The name of an enumerated type is prefixed with 'T' and its members' names are prefixed with 'E'.

```
enum TGameStates (EPlaying, EPaused, EFinished);
```

Suffixes

Single-letter suffixes are only used in function names. The suffix 'L' is used to indicate that the function in question may leave. A leaving function may not complete successfully due to conditions such as unsuccessful memory allocation. If there are not enough resources available then the function will cause a leave. As programmers, we are able to handle events that may cause a leave by using trap harnesses (see Chapter 3). However, knowing which particular functions may leave is useful to a programmer and you should always append the letter 'L' to a function name if its actions may cause a leave.

```
void FunctionMayLeaveL()
```

The suffix 'C' indicates that the function will return a pointer that has been pushed onto the cleanup stack. The cleanup stack is used to store pointers that may become orphaned so that if a leave occurs, cleanup can still be carried out. Chapter 3 gives a more detailed overview of the cleanup stack and other memory issues.

```
CMyClass* NewLC()
```

The suffix 'D' indicates that the object associated with the function will be deleted. In the example below, `ExecuteLD()` will delete `CAknInformationNote` once it has finished.

```
CAknInformationNote* note = new(ELeave) CAknInformationNote;
note->ExecuteLD(KNoteMessage);
```

Underscores

The use of underscores should generally be avoided. When naming functions or variables, capitalization and joining of the words is recommended. Underscores may be used in the definitions of resource names (which are always in lower case) and macro names (which are normally written in upper case).

```
RESOURCE my_dialog
```

Type Definitions

Symbian OS provides a number of type definitions that should be used instead of standard C++ types (such as `int`, `float` and `char`). These definitions are guaranteed to be compiler-independent and therefore should always be used.

Integers

An integer value is defined by its size and whether it is signed or unsigned. A signed integer will hold any number between -2^{n-1} and $2^{n-1}-1$ and an unsigned integer will hold a value between 0 and $2^{n}-1$, where n is the number of bits.

A `TInt` is a signed 32-bit integer that should be used in preference to other defined integers. The unsigned equivalent is a `TUint`, where 'U' indicates unsigned. Smaller signed integers can be defined to save resources: `TInt8`, `TInt16` and `TInt32` are signed 8-, 16- and 32-bit integers, respectively. Unsigned 8-, 16- and 32-bit integers are named appropriately: `TUint8`, `TUint16` and `TUint32`. A larger 64-bit signed integer, `TInt64`, is also available but there is no `TUint64`. All the integer types are defined in `e32def.h` apart from `TInt64`, which is defined in `e32std.h`.

Floating-point numbers

The use of floating-point numbers should be avoided where possible as they are not natively supported. An application is much slower when it uses floating-point numbers on a mobile phone. However, a number of floating-point types are defined in `e32def.h`:

- `TReal`: 64-bit floating-point number providing double precision

- `TReal32`: single-precision floating-point number

- `TReal64`: double-precision floating-point number (the same as `TReal`).

Characters

`TText` is an independent general unsigned character which can be used to store narrow or wide characters. Non-Unicode builds map `TText` to `TText8` (narrow characters) whereas Unicode builds map to `TText16` (wide characters). All versions of Symbian OS are now Unicode builds. `TChar` holds a character value stored as a 32-bit unsigned integer. More frequently, and for general use, `TText` is used in preference to `TChar`.

Boolean values

`TBool` defines a Boolean value where `ETrue` means logical truth (1) and `EFalse` means logical falsity (0). Comparisons with `ETrue` should be avoided, because any non-zero value evaluates to true but `ETrue` is only ever 1.

Classes

Class names are defined by a prefix followed by a useful name for the class and then by a suffix, if it is required. We have already discussed the suffixes and a number of prefixes, however classes have their own prefixes, C, T, R and M, that denote the nature of the class.

C classes

A C class derives from `CBase` or any class already derived from `CBase`. The 'C' indicates that the class is constructed on the heap and will need a 'cleanup'. The class overloads the `new` operator to initialize the object data to zero, thus initialization of member data is not necessarily required. `CBase` also includes a virtual destructor to allow the safe deletion of objects through a base-class pointer. The class should be accessed by a pointer owned by another object, a local pointer variable or by reference.

T classes

A T class does not use dynamic data (heap-allocated memory). As no cleanup is required, there is no need for a destructor. All data is contained internally or refers to external data that is 'used' rather than 'owned'. T class objects are returned from methods by value and are passed by value or reference.

R classes

A resource class, or R class, owns a resource. An R class will typically have a constructor to set its resource handle to null. The object must be associated with a resource via methods such as `Open()`, `Create()` or `Initialize()`. There should also be a corresponding `Close()` or `Reset()` method to free resources.

M classes

A mixin class is an abstract interface often used to define callback interfaces or observer classes. This is the only type of class in Symbian OS that allows multiple inheritance. Mixin classes will be discussed further in Chapter 4.

Structs

Structs are rarely seen in Symbian OS as the T class should be used in preference. The structure has no member functions and can be declared as:

```
typedef struct linked_list_node
  {
  UInt16 top;
  UInt16 left;
```

```
UInt16 bottom;
UInt16 right;
} NPRect;
```

Static classes

Static classes have no prefix letter. The class contains only static functions that cannot be instantiated into an object. An example is the `User` class which contains a number of functions related to the component APIs.

2.4   Tool Chains

For developing Symbian OS software, the use of Symbian's standard tool chain is essential. In theory, one could develop perfectly satisfactory code with nothing more than a text editor and a Software Development Kit (SDK). In reality, the situation is more complex and a rather richer set of tools is required. In order to quickly produce effective code, an Integrated Development Environment (IDE) is critical. Depending on the particular IDE and the target platform chosen, the IDE will perform simple functions such as color-coding the source code as it is entered, grouping together files, compiling code and interpreting error messages from the compiler. The more advanced IDEs provide debugging tools on the emulator or the target device. An IDE may also provide access to additional tools, for example project wizards that aid in the creation of new projects. In this section, we shall consider a tool chain which provides an adequate set of tools to develop S60 C++ applications. This list is by no means comprehensive and is subject to change as new tools emerge and old ones become redundant.

Software Development Kits

The SDK provides the basic Application Programming Interface (API) functions for use in Symbian OS programs, as well as the compilation tools needed to compile software for mobile phones and tools to package up files into the required formats for transfer to the phone.

The S60 SDKs can be downloaded from ***www.forum.nokia.com***. When choosing an SDK to use, you need to know which version of Symbian OS and which edition of S60 you wish to target, and which feature packs are required for your application. Feature packs are additional libraries that are added to support new functionality as it appears on phones, for example, 3D libraries supporting OpenGL ES were introduced in 2nd Edition, Feature Pack 2.

For example, if you are creating a basic application that uses only simple graphic elements, then you will need to download, install and compile with the SDK for S60 1st Edition, Feature Pack 1. Your application will then support the widest range of devices up to (but not including) S60 3rd Edition. If you want to develop an application that uses the camera, then you will need to install the 2nd Edition SDK, as the camera APIs changed in this version (if you wish to support older mobile phones, then you will need to develop two versions of your application). If you wish to use 3D features, then you will need S60 2nd Edition, Feature Pack 2.

Your choice of SDK determines the size of the target market for your application. When selecting a version of Symbian OS and S60 to target for your application, you should be aware that the application structure changes fundamentally between S60 2nd Edition and S60 3rd Edition (Symbian OS v9). You will need to develop separate versions of an application if you wish to support phones that use S60 3rd Edition and also phones that use earlier versions of S60.

To add further complexity, you may also require different SDKs for each IDE that you use. A minimal set of SDKs would be 1st Edition Feature Pack 1, 2nd Edition Feature Pack 2, and 3rd Edition (although it is advisable to install all available SDKs for your preferred IDE).

Integrated Development Environments

There are three IDEs available to Symbian OS C++ developers:

- Carbide.C++, based on the open source IDE called Eclipse

- Microsoft Visual Studio, the IDE of choice for most Windows programmers

- CodeWarrior, formerly the IDE of choice for Palm programmers and for PlayStation development and which is now being deprecated.

Carbide.C++ is an IDE available from Nokia. The Express version is available for free and provides the necessary functionality to build and compile applications. The Developer version has additional tools for on-device debugging and graphical tools for Rapid Application Development

(RAD), such as drag-and-drop creation of the user interface. The Professional version is geared towards developing new Symbian OS devices, supporting the use of development hardware.

Visual Studio and CodeWarrior are commercial applications, although both are available at preferential rates to academic institutions for non-commercial application development. CodeWarrior is available in three flavors: Personal Edition for developing applications; Professional Edition, which allows development on pre-release hardware; and the OEM edition, which enables development on custom development boards.

The choice of IDE is not necessarily simple. Initially, Carbide.C++ supported only the Symbian OS v9 SDKs (for example, S60 3rd Edition and UIQ 3), with support for older SDKs being introduced later. Developers may still need CodeWarrior or Visual Studio for developing applications on older SDKs (having said this, the main market for applications is increasingly Symbian OS v9 and later). Of the two, CodeWarrior is the better environment for Symbian OS development, although Visual Studio has a better application wizard. So, at least for now, it may be appropriate to have all three IDEs (and a selection of SDKs supporting each of the IDEs). For beginners, however, Carbide.C++ Express is obviously the cheapest solution.

Utilities

In addition to the core tool chain of IDE and SDK, a number of other utilities are useful. These utilities are necessary for basic image manipulation, quality assurance, or prototyping. This list is by no means exhaustive and the choice of tools is very much a matter of personal preference and the requirements of the particular applications being developed.

Leavescan

Leavescan is a tool developed by Symbian. It checks that functions that may leave are correctly named, with the letter 'L' appended to the function name. Whilst applications will run and compile with incorrectly named functions, this provides a useful signifier that the potential leave may not have been handled safely, leading to potential memory leaks in the application.

Automated Test Tool

A number of tools are available for testing applications prior to submission for the Symbian Signed test process. The most useful of these is the

Automated Test Tool, developed by SysOpen Digia. At the time of writing, a beta version was available for download from the Symbian Signed website (***www.symbiansigned.com***). The Automated Test Tool takes your application through a series of tests to check for compliance against the Symbian Signed test criteria, such as low-memory start-up, unexpected reboot and more.

Vector-drawing and image-editing packages

Developers will inevitably need to create, modify, convert and manipulate images for use in their applications. Such packages come in two flavors: vector-drawing packages, which create images from primitive shapes and objects, and image-editing packages, which manipulate images at a pixel level. The choice of package is a matter of personal taste and a matter of much debate amongst the authors of this book. We recommend the following three vector-drawing packages: Adobe Illustrator, Macromedia Freehand and CorelDRAW. As ever when dealing with software packages, nothing stands still; at the time of writing, Adobe and Macromedia are in the process of merging, casting some doubt on the future of Freehand. There are also three image-editing packages to consider: Adobe Photoshop, Corel Photopaint and Corel Paint Shop Pro.

Rapid Prototyping

It is often useful to be able to develop a prototype application quickly in a scripting language before developing a full version of the application in C++. There are two scripting languages which provide useful features and functionality for rapid prototyping: Macromedia Flash 8 and Python.

Flash 8

Flash 8 provides a graphical approach to application development and targets the Flash Lite environment which is increasingly available on mobile phones. The Flash Lite currently supports a limited set of ActionScript commands but it can still provide a powerful framework for application development and prototyping. In fact, it is quite easy to develop sophisticated games and applications in Flash Lite. Flash Lite 2, which will be available from 2006, will support more advanced ActionScript features such as XML objects, turning it into a far more serious proposition for Symbian OS application development. HTTP access is straightforward but as yet there are no plans for Bluetooth support.

Python

Python is an open-source scripting language, popular on the web, which has been ported onto Symbian OS. Python is somewhat limited graphically when compared to Flash Lite but it does provide greater underlying functionality in its communications capabilities. For developing Bluetooth applications, Python is by far the easiest of all the available languages.

3

The Console Application

Introduction

It is traditional for programming books to start with a 'Hello World' application and this book is no exception, as there is still something reassuring about being able to print a couple of words to the screen. Although a Symbian OS device is a based on a graphical user interface (GUI), we are going to start with a console-based version of 'Hello World', as it is both simple and a useful tool for testing an application engine.

An application's engine is the core logic at the heart of the application, where all the information or data processing is carried out as directed by the user interface. Examples are a game's algorithm processing, the storage and retrieval of data in a database application and the message processing of a chat application. The code is independent of the GUI and so the code is the same across devices – a chess game has the same logic regardless of the specific Symbian GUI used (for example, S60 or UIQ).

3.1 Creating a Console Application

For a basic (minimal) 'Hello World' application, we need three files: `bld.inf`, `helloworld.mmp`, and `helloworld.cpp`.

The `bld.inf` file contains information about where to find the individual components of an application, as well as the platforms supported (for example, emulator or target). For simple applications, there will be only one component and so the `bld.inf` file may simply point to the `.mmp` file.

The `.mmp` file is the project definition file. This file lists and describes each of the individual source code files and libraries required by the application or component, as well as directory locations and other project-defined assets. This file can be used to generate the appropriate project files for your chosen Integrated Development Environment (IDE), and so allows for a software-independent definition of your application.

The `.cpp` file contains the source code for the console application. This is the part of the code that tells the compiler what function we want the phone to perform.

The console application we are going to develop is an executable (EXE) file. Symbian OS applications are usually a special form of dynamic link library (DLL). A DLL is a dynamic link library that contains functions available for use by other applications. DLLs are more rigid than EXEs in their use of memory (an advantage on a memory-limited device) and are, for example, not allowed to contain global variables.

On Symbian OS, an application is a DLL with file extension `.app` for OS versions prior to Symbian OS v9. From version 9 onwards Symbian applications are executable files with extension `.exe`. However, in both cases, console applications are compiled as `.exe` files, so our first example is fairly straightforward.

In order to prevent malicious applications from accessing low-level features in the phone, Symbian OS v9 introduces a strict security model that requires applications to be signed. A distributable application must go through the full Symbian Signed (***www.symbiansigned.com***) signing process (see Chapter 8) and development versions can be signed using a certificate generated by the user for a specific phone by linking the certificate to the IMEI number. At this basic level of certification, applications can access local services (such as Bluetooth and location APIs), read and write user data, access network features, etc. However, applications cannot access the file system, DRM APIs or other sensitive functionality without having the application approved and signed by a mobile-phone manufacturer.

This is quite enough of the preamble, so let's get started on our first application. It is a good idea to practice good development techniques, even with relatively trivial applications such as this. The three files should therefore be stored in separate subdirectories that can then provide additional information to help other developers understand their purpose.

Note that directory names and the paths to them should not contain spaces since the Symbian OS toolset relies heavily on command-line tools, which make it difficult to deal with such directory names.

The project should be placed in a directory called `helloworld`. Within this directory, there should be two further subdirectories, called `group` and `source`. There are no hard and fast rules as to what subdirectory names to use and which files to place within each, but we will aim to use a set of names and locations that are used commonly in Symbian OS development. The `bld.inf` and `helloworld.mmp` files should be placed in the `group` directory and the `helloworld.cpp` file should be placed in the `source` directory. The code listings for these files are as follows.

bld.inf

```
PRJ_MMPFILES
helloworld.mmp
```

The first line's label, `PRJ_MMPFILES`, indicates that a list of the `.mmp` files contained in the project will follow, and sure enough, the second line lists this project's single `.mmp` file.

helloworld.mmp

```
TARGET          helloworld.exe
TARGETTYPE      exe
SOURCEPATH      ..\src
UID             0
SOURCE          helloworld.cpp
USERINCLUDE     ..\inc
SYSTEMINCLUDE   \epoc32\include
LIBRARY         euser.lib
```

This is the project definition file, which lists the name of the compiled application (the target), the target type (in this case, an EXE), the directory that contains the `.cpp` files for the project (the source path), the unique identifier for the application, the directory that contains the `.h` files (the user include directory), the directory that contains the API header files (the system include directory), and a list of library files to be compiled against. In this case, we are using only one library, `euser.lib`.

helloworld.cpp

```
#include <e32base.h>
#include <e32cons.h>
LOCAL_D CConsoleBase* gConsole;
// main function
LOCAL_C void MainL()
  {
  _LIT(KHelloWorldString, "Hello World\n");
  gConsole->Printf(KHelloWorldString);
  }
// Console Harness
LOCAL_C void ConsoleMainL()
  {
  _LIT(KConsoleTitle,"Hello World!");
  gConsole = Console::NewL(KConsoleTitle, TSize(KConsFullScreen,
                                                KConsFullScreen));
  MainL();
  }
// EPOC's main entry point
GLDEF_C TInt E32Main()
  {
  ConsoleMainL();
  User::After(5000000);
  return 0;
  }
```

This is the source code for the application. The first function called by a Symbian OS phone when an application is started is the E32Main() function, which builds the rest of the application. This example is very simple: the main function uses the console harness, ConsoleMainL(), to create a console for the application, waits for 5 000 000 microseconds, and then exits the program.

The console harness creates a console, gConsole (the g indicates that it is a global variable, which is permitted in an EXE although not in a DLL). This console is titled 'Hello World' and the _LIT macro, KConsoleTitle, turns the name into a literal string, which we will talk about later. The console is set to the full size of the screen.

After creating the console harness, it calls the main function, MainL(), which simply prints 'Hello World' to the screen. Note that the Symbian OS implementation of Printf() requires a literal string as a parameter.

Building the Application

The only viable option for Symbian C++ application development is Carbide.C++. As we mentioned previously, it is recommended that beginners use the free Carbide.C++ Express edition and then migrate to Carbide.C++ Developer edition as required. It is also useful to gain a basic understanding of the command-line tools, particularly when it comes to getting the application onto the phone.

A couple of command-line tools you should become familiar with are `bldmake` and `abld`. The `bldmake` tool processes the `bld.inf` file and the corresponding `.mmp` files in the current directory to generate the batch file, `abld.bat`, and a number of makefiles.

The easiest way to use `bldmake` is:

```
bldmake bldfiles
```

This creates the project directory within the `\epoc32\build` directory. It generates target-specific makefiles for the component in this directory and finally creates the batch file, `abld.bat`, in the current directory.

The `abld.bat` file is used to control the building process of the project. Before building the application, it is useful to clean (remove) the previous binary files from the project:

```
abld clean
```

To remove the intermediate files, such as those from the `\epoc32\build` directory use the following command:

```
abld reallyclean
```

This command is the same as `abld clean`, but it also removes files exported by `abld export` and the makefiles generated by `abld makefile`.

The simplest method for building the project is:

```
abld build
```

This will build the project for all possible build variants. However, it is possible to build for a specific platform. The following command will build a WINSCW platform version for debug:

```
abld build winscw udeb
```

An easier method of compiling and running the application is to import it into an IDE. Having imported your application into Carbide.C++, you can compile it and run your project in the emulator.

We have now created a basic framework with which we can test the logical engines for our games and applications. (At this stage we have not begun to worry about memory checking or the cleanup stack, because the size and complexity of the application is trivial and, furthermore, a console application is not intended to be run on a phone.)

3.2   CBase Classes

Before we can go much further, we need to think a little more about one of the Symbian OS coding idioms. Usually, when we create a class, in this case to provide the application's engine, it will be instantiated on the heap. Such classes must inherit either from the base class, CBase, or from a class that itself inherits from CBase. Classes that inherit from CBase are recognized by the fact that their name begins with the letter C. It is obviously quite important that we also name classes that derive from CBase with an initial letter C.

CBase objects are initialized to zero. That is, any member variables within the class are initialized by the new operator of the CBase class. A key reason for this zero initialization is to aid in the way compound objects are created using two-phase construction. It also means that a programmer does not need to initialize variables to zero in the constructor.

The CBase class has a virtual destructor. This means that derived classes can be destroyed and cleaned up through a CBase* pointer. The CBase* pointer can be pushed onto the cleanup stack and destroyed via the cleanup stack.

3.3   Protecting Memory

In any limited-hardware device, memory management is critical. Windows programmers can be wasteful as it is relatively simple to add more memory into a computer, or failing that, with modern hard drives, virtual memory is practically unlimited.

In a mobile phone, however, memory resources are not just limited but also relatively small. Memory is particularly limited on the stack, and so it is important that software development continuously takes into account the potential for failing to allocate resources. Such issues are dealt with in Symbian OS using two concepts: leaves and the cleanup stack. Leaves provide a lightweight exception-handling mechanism that is lighter on resources than more conventional C++ exception-handling mechanisms. The cleanup stack is a static resource that can be used to clean up dynamically allocated resources on the heap in the event of a leave. If resources are not properly cleaned up in the event of a leave, then memory leaks will occur. These leaks can only be freed up by rebooting the phone (i.e. turning it off and on again). Rebooting a PC is a fairly regular occurrence that usually happens at least once a day. However, phones may be left on for weeks at a time between reboots and so leaked resources may not be reclaimed for long periods of time, impacting the amount of memory available in the system.

The Cleanup Stack

The cleanup stack provides a mechanism for saving pointers that may be orphaned in the event of a leave (we will look at this in more detail later in our examples). Pointers are pushed onto the stack using the `PushL()` function. In the event of a Leave, each of the items on the cleanup stack is freed up either by calling `delete`, in the case of `CBase`-derived classes, or by calling the static function `User::Free()`, in the case of untyped objects. When `delete` is called on a `CBase`-derived class, the destructor is called and the object can be properly destroyed. `User::Free()`, however, only implements a limited form of cleanup and does not call the destructor, hence the importance of inheriting objects properly from `CBase`.

Once it is safe to remove a pointer from the cleanup stack, the `Pop()` method can be called. If the resource is no longer required, you can call the `PopAndDestroy()` method, which also cleans up the resources to which the pointer refers. If a number of items have been pushed onto the stack, then a `TInt` parameter can be passed to these methods specifying how many objects are to be popped or popped and destroyed.

```
CBtEngine* self = new (ELeave) CBtEngine();
CleanupStack::PushL(self);
self->ConstructL();
CleanupStack::Pop(self);
```

Leaves

Leaves are the way of dealing with exception handling in Symbian OS. Exceptions are errors that occur at run time, but in such a way that the application developers or the operating system developers have predicted may occur. The application developer has the option as to how to deal with the exception, for example, to ask the user to close other applications before trying again to run the application.

Symbian OS did not initially use C++ exceptions since they were not well supported at that time. While later versions of Symbian OS do support try...catch exception handling, it is necessary for Symbian OS programmers to grasp the Symbian OS error-handling framework so that they can design and implement applications that will support as wide as possible a range of mobile phones.

For consistency, the traditional exception-handling mechanisms of Symbian OS should not be mixed with try...catch methods.

When an exception occurs, a leave is triggered and the exception is caught in a trap harness. That is, code execution ends at the leave and resumes at the trap harness.

Leaving Functions

A leave is triggered by calling the static system function `User::Leave()`. This function raises an exception and propagates an error value until it can be caught by a trap harness. If we fail to deal with the leave appropriately then either there will be a memory leak or a resource, for example, the phone's camera, will not be released properly, preventing other applications from using it. Since it is vital that we recognize when a function may leave, it is important that, as with `CBase`-derived classes, we label our functions appropriately. Functions that may leave are labeled with an 'L' at the end of their names. Leaving functions perform an operation that is not guaranteed to succeed, such as memory allocation, and the label reminds us that we need to take care of pointers or resource handles that may be orphaned by that function leaving.

Functions may leave if they call functions that may leave without surrounding the code with a trap harness. Similarly, they can leave if they call a system function that initiates a leave, for example, `User::Leave()` or `User::LeaveIfError()`, or if they use `new (ELeave)` for heap allocations.

In Symbian OS, the `new` operator has been overloaded with another version `new (ELeave)`. This operator calls the default constructor of an object, but also triggers a leave if there is insufficient memory to create the object, thus removing the need for the developer to check explicitly for a NULL pointer when allocating memory on a heap.

As with naming CBase-derived classes with a letter 'C' and leaving functions with the letter 'L', it is important that Symbian OS programmers get into the habit of calling new (ELeave) rather than new(). For example:

```
CClass object = new (ELeave) CClass;
```

Construction and Destruction

Hopefully, you are beginning to get a feel for some of the problems associated with memory resources on a mobile phone. This leaves us with a hard and fast rule when creating classes: constructors and destructors should never leave.

If a constructor leaves, then we risk orphaning any dynamic resources that have been allocated during the partial construction. If the destructor leaves then the object will not have been fully destroyed, and again resources will have been orphaned. Both cases will result in a memory leak.

However, this rule causes us problems in designing objects, as we usually need to dynamically allocate resources during the creation of an object. In order to obey the rule, we must use a two-phase process for construction and destruction. We will focus on the two-phase construction process in the remainder of this chapter, as this is the more common scenario that you will need to deal with. Suffice it to say that if you need to call any leaving functions to free up resources, then these operations should be wrapped up in a separate leaving function, for example, PrepareForDestructionL(), which is called before deleting the object.

The class definition below provides a basic template for a two-phase construction process:

```
class CExample : public CBase
  {
  public:
    static CExample* NewL();
    ~CExample();
  private:
    CExample();
```

```
  void ConstructL(); // instantiated through NewL
  ...
}
```

The class definition contains a static method `NewL()` as well as the default constructor and destructor. In addition there is a leaving function, called `ConstructL()`, that by convention provides a second-phase constructor. The `ConstructL()` method is only called once the resources for the object have been successfully allocated and pushed onto the cleanup stack. If the `ConstructL()` method leaves, the parent object can safely be destroyed. The destructor must be able to cope with destroying the object if the `ConstructL()` method fails part way through, as the destructor will be called in the event of a leave. It is good practice to set deleted objects to `NULL` to avoid deleting them twice and also, before deleting, to check that the object exists. Note that the default constructor is declared private, which means that the object must be created using the `NewL()` function:

```
CExample* CExample::NewL()
  {
  CExample* self = new (ELeave) CExample();
  CleanupStack::PushL(self);
  self->ConstructL();
  CleanupStack::Pop(self);
  return self;
  }
```

The `NewL()` function creates an object of its own type on the heap, calling the `new (ELeave)` operator. If there is insufficient memory to allocate the object, the function will leave without having allocated any resources. If the first-phase (safe) construction is successfully completed, we call the second-phase (unsafe i.e. liable to leave) constructor. However, if the second-phase constructor were to leave, the pointer `self` could be orphaned, so we must protect the pointer by placing it on the cleanup stack. Then, if the second-phase constructor `ConstructL()` were to leave, the object can be deallocated via the cleanup stack. Once the second-phase constructor has completed successfully, we can pop the pointer from the cleanup stack and return a reference to the location of the object on the heap. In this way, an object can be created and destroyed as shown:

```
CExample* example = CExample::NewL();
...
delete example;
```

However, if the CExample object is to be used through an automatic variable for the lifetime of the project, this would also require the use of the cleanup stack throughout the lifetime of the project. The pointer could be pushed onto the cleanup stack on return but we have already pushed and popped the pointer off the cleanup stack once, so this does not seem like an efficient method. An alternative method, NewLC(), has the same functionality as NewL() but leaves a pointer on the cleanup stack, hence the 'C' appended to the function name.

```
CExample* CExample::NewLC()
  {
  CExample* self = new (ELeave) CExample();
  CleanupStack::PushL(self);
  self->ConstructL();
  return self;
  }
```

When using NewL() and NewLC() together, it is necessary to modify NewL() as follows:

```
CExample* CExample::NewL()
  {
  CExample* self = CExample()::NewLC();
  CleanupStack::Pop(self);
  return self;
  }
```

Examples of Leaving Functions

It is difficult to progress very far in Symbian OS programming without properly getting to grips with leaving functions, so we will consider a number of examples that further illustrate the operation of functions that may leave.

The example below illustrates a function that may leave as a result of calling another leaving function:

```
void FunctionThatMayLeaveSafelyL()
```

```
{
CClass* object = CClass::NewL();
object->NonLeavingFunction();
delete object;
}
```

In this function, an object of type CClass is allocated on the heap by calling the object's NewL() method. If the NewL function leaves, no memory will be orphaned and the function may leave safely. It may be noted that the pointer to this object is potentially vulnerable until the end of the function. But, since the only other function does not have the potential to leave, there is no danger of the pointer being orphaned. The function below, however, is potentially unsafe:

```
void UnsafeFunctionL()
  {
  CClass* object = CClass::NewL();
  object->FunctionThatMayLeaveL();
  delete object;
  }
```

In this example, an object is created on the heap and then a function that may leave is called. If this function were to leave, then the pointer object would be orphaned and a memory leak would ensue. The following code uses the cleanup stack to make this function safe:

```
void SafeFunctionL()
  {
  CClass* object = CClass::NewL();
  CleanupStack::PushL(object);
  object->FunctionThatMayLeaveL();
  CleanUpStack::Pop(object);
  delete object;
  }
```

The pointer object is now protected by being stored on the cleanup stack while the leaving function is called. If a leave occurs, object can safely be deleted by means of the reference stored on the stack. NewLC() would be more efficient and there would be no need to do the additional push and pop:

```
void SafeFunctionL()
  {
```

```
CClass* object = CClass::NewLC();
object->FunctionThatMayLeaveL();
CleanupStack::PopAndDestroy(object);
}
```

The following example shows an alternative version of this function that uses a member variable to store the pointer to the object created. The cleanup stack is no longer necessary since the location of the object is stored within the class and the object can be freed by using its owner's destructor.

```
void CClass1::SafeFunctionL()
{
// allocate heap member
iObject = CClass2::NewL();
iObject->FunctionMayLeaveSafelyL();
}
```

The 'L' suffix is not checked during compilation and so you may forget to append 'L' to a function that leaves, especially when modifying previously non-leaving functions. Symbian provides a tool called LeaveScan that checks code for incorrectly named leaving functions and this should be used regularly on large projects since correct labeling of leaving functions is critical to the readability of Symbian OS applications by other developers.

Trapping Leaves

We have now looked in some detail at leaving functions, which leads to the final ingredient, the trap harness. Two macros have been defined to trap a leave: TRAP and TRAPD. The TRAP harness requires a predefined variable in which to store the error code; the TRAPD harness creates the variable itself from a name provided. There is relatively little difference between the two in practice:

```
Tint result;
TRAP(result, MayLeaveL());
if (KErrNone!=result)
  {
  // handle error
  }
TRAPD(secondResult, MayLeaveL());
if (KErrNone!= secondResult)
  {
```

```
// handle error
}
```

Every program must have at least one TRAP (at the topmost level), to catch leaves that have not been trapped elsewhere. However, the total number of TRAPs should be minimized as they have a performance impact on both size and speed. The example below demonstrates how a function may implement a trap harness to deal with insufficient memory:

```
void FunctionL()
  {
  CClass* object;
  TRAPD(result, object=CClass::NewL());
  switch (result)
    {
    case (KErrNoMemory):
      // free up memory and try again...
      break;
    default:
      User::Leave(result);
      break;
    }
  delete object;
  }
```

If all possible exceptions are handled then the function will no longer be a leaving function. However, in this case, if we fail to deal with the error code, it is passed to the next trap harness up the chain and so the function may still leave.

3.4   Putting It Into Practice: An Engine for a Simple Card Game

In this section we will put the ideas previously discussed in this chapter into practice by producing an engine class for a simple card game, Blackjack.

Building the Engine

We will use the console harness to create and test the engine that is to form the basis of the Blackjack game. The engine will use a new class called CCards, representing a deck of cards. The class will, initially at least, contain a deck of 52 cards, a pointer to the next card to be dealt and a `Deal` method that will allow us to take a card from the pack.

The header file, `cards.h`, is shown below:

```
#ifndef __CARDS_H__
#define __CARDS_H__
#include <e32base.h>
class CCards : CBase
  {
  public:
    static CCards* NewL();
    static CCards* NewLC();
    TInt Deal();
  private:
    void ConstructL();
    CCards();
  private: //data
    TInt iDeck[52];
    TInt iNextCard;
  };
#endif
```

This class contains an array of integer values to represent each card in the deck, two-phase construction and destruction and a `Deal()` function. The class is derived from `CBase`, therefore `iDeck` and `iNextCard` are zero-initialized and there is no need to initialize them in the constructor.

The class is implemented in the source file, `cards.cpp`:

```
#include "cards.h"
CCards* CCards::NewL(TInt aNumPacks)
  {
  CCards* self = CCards::NewLC(aNumPacks);
  CleanupStack::Pop(self);
  return(self);
  }
CCards* CCards::NewLC(TInt aNumPacks)
  {
  CCards* self = new (ELeave) CCards(aNumPacks);
  CleanupStack::PushL(self);
  self->ConstructL();
  return(self);
  }
void CCards::ConstructL()
  {
  }
CCards::CCards()
  {
  for (Tint i=0; i<52; i++)
```

```
   iDeck[i] = i;
 }

CCards::~CCards()
  {
  }
TInt CCards::Deal()
  {
  TInt card = iDeck[iNextCard];
  iNextCard = (iNextCard+1)%52;
  return card;
  }
```

This is a very simple implementation, but sufficient for now to demonstrate the steps necessary to link a new class into a Symbian OS project. This class can be linked into the project by modifying the `helloworld.mmp` file:

```
TARGET          helloworld.exe
TARGETTYPE      exe
UID             0
SOURCEPATH      ..\src
SOURCE          helloworld.cpp
SOURCE          cards.cpp
USERINCLUDE     ..\inc
SYSTEMINCLUDE   \epoc32\include
LIBRARY         euser.lib
```

Note that we have now included two source files in the project. The Carbide.C++ IDE should automatically be aware that changes have been made.

Finally, we can modify the previous `MainL()` function to test the class (remember to include `cards.h` into the `helloworld.cpp` file):

```
_LIT(KAce, "Ace");
_LIT(KJack, "Jack");
_LIT(KQueen, "Queen");
_LIT(KKing, "King");
_LIT(KOf, "of");
_LIT(KHearts, "Hearts");
_LIT(KClubs, "Clubs");
_LIT(KDiamonds, "Diamonds");
_LIT(KSpades, "Spades");
// main function
void MainL()
  {
  CCards* deckOfCards = CCards::NewL();
```

```
TInt i, card;
for (i=0; i<15; i++)
  {
  card = deckOfCards.Deal();
  TInt suit = card/13;
  card%=13;

  if (0==card)
    gConsole->Printf(KAce);
  else if (10==card)
    gConsole->Printf(KJack);
  else if (11==card)
    gConsole->Printf(KQueen);
  else if (12==card)
    gConsole->Printf(KKing);
  else
    gConsole->Printf(_L("%d"), card+1);

  gConsole->Printf(KOf);
  if (0==suit)
    gConsole->Printf(KHearts);
  else if (1==suit)
   gConsole->Printf(KClubs);
  else if (2==suit)
   gConsole->Printf(KDiamonds);
  else
   gConsole->Printf(KSpades);
  }
delete deckOfCards;
}
```

A number of literals are defined to represent the card names. The results of running the program in the emulator are shown in Figure 3.1.

Shuffling the Cards

In its current form, the card class isn't particularly useful. What we need next is a Shuffle function to randomize the position of our cards in the deck before we start a game. The Shuffle function will make use of the e32Math.h library, which provides a random function:

```
void CCards::Shuffle()
  {
  TTime time;
  time.UniversalTime();
  TInt64 seed = time.Int64();
  TInt temp;
```

```
TInt swap;

for (TInt i=0; i<KNoOfCardsInPack; i++)
  {
  swap = Math::Rand(seed)%(KNoOfCardsInPack); // create random
                                              // swap position
  temp = iDeck[i]; // puts the ith card in a temp variable
  iDeck[i] = iDeck[swap]; // swap the two cards
  iDeck[swap] = temp;
  }
 }
```

There are a number of ways of shuffling the cards; we have chosen to take a random number from 0 to 51 for each of 52 times and then for each card in turn to swap the *i*th card with the card corresponding to the random number. The Rand() function used requires a 64-bit seed, which in this instance has been set using the UniversalTime() method to retrieve the current time thus ensuring that the random number is different each time the game is played.

Figure 3.1   Console application showing basic card game class

Generating Card Names

The current method of printing the card names to screen is ungainly and inflexible and so the next stage is to add to the CCards class a method to generate a string name. In Symbian OS, the type used to generate a name is a text buffer rather than a string. In this instance, we will use a text buffer with a limit of 20 characters, TBuf<20>. The function's logic, however, is the same as we developed previously:

```
_LIT(KAce, "Ace");
_LIT(KJack, "Jack");
_LIT(KQueen, "Queen");
_LIT(KKing, "King");
_LIT(KOf, "of");
_LIT(KHearts, "Hearts\n");
_LIT(KClubs, "Clubs\n");
_LIT(KDiamonds, "Diamonds\n");
_LIT(KSpades, "Spades\n");
const TBuf<KCardNameLength>& CCards::CardName(TInt aCard)
  {
  TInt card=aCard;

  TInt suit = card/13;
  card%=13;

  if (0==card)
    iCardName.Format(KAce);
      // Format re-formats the string to the new card name
  else if (10==card)
    iCardName.Format(KJack);
  else if (11==card)
    iCardName.Format(KQueen);
  else if (12==card)
    iCardName.Format(KKing);
  else
    iCardName.Format(_L("%d"), card+1);

    iCardName.Append(KOf);
      // Append characters to the end of the current string
  if (EHearts==suit)
    iCardName.Append(KHearts));
  else if (EClubs==suit)
    iCardName.Append(KClubs);
  else if (EDiamonds==suit)
    iCardName.Append(KDiamonds);
  else
    iCardName.Append(KSpades);

  return iCardName;
  }
```

This produces a simplified `MainL()` function:

```
LOCAL_C void MainL()
  {
  CCards* deckOfCards = CCards::NewL(2);
  deckOfCards->Shuffle();

  TInt i, card;
  for (i=0; i<6; i++)
    {
    card = deckOfCards->Deal();
    TBuf<KCardNameLength> theCard=deckOfCards-> CardName(card);
    gConsole->Printf(theCard);
    }
  delete deckOfCards;
  }
```

Dynamic Deck Size

The next stage, and possibly the most difficult, is to modify the deck so that we have the ability to add more than one pack of cards. In order to do this we need to make `iDeck` a variable-length array, which means using dynamic memory.

First we need to create a `TRAP` harness to deal with any leaves that may have been caused further down the program structure. This is dealt with in the `E32Main()` function, which has the highest level control of the application:

```
// Epoc main function
GLDEF_C TInt E32Main()
  {
  __UHEAP_MARK;
  TInt error = KErrNoMemory;
  CTrapCleanup * cleanupStack = CTrapCleanup::New();
  if(cleanupStack != NULL)
    {
    TRAP(error, ConsoleMainL());
    delete cleanupStack;
    }
  _LIT(KProgramError, "Program Error");
  __ASSERT_ALWAYS(!error, User::Panic(KProgramError, error));
  __UHEAP_MARKEND;
  return error;
  }
```

We create an instance of the `CTrapCleanup` class to delete items from the cleanup stack on its own deletion. We then call `ConsoleMainL()`, trapping any unhandled errors that have propagated back this far. In the case of an error we create a panic, which quits the program with a message. Finally we delete the cleanup stack before quitting the program.

We must then modify the `ConsoleMainL()` function. If the `MainL()` function leaves, then the pointer to the console, `gConsole`, will be orphaned (left allocated in memory) so we need to push this pointer onto the cleanup stack first:

```
void ConsoleMainL()
  {
  _LIT(KConsoleTitle,"Hello World!");
  gConsole = Console::NewL(KConsoleTitle, TSize(KConsFullScreen,
                                                KConsFullScreen));
  CleanupStack::PushL(gConsole);
  MainL();
  CleanupStack::PopAndDestroy(gConsole);
  }
```

The `ConstructL()` method is responsible for allocating the dynamic array, which may cause a leave, and as it follows the call to the default constructor it now includes the initialization of the array. In more complex classes, it may be useful to add a further method, `CompleteConstruct()` or `CompleteConstructL()`, to perform such operations. The code for the `ConstructL()` function is below (note that the default constructor is now empty):

```
void CCards::ConstructL()
  {
  iDeck = new (ELeave) TInt[52];
  TInt i;
  for (i=0; i<52; i++)
    iDeck[i] = i;
  }
CCards::CCards()
  {
  }
```

Multiple Packs

While we now have a more flexible, safer and more dynamic implementation, it still performs exactly the same way as our previous version. The next stage is to add support for multiple packs of cards, exploiting the

dynamic nature of our deck of cards. This involves a modification to the
CCards class constructors:

```
class CCards : CBase
  {
  public:
    static CCards* NewL(TInt);
    ~CCards();
    TInt Deal();
    void Shuffle();
    TBuf<20> CardName(TInt);
  private:
    CCards(TInt);
    void ConstructL();
    TInt* iDeck;
    TInt iNextCard;
    TInt iNumPacks;
  };
```

The NewL constructor takes a TInt variable which is passed to the
first-phase constructor:

```
CCards::CCards(TInt aNumPacks)
  {
  if (aNumPacks>0)
    iNumPacks = aNumPacks;
  else
    iNumPacks = 1;
  }
```

The second-phase constructor can now make use of the new
iNumPacks variable to create a multi-pack deck of cards:

```
void CCards::ConstructL()
  {
  iDeck = new (ELeave) TInt[iNumPacks*KNoOfCardsInPack];
  for (TInt j=0; j<iNumPacks; j++)
    for (TInt i=0; i<KNoOfCardsInPack; i++)
      iDeck[KNoOfCardsInPack*j+i] = i;
  }
```

This propagates further changes to the Deal() and Shuffle()
functions as shown:

```
TInt CCards::Deal()
```

```
    {
    TInt card = iDeck[iNextCard];
    iNextCard = (iNextCard+1)%(52*iNumPacks);

    return card;
    }
void CCards::Shuffle()
    {
    TTime time;
    time.UniversalTime();
    TInt64 seed = time.Int64();
    TInt temp;
    TInt swap;

    for (TInt i=0; i<iNumPacks*KNoOfCardsInPack; i++)
      {
      //create random swap position
      swap = Math::Rand(seed)%(iNumPacks*KNoOfCardsInPack);
      temp = iDeck[i]; //Puts first card in a temp variable
      iDeck[i] = iDeck[swap]; //Swap the cards
      iDeck[swap] = temp;
      }
    }
```

Incorporating User Input

Finally, we need to emulate some user interaction – otherwise we have to rely on programming our test cases. To do this we can use the `Getch()` function, which is a member of the `Console` class. The `Getch()` function returns a value of type `TKeyCode`, which contains enumerated values representing both keyboard and phone keys. In this example, we set up a loop which terminates when the '0' key is pressed. If the '1' key is pressed, then a new card is dealt:

```
void MainL()
    {
    CCards* deckOfCards = CCards::NewL(2);
    deckOfCards->Shuffle();
    deckOfCards->Shuffle();
    deckOfCards->Shuffle();

    gConsole->Printf(KStart);
    TInt card;
    TKeyCode inputKey;
    while ((inputKey = gConsole->Getch()) != '0')
      {
      if (inputKey == '1')
        {
        card = deckOfCards->Deal();
```

```
    TBuf<KCardNameLength> theCard=deckOfCards->CardName(card);
    gConsole->Printf(theCard);
    }
  }
 delete deckOfCards;
 }
```

Summary

In this section we have built an application that is both simple and sophisticated. It is simple in terms of operation, but sophisticated in terms of the concepts it introduces. This application has demonstrated the implementation of a console application, how to create an engine class and test it within the console application, how to use and manage a cleanup stack and trap potential errors, how to use a two-phase construction process to dynamically create resources and how to handle input from the user.

Before continuing to the more advanced chapters of this book please ensure that your application runs. Test for different numbers of packs of cards (you might even want to ask the user how many packs of cards to use) and make sure that you understand each of the steps that we have introduced.

4

A GUI Application

Introduction

A badly designed interface can 'make or break' any mobile application. A well-designed graphical user interface (GUI) enables us to enhance the user experience by allowing the user to interact through graphical images and menus, in addition to text. In Chapter 1, we discussed some of the limitations of the mobile phone in terms of input and display mechanisms. This chapter is less concerned about the philosophy of human–computer interface design but more about how it can be implemented. We start with an introduction to descriptors, a fundamental part of Symbian OS coding which is needed for text manipulation and display. The following section discusses how to enhance the display with graphics. We then introduce more complex images, such as bitmaps, as well as the conversion of these images utilizing mixins. Finally, we show you how to handle user input from the keypad before enabling you to enhance the simple text-based card game. The game project is enhanced in this chapter with a much richer graphical environment, by incorporating a menu structure to simplify game play and the use of card images to enhance the look and feel of the application.

4.1 The Structure of a Symbian OS Application

The S60 App Wizard (supplied with the S60 SDK) is the recommended way to start a new application project. The wizard creates an empty application with a menu, which is ready for you to add features and run. The wizard removes the repetitive task of creating concrete instances of the foundation base classes of the Symbian OS application framework. Figure 4.1 demonstrates the structure of a Symbian OS application.

The structure contains the following classes:

- The **application class** is responsible for setting up and executing the application. It supplies a globally unique 32-bit identifier (UID) which is always associated with the application (both in the build project and at run time). Changing the UID during the lifetime of the project is not advisable since it is used in a number of places through the application source files.

- The **document class** is created by the application class. It usually has strong ownership of application data and is responsible for persisting and internalizing the data. This class also instantiates the application user interface (AppUi) class. It is feasible for the document class not

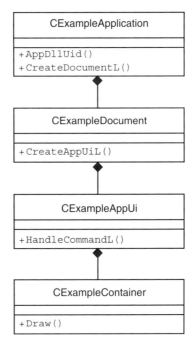

Figure 4.1   Application structure

to implement anything other than creating the application's instance of the AppUi.

- The **application user interface** is used for event handling. The AppUi acts as a global event, and command, handler. It processes key presses and menu selections and can pass these events on to the views and container classes that make up an application. The AppUi is a controller that has no visible presence on the screen.

- **Views and container classes** provide the screens of the application. They are handled by the view architecture. A view is essentially a container class associated with an ID. A particular view can be activated from within the application or from another application by supplying the UID of the application and the ID of the view. For very simple applications, a single container class is used, rather than a view. (See Chapter 6 for more information on views and containers.)

Figure 4.1 shows the minimum number of classes that need to be created to run an application. More classes may be added as the application evolves and other screens or views are needed.

As well as the source files, a fully fledged application includes `.hrh` files, `.rss` application resource files (see Chapter 5) and files for building the application installer package (the SIS file).

Directory Structure

A standard directory structure for your application is recommended, in order to maintain clarity as the application evolves. If we use a common structure for the project we will have at least six folders and a build description file:

- The **application interface** (`/aif`) directory contains two icons and their masks. One icon, a 42 × 29-pixel image, is for the main menu and a larger 44 × 44-pixel icon is for the application's context pane. A resource file is also stored here for the icons.

- The **data** directory holds files that define the specific resources utilized by the application. For applications using Symbian OS v9 and higher, these files address the new security implications.

- The **group** directory holds the resource files for each of the compilers, a UID source file, the `bld.inf` file (which tells the compiler where the project file is) and the project file itself.

- The **include** directory holds the header files, global files and localization files.

- The **install** directory contains the package file (`.pkg`) and Symbian installation file (`.sis`). The package file lists all the resources and files required by the project. When compiled, using the `makesis` command, the installation file is created.

- The **source** directory stores all the source files (`.cpp`) which implement the functionality of the system. Other folders to store graphics and sounds may also be added here.

Project File Structure

In Chapter 3, we briefly looked at the structure of a project file (`.mmp`) for creating a console application. When creating a graphical application, the `.mmp` file is used in the same way but contains additional information to describe the application.

The project file defines all the components that the project requires, source files, bitmap and library files are examples of a view. Consider the following `cardgame.mmp` file:

```
TARGET          CardGame.app
TARGETTYPE      app
UID             0x100039CE 0x0F67D003
TARGETPATH      \system\apps\CardGame
SOURCEPATH      ..\source
SOURCE          CardGameApp.cpp
SOURCE          CardGameAppUi.cpp
SOURCE          CardGameDocument.cpp
SOURCE          CardGameContainer.cpp
SOURCE          cards.cpp
RESOURCE        ..\data\CardGame.rss
RESOURCE        ..\data\CardGame_caption.rss
LANG            SC
USERINCLUDE     ..\include
SYSTEMINCLUDE   . \epoc32\include
LIBRARY         euser.lib apparc.lib cone.lib eikcore.lib eikcoctl.lib
LIBRARY         avkon.lib fbscli.lib eikdlg.lib efsrv.lib estor.lib
AIF             Bacarat.aif ..\aif Bacarataif.rss c8 context_pane_icon.bmp
                context_pane_icon_mask.bmp list_icon.bmp list_icon_mask.bmp
```

- TARGET gives the name of the application including its extension, which is also defined under TARGETTYPE.

- TARGETTYPE gives the extension for the application. In this instance, it is 'app'. This tells the system to build a special DLL with an entry point which, when called, starts the execution of the standard Symbian application class. Applications written for versions of Symbian OS before v9 use the special `.app` DLL. Applications written for versions of Symbian OS from v9 are declared as EXE files with an `.exe` extension. A TARGETTYPE of 'exe' is also used for console applications, unit test code, and for servers and system services. A TARGETTYPE of 'dll' is used to share common code between several applications or to provide an interface for accessing a service.

- UID specifies the identifiers for the application. The first number indicates the type of the DLL (for a Symbian OS application this is always `0x100039CE`). The second number must be unique (if it isn't, your application is not guaranteed to be recognized by the system).

- TARGETPATH defines the location of the built application, which has to be in `\system\apps` in versions of Symbian OS before v9.

- SOURCEPATH is the location of the source file. If you use common project structure described above, it should always be the same.

- Successive SOURCE lines define each source file.

- RESOURCE defines the resource files in the application (usually the files in the `data` directory are defined here).

- LANG defines the languages supported by the application. This two-character code is required as the extension to the resource files.

- USERINCLUDE defines the path for the include directory. For instance, when header files are included within the project, with code such as `#include "cards.h"`, the linker looks here to find out where they are stored.

- LIBRARY is a list of the files that the application uses at run time. For example, if Bluetooth sockets are being used, `Bluetooth.lib` must be included. Unfortunately, not all the names of the libraries are this obvious! (The Symbian Developer Library tells you which libraries to include for a given API, as shown in Figure 4.2.)

- AIF defines the icons and captions used by an application written for versions of Symbian OS before v9. It also has options to specify mime type associations and whether or not the application can be embedded. Applications written for versions of Symbian OS after v9 define the captions and icons in the `.loc` resource script; their ability to be embedded is defined within the `.reg` resource script.

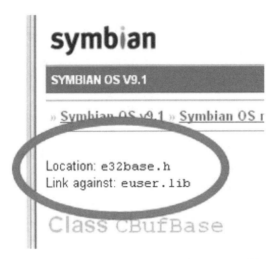

Figure 4.2 Symbian Developer Library showing the library required by an application

In addition, applications written for versions of Symbian OS after v9 can also have a CAPABILITY attribute to indicate permissions that are required in the applications certificate. For example, the following code provides access to local, typically non-chargeable, services, such as Bluetooth:

```
CAPABILITY LocalServices
```

A Developer Certificate Request plugin is available for integration with Carbide.C++ and can be downloaded from ***www.symbian.com***. The plugin enables the creation of a password key file and a developer certificate (a publisher certificate from VeriSign is required for release applications). The plugin produces a certificate request file (`.csr`) which can be used to request a certificate from ***www.symbiansigned.com*** (note that this step requires registration on the site). For development purposes, the certificate is linked to a single IMEI, so a new certificate file must be generated for each phone on which the application is to be tested. Once a certificate file is obtained, the SIS file can be signed using the command-line tools:

```
signsis unsigned_app.sis signed_app.sis DevCert.cer DevCert.key password
```

Remember, the final release version of the application must be certified by Symbian Signed. It can then be installed on any compatible device.

You will have to develop two versions of most applications: one for phones using versions of Symbian OS before v9 and one for phones using versions of Symbian OS v9 and higher.

4.2 Descriptors

Descriptors enable the manipulation of text strings and binary data stored in memory. A descriptor may be stack-, heap- or pointer-based. Strings can also be categorized as modifiable or non-modifiable. This can be slightly daunting at first, so take a look at the descriptor hierarchy in Figure 4.3.

TDesC is a non-modifiable abstract class used as the base class for all descriptors and contains non-modifiable methods. As the class is abstract, it cannot be instantiated; it should, however, be used when passing non-modifiable data to functions. For example, a const TDesC& parameter can be used to provide read-only access to a descriptor's data.

TDes is similar to TDesC as it is also abstract, but it has a maximum length. This allows data to be modified as long as the new descriptor does not exceed this length. This modifiable class contains methods that can edit the descriptor's content.

TPtrC and TPtr are pointer descriptors. The 'C' in TPtrC defines this as constant and, hence, non-modifiable. This pointer has length and address parameters, as shown in Figure 4.4.

TPtr has an additional parameter that indicates how long the descriptor is, allowing modification, as shown in Figure 4.5.

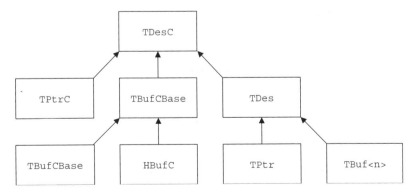

Figure 4.3 Descriptor hierarchy

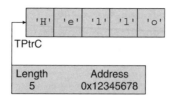

Figure 4.4 `TPtrC` structure

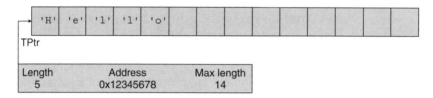

Figure 4.5 `TPtr` structure

As the length of the string is contained in the descriptor, there is no need to include a null terminator.

`HBufC` descriptors are allocated on the heap (notice the prefix letter 'H'). They are used for fixed-length text and binary data descriptors, however the size may not be known until run time. The 'C' indicates that the descriptor is constant and cannot be modified. If modification is required, a pointer to the descriptor should be constructed using the `Des()` method, for example:

```
_LIT(KMessage, "Hello");
HBufC* aMessage = HBufC8::NewL(KMaxItemLength);
aMessage->Des().Append(KMessage);
```

This allocates a new `HBufC` on the heap and adds a temporary variable. `Des()` creates a modifiable pointer descriptor and appends the literal text `KMessage`, which could be a `TBuf` or literal.

To enable a larger string to be used within the descriptor, use `ReAllocL()` to extend the size of the descriptor, instead of allowing overflow and causing a panic:

```
aMessage = aMessage->ReAllocL(25);
```

Heap descriptors can also be constructed using `New()` and `NewLC()`. If a descriptor already exists, the current descriptor can use the `Alloc()`, `AllocL()` and `AllocLC()` methods to assign the new descriptor.

```
TBuf<KMaxLength> temp;
temp.Append(_L("Hello Mum"));
HBufC* hPtr;
hPtr = temp.AllocL();
```

`TBuf` and `TBufC` are modifiable and non-modifiable descriptors, respectively, with an integer size template. These descriptors are best described by their methods.

Non-Modifiable Descriptor Methods

Listed below are a few of the more common `TDesC` and `TBufC` methods. Other methods that allow the manipulation of descriptors without modification can be found in the SDK documentation.

`Alloc()`, `AllocL()` and `AllocLC()` create a new 16-bit heap descriptor that contains a copy of the data. Note the naming conventions, where 'L' states that the function may leave and 'LC' further indicates that if the function does not leave, it pushes a pointer to the descriptor onto the cleanup stack.

`Compare()`, `CompareC()` and `CompareF()` compare two strings and return an integer value. Note that the appended 'C' and 'F' refer to collated and folded comparisons. The return value from the `Compare()` methods is 0 if the two strings are the same. A positive value is returned if the main descriptor is larger than its parameter and a negative value if the main descriptor is smaller.

```
TBufC<KMaxLength> descriptorOne;
descriptorOne = _L("One");
TBufC<KMaxLength> descriptorTwo;
descriptorTwo = _L("Two");
TInt result;
result = descriptorOne.Compare(descriptorTwo);
```

The variable `result` contains −5. Rarely are we interested in the number, just the sign that it returns. Here `"Two"` is greater than `"One"`, therefore a negative is returned.

Find(), FindC() and FindF() search for substrings. They each return an integer value that defines the offset of the first instance of the string's location. If no string is found, KErrNotFound is returned. Strings are always searched from the start. To search from another point, the Left(), Right() and Mid() methods can be used to extract a section of string.

- Left(TInt aLength) returns a TPtrC to the leftmost part of the descriptor.

- Right(TInt aLength) returns a TPtrC to the rightmost part of the descriptor.

- Mid(TInt aPos) returns a TPtrC to a defined section of string, starting from aPos to the end of the string.

- Mid(TInt aPos, TInt aLength) returns a TPtrC to a defined section of string, starting from aPos to the specified length.

Length() returns the number of characters in the string and Size() returns the number of bytes in the descriptor.

Locate(), LocateC() and LocateF() are similar to Find() but search for a single character rather than a string. The position of the first character that is located from the start of the string is returned. For example, the following code returns 1 in result.

```
TBufC<KMaxLength>descriptorOne;
descriptorOne = _L("One");
TChar aChar;
aChar = 'n';
result = descriptorOne.Locate(aChar);
```

LocateReverse() has the same functionality as Locate() but searches from the end of the string. In either case, if no match is found, KErrNotFound is returned.

Operator functions such as !=, <, >, <=, >=, == and [] are overloaded to allow text comparison. These are defined in TDesC. TBufC introduces the = operator, but remember that it is a constant class! It copies and replaces the existing data; therefore one might say it is not 'modifying' the data but replacing it entirely.

```
TBufC<5> descriptorOne;
descriptorOne = _L("One");
```

```
TBufC<5> descriptorTwo;
descriptorTwo = _L("Two");
if (descriptorOne <= descriptorTwo)
    descriptorTwo = descriptorOne;
```

Modifiable Descriptor Methods

TBuf and TPtr descriptors allow modification by the following methods.
Append() allows the addition of a character or a descriptor:

```
TBuf<KMaxLength> aDescriptor;
aDescriptor.Append(_L("Hello"));
```

If the new descriptor and the current contents of aDescriptor are
greater than KMaxLength, the application raises a USER 11 PANIC (even
a copy of the *Hitchhiker's Guide to the Galaxy* won't help). Other types
of Append methods that can be found in the SDK documentation.

Capitalize(), UpperCase() and LowerCase() are self-
explanatory and it is useful to know they exist. Other useful Append
methods can be found in the SDK documentation.

A number of overloaded Copy() methods take a variety of types of
data. This data is copied from source to destination descriptor, replacing
any existing data.

Delete() removes a specified subsection from the string. On execution of the following code, aDescriptor contains "Hello Peace":

```
TBuf<20> aDescriptor;
aDescriptor.Append(_L("Hello World Peace"));
TChar aChar = 'W';
TInt aPos = aDescriptor.Locate(aChar);
TInt aLength = 6;
aDescriptor.Delete(aPos, aLength);
```

A number of Fill() functions allow descriptors to be filled with
characters or zeros.

Format() copies formatted data into the descriptor:

```
aDescriptor.Format(_L("%S\t%S"), aDes1, aDes2);
```

See the SDK documentation for a list of conversion specifiers.

`Num(TInt aNum)` formats the descriptor to the integer parameter. This does not work if the descriptor is already formatted.

The above methods are just a few of the methods that descriptors allow. If you are using Carbide.C++, you can type the variable name and hold down '.' to display a list of possible methods for it.

Note that descriptors need to be linked against `euser.lib` and `estor.lib`. You also need the header files `e32des8.g` and `e32std.h`.

4.3   Literals

Literals provide a simple method of defining strings in a program. They can be defined and used as follows:

```
_LIT(KMyName, "Helen");
TBuf<KMaxItemLength> myName;
myName.Append(KMaxItemLength);
```

Literals are easily changed if they are situated at the top of a `.cpp` file, just like macro definitions. The predecessor to `_LIT` was `_L`; you may see it being used as:

```
myName.Append(_L("Helen"));
```

`_L` can still be used in test programs (non-release versions) where clarity is more important than efficiency but it has now been deprecated as `_LIT` is more efficient. The string supplied to `_LIT` is stored once per unit of compilation (`.cpp` file) unlike the string supplied to `_L`, which is inserted in the code each time it is used. Therefore `_LIT` consumes less memory if the string is used more than once and its use is encouraged by Symbian in creating memory-efficient applications.

4.4   Simple Graphics

Graphics play a major part in achieving an attractive, clear application display. Adding styled text with different fonts and colors can really add a professional feel to the application. We look at formatting text before moving onto richer graphic displays.

Each rectangular area of the screen is owned by a CCoeControl object, generally referred to as a control. A control is responsible for drawing the contents of that area of the screen.

The Draw() method, inherited from CCoeControl, allows access to an area of screen defined by TRect. All CCoeControl-derived classes have a Draw() function, which can be overwritten in the derived class. A control needs a window to draw to and the correct window is set up during ConstructL(). You need to include coecontrol.h and link against cone.lib.

As an example, here is a new class derived from CCoeControl which draws to an area of the screen:

```
class CStartContainer : public CCoeControl
  {
  public:
    CStartContainer();
    ~CStartContainer();
  private:
    void ConstructL(const TRect& aRect);
    // from CCoeControl
    void Draw(const TRect& aRect) const;
  };
```

The basic class declaration has a default constructor, a destructor and a second-phase constructor, ConstructL(). Draw() is inherited from CCoeControl to enable drawing to the screen.

ConstructL() needs to be passed the size of the window, the control, that the application can access. Usually this is the client area, which can be accessed through ClientRect(). Figure 4.6 shows the areas we are accessing.

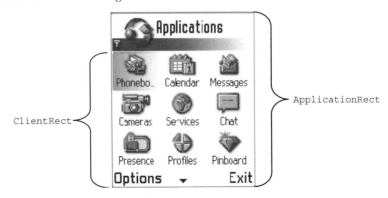

Figure 4.6 Screen areas

Passing `AppUi()->ApplicationRect()` to `ConstructL()` allows access to all of the screen, including the context pane. Of course, you can use a customized size, `TRect`, thus allowing other `Draw()` methods to access separate sections of the screen. `ConstructL()` needs three methods to allow control of the screen:

```
void CStartContainer::ConstructL(const TRect& aRect)
  {
  CreateWindowL();
  SetRect(aRect);
  ActivateL();
  }
```

- `CreateWindowL()` creates the control window

- `SetRect()` sets the control's extents to the size of `TRect`

- `ActivateL()` informs the framework that it may access the screen, once the control has been set.

In order to draw to the screen, a graphics context must be fetched. All drawing (i.e. texts, lines or shapes) is done through a graphics context, `CWindowGc`.

```
void CStartContainer::Draw(const TRect& aRect) const
  {
  CWindowGc& gc = SystemGc();
  gc.Clear(aRect);
  ...
  }
```

`SystemGc()` returns the standard graphics context to the `gc` variable. The control area is then cleared before any updates to the screen are made.

`Draw()` has a specific contract with the application framework: it is constant and it must not leave. This means that you cannot create a dynamic element within `Draw()` and you cannot alter the state of any data.

The best way to look at this is to consider what happens if you call `Draw()` twice in succession (without any calls in between). What is drawn to the screen should be identical in each call. Note that we use

`DrawNow()`, which is implemented by `CCoeControl` and calls the `Draw()` function itself.

Writing Text

The theory of writing text to the screen is pretty simple but the formatting can become a nuisance.

```
_LIT(KExampleText, "Chocolate Cake"));
gc.DrawText(KExampleText, TPoint(80,40));
```

The position parameter is relative to the control, so `TPoint(0,0)` is the top left corner of the screen of which we have control. The position may vary on different devices so be careful when hard-coding positions such as `TPoint`. Luckily there are a number of functions, such as `CGraphicsContext::ECenter`, which center the text depending on the size of the screen. Other useful techniques include changing the color and font of the text.

To change the color of the text, use:

```
gc.SetPenColor(KRgbRed);
```

There are a number of colors predefined as `TRgb` parameters:

- `KRgbBlack`
- `KRgbDarkGreen`
- `KRgbDarkMagenta`
- `KRgbGreen`
- `KRgbMagenta`
- `KRgbWhite`

- `KRgbDarkGray`
- `KRgbDarkYellow`
- `KRgbDarkCyan`
- `KRgbYellow`
- `KRgbCyan`

- `KRgbDarkRed`
- `KRgbDarkBlue`
- `KRgbRed`
- `KRgbBlue`
- `KRgbGray`

It is useful to know how to create custom `TRgb` colors to allow an extended color scheme. The `TRgb` constructor takes three parameters: red, green and blue values represented as numbers between 0 and 255. This can be constructed as a hexadecimal number: `TRgb(0x00112387)` or by using the separate components, `TRgb(50, 50, 0)`. There are also methods to alter the color, such as `SetRed()`; to set a grayscale level, such as `Gray16()`; and to alter the number of colors.

To change the font:

```
const CFont* font = iEikonEnv->AnnotationFont();
gc.UseFont(font);
```

There are a number of predefined fonts available:

Annotation Font
Title Font
Legend Font
Symbol Font
Dense Font

To return to normal font:

```
gc.UseFont(iCoeEnv->NormalFont());
```

Remember, once you have finished using a font, call:

```
gc.DiscardFont();
```

Layout of elements on a variable size screen with variable fonts is a complex task. One option is to move away from direct drawing functions and use a `CRichText` class (as described in the section on text editors). This allows much easier formatting and the insertion of images.

Drawing Shapes

As we have seen with text, the `gc` pen can be used to change color. The style and size of the pen can also be changed and used to draw shapes. The following code sets the pen style to dash and the size of the dash to `aSize`:

```
gc.SetPenStyle(CGraphicsContext::EDashedPen);
gc.SetPenSize(aSize);
```

The `TPenStyle` enumeration defines the following types of pen:

- `ENullPen`
- `ESolidPen`

- `EDottedPen`

- `EDashedPen`

- `EDotDashPen`

- `EDotDotDashPen`

The size of the pen is determined by a `TSize(width, height)`, measured in pixels. To draw a line, two `TPoints` need to be defined for start and finish:

```
gc.DrawLine(aPoint, bPoint);
```

Rectangles can be drawn in a similar way using `DrawRect()`:

```
gc.DrawRect(rect);
```

where `rect` may be the `TRect` parameter passed to the Draw function, or an instance of `TRect` which can be manipulated by methods such as `Shrink()`.

The pen is used to outline shapes and text. You need the brush to fill areas. The brush has a `TBrushStyle` parameter, which can be set by using `SetBrushStyle()`. The color of the brush can be set using `SetBrushColor()`.

Other shape methods, such as `DrawEllipse()` and `DrawPolygon()`, are defined. They are filled using the brush and outlined using the pen.

Using Text Editors

A text editor provides a means of displaying formatted text on the screen. S60 on Symbian OS supports three types of text editor: plain, global and rich text. Other editors, such as numeric, secretive and date editors, are also available. We start by looking at the plain-text editor, as this is the basis for the global and rich-text editors.

Plain-text editor

Plain-text editors use an Edwin control that allows unformatted text to be written to the screen. One use of a plain-text editor is for creating

Figure 4.7   Plain-text editor

customized forms, where each input is a separate control. Each editor
is manipulated in the same way as the Edwin control, allowing them
to be displayed on screen at the same time and handled individually.
The screen in Figure 4.7 shows two plain-text editors, each with separate
resources.

Before continuing to look at implementing a plain-text editor, it must
be noted that the Edwin resource is discontinued from S60 SDKs for
Symbian OS v7.0s, so you should not use it in applications targeting
Symbian OS v7.0s onwards.

The easiest method of implementing a plain-text editor is through a
resource. We can define this in the resource file:

```
RESOURCE EDWIN r_basic_edwin
  {
  flags = EAknEditorFlagDefault;
  width = 10;
  lines = 1;
  maxlength = 60;
  allowed_input_modes =
      EaknEditorTextInputMode|EAknEditorNumericInputMode;
  default_input_mode = EAknEditorTextInputMode;
  numeric_keymap = EAknEditorPlainNumberModeKeymap;
  avkon_flags = EAknEditorFlagNoT9;
  default_case = EAknEditorLowerCase;
  allowed_case_modes = EAknEditorUpperCase|EAknEditorLowerCase;
  special_character_table = R_AVKON_URL_SPECIAL_CHARACTER_TABLE_DIALOG;
  }
```

The Edwin structure has a number of fields that define the behavior of the resource. All the predefined numbers can be found in uikon.hrh.

- flags are used to define the action of the dialog.

- width is the actual length of the editor on screen, in characters.

- lines defines the number of lines the editor uses; Figure 4.7 shows two editors, the first with one line and the second with five lines.

- maxlength is the maximum number of characters allowed in the editor.

- allowed_input_modes defines the types of input allowed, such as text, numeric, or both. If more than one input mode is defined, default_input_mode declares the default.

- numeric_keymap sets the keymap to be used when the editor is in numeric mode.

- avkon_flags can be used to help the user input data in a certain manner (e.g., using predictive input).

- default_case and allowed_case_modes define whether the input is to be in upper or lower case.

- special_character_table is used if unusual characters are needed, for example, to allow entry of a URL.

Note that not all of the fields are required for the resource to be functional. A simple resource could be defined:

```
RESOURCE EDWIN r_numeric_edwin
  {
  flags = EAknEditorFlagDefault;
  width = 10;
  lines = 1;
  maxlength = 15;
  allowed_input_modes = EAknEditorNumericInputMode;
  default_input_mode = EAknEditorNumericInputMode;
  }
```

The editor can now be created from the resource. This requires the inclusion of barsread.h for the resource reader and eikedwin.h for the Edwin resource.

```
TResourceReader reader;
iCoeEnv->CreateResourceReaderLC(reader, R_BASIC_EDWIN);
iEdwinTitle = new(ELeave) CEikEdwin;
iEdwinTitle->SetContainerWindowL(*this);
iEdwinTitle->ConstructFromResourceL(reader);
CleanupStack::PopAndDestroy();
```

TResourceReader provides a means of interpreting the Edwin editor defined in the resource file. CCoeEnv provides a way to set the resource file through CreateResourceReaderLC(). This method puts a pointer to the resource reader onto the cleanup stack. The next step is to create and construct the Edwin editor itself, using the new(ELeave) method. The focus of the Edwin control is then set to this class using SetContainerWindowL(), with a pointer to the container class. The control then uses the resource reader to construct the Edwin resource so that it can be used. Remember to pop the reader from the cleanup stack once the editor has been constructed.

SetExtent() can be used to set the position of the editor on screen:

```
iEdwinTitle->SetExtent(TPoint(10,10), iEdwinTitle->MinimumSize());
```

where TPoint(10, 10) refers to a set of co-ordinates, in pixels, from the top left corner of the screen control and MinimumSize() is called to allow the framework to take the size of the control into consideration. If MinimumSize() is not called, no space is allocated to the control and the caption does not appear.

If a number of controls are being used in the same container, SetFocus() can be used to determine which control is in view (focus). SetFocus() can be used alongside an event handler to move the focus from control to control, determined by key events. For example:

```
TKeyResponse CRecipeEditorView::OfferKeyEventL
                         (const TKeyEvent& aKeyEvent, TEventCode aType)
  {
  if (aType == EEventKeyDown)
    {
    switch (aKeyEvent.iScanCode)
      {
      case EStdKeyUpArrow:
        if (iEdwinTitle->IsFocused())
          {
          iEdwinTitle->SetFocus(EFalse);
          iEdwinDescription->SetFocus(ETrue);
```

```
        return EKeyWasConsumed;
      }
    ...
      }
    }
  }
```

Using an OfferKeyEventL() method to trap key events, we can check the navigation key events. If an Up event is caught, we can set the focus of the Edwin (and the cursor) to the other control. Obviously, there can be more controls on the screen, which involves a little more logic when handling the focus.

Rich-text editor

A global editor is a stepping stone between a plain-text editor and a rich-text editor. It adds inclusive formatting, such as paragraphs. However, if you need a text editor for formatted text, you may as well use a rich-text editor.

The CRichTextEditor class provides the functionality to format paragraphs of text, allowing font, color and size attributes to be set. A rich-text editor allows objects such as pictures to be embedded in line with the text. Figure 4.8 shows some of these facilities.

As with the plain-text editor, we start by defining the editor as a resource:

```
RESOURCE RTXTED r_richtexteditor
  {
  width = 176;
  height = 180;
  textlimit = 500;
  flags = EEikEdwinReadOnly | EEikEdwinAvkonDisableCursor;
  avkon_flags = EAknEditorFlagEnableScrollBars;
  }
```

Most of the field names are familiar from the definition of the plain-text editor, however the resource is of the type RTXTED, which adds a textlimit field.

The easiest way to encapsulate all the rich text functionality is by writing our own class that inherits from CEikRichTextEditor. This provides lots of public member functions which can be accessed to change the formatting and content.

Figure 4.8   Rich-text editor

We now need to design the class. Do we want the option to make the fonts bold or underlined? Are these actions to be performed together or separately? These are decisions that are made by the designer.

Here we implement a basic, portable rich-text-editor class that can be used in various applications. First, as usual, two header files need to be included:

- `eikrted.h` provides the `CCEikRichTextEditor` (from which we inherit the class)

- `txtfrmat.h` enables formatting by accessing `TCharFormatMask`.

The editor is constructed from the resource that we defined above, using a `TResourceReader` to read the resource. `SetFocus()` is set to `ETrue`: the whole class is in effect a control, so focus is set to the class.

The position of the cursor changes in a response to a key event, for example, specific keys may move pages up and down. Cursor position can also be changed directly by the application. `CEikRichTextEditor` provides a `MoveCursorL()` method, which can be used to move the cursor to a new position or page.

```
TKeyResponse CRTextEditor::OfferKeyEventL(const TKeyEvent& aKeyEvent,
                                          TEventCode aType)
  {
  if (aType == EEventKey)
    {
    if (aKeyEvent.iCode == EKeyDownArrow)
      {
```

```
    MoveCursorL(TCursorPosition::EFLineDown, EFalse);
    return EKeyWasConsumed;
    }
  else if (aKeyEvent.iCode == EKeyUpArrow)
    {
    MoveCursorL(TCursorPosition::EFLineUp, EFalse);
    return EKeyWasConsumed;
    }
  else
    return CEikRichTextEditor::OfferKeyEventL(aKeyEvent, aType);
  }
return EKeyWasNotConsumed;
}
```

The event handler takes a key event and code and uses the `if` statement to determine which key was pressed. `MoveCursorL()` takes a `TCursorPosition`, which indicates the position and manner in which to move the cursor. The `TCursorPosition` is a `TMovementType` enumeration as defined in Table 4.1.

Table 4.1 `TMovementType` enumerations

TMovementType	Description
EFLeft	Cursor moves a single character to the left
EFRight	Cursor moves a single character to the right
EFLineUp	Moves the cursor up a line
EFLineDown	Moves the cursor down a line
EFPageUp	Moves the cursor up a page
EFPageDown	Moves the cursor down a page
EFLineBeg	Moves cursor to start of line
EFLineEnd	Moves cursor to end of line
EFNoMovement	No cursor movement

The second parameter for `MoveCursorL()` determines whether the text between the old and new cursor positions is selected: `EFalse` means it is not selected and ETrue means it is selected. If the editor uses the event, it returns EKeyWasConsumed to ensure the event is not re-handled elsewhere in the application otherwise it returns EKeyWasNotConsumed so that the event can be handled.

Adding text requires the use of a CRichText object, which allows the formatting of every character (if you need that level of granularity). Theoretically it works on 'paragraphs', chunks of text passed to its InsertL() method. Styles are also supported and these are a collection of character- and paragraph-formatting attributes. Note that the style is applied to the whole paragraph, not to single characters, although the style may alter character attributes. Object embedding is also permitted, which allows the use of inserted pictures (discussed towards the end of this section).

```
void CRTextEditor::AddTextL(const TDesC& aText)
  {
  CRichText* richText = RichText();
  TInt documentLength = richText->DocumentLength();
  richText->InsertL(documentLength, aText);
  richText->ApplyCharFormatL(iCharFormat, iCharFormatMask,
                          documentLength, aText.Length());
  HandleTextChangedL();
  }
```

An AddTextL() method receives a text descriptor (the text that is added to the editor). An instance of the rich-text editor is created so that we can access methods to insert the text into the editor. DocumentLength() returns the position of the last character, plus one, in the editor. This is used as the position to add the new text. The text is then inserted into the editor and any formatting attributes are applied (we will see how to do this next). HandleTextChangedL() updates the screen so that the user can see the change.

In a similar manner we can add a carriage return to the text using CEditableText::ELineBreak.

```
void CRTextEditor::AddCarriageReturnL()
  {
  CRichText* richText = RichText();
  richText->InsertL(richText->DocumentLength(), EditableText::ELineBreak);
  }
```

The formatting of attributes is performed using a TCharFormat and TCharFormatMask. The TCharFormat is used to save the values of the attributes, such as bold, italic and color. `TCharFormatMask` is used to specify which attributes are relevant at that time. For example:

```
void CRTextEditor::SetUnderlineOn(TBool aOn)
  {
  iCharFormatMask.SetAttrib(EAttFontUnderline);
  if (aOn)
    iCharFormat.iFontPresentation.iUnderline = EUnderlineOn;
  else
    iCharFormat.iFontPresentation.iUnderline = EUnderlineOff;
  }
```

`SetUnderlineOn()` takes a Boolean value: if `ETrue`, the underline is turned on and, if `EFalse`, the underline is turned off. The attribute stays with its value throughout the duration of the editor, unless this function is called again.

The character format mask defines the attribute which is to be changed, in this instance `EAttFontUnderline`. Note that `TTextFormatAttribute`, found in `txtfrmat.h`, defines all the attributes. The character format can then use `iFontPresentation` to access the attribute and assign it a new value.

This same method is used to set the font to italic, to bold, or to a specific color:

```
iCharFormatMask.SetAttrib(EAttFontPosture);
iCharFormat.iFontSpec.iFontStyle.SetPosture(EPostureItalic);

iCharFormatMask.SetAttrib(EAttFontStrokeWeight);
iCharFormat.iFontSpec.iFontStyle.SetStrokeWeight(EStrokeWeightBold);

iCharFormatMask.SetAttrib(EAttColor);
iCharFormat.iFontPresentation.iTextColor = aColor;
```

To clear the screen (and the contents of the editor), use the `DeleteL()` method. This takes a start and end point between which the text is deleted, so we can delete small sections of text or all of it.

```
void CRTextEditor::ClearAllL()
  {
  CRichText* richText = RichText();
  richText->DeleteL(0, richText->DocumentLength());
  }
void CRTextEditor::DeleteSection(TInt startPos, TInt endPos)
  {
```

```
CRichText* richText = RichText();
richText->DeleteL(startPos, endPos);
}
```

The editor object is usually paired with an application-specific class which controls the Edwin and filters key events. To allow the editor to be seen, its window needs to be set to the window of the containing class:

```
CRTextEditor* iEditor;
Editor = CRTextEditor::NewL();
iEditor->SetContainerWindowL(*this);
```

To add text to the editor use `AddTextL()`. If any formatting is required, the formatting methods should be called prior to `AddTextL()`. Figure 4.9 shows an example of the effects of text formatting on the screen. The code clears the screen and writes a name in black, with bold and underline set. On the following line, a description is written in italic.

Adding a picture

Pictures are represented by a `CPicture` object that can be used by an `RTextEditor`. `CPicture` is an abstract class that provides a `Draw()` method to draw the picture and a number of virtual functions to handle the picture. To start, we need to implement a new class that inherits from `CPicture` so we can implement these virtual functions.

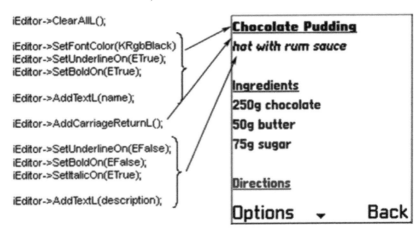

Figure 4.9 Formatted recipe for chocolate pudding

```
class CEditorPicture : public CPicture
  {
public:
  CEditorPicture(TSize aSize, CFbsBitmap& aBitmap);
  TBool LineBreakPossible(TUint aClass, TBool aBeforePicture,
                                TBool aHaveSpaces) const;
  void Draw(CGraphicsContext& aGc, const TPoint& aTopLeft,
      const TRect& Rect, MGraphicsDeviceMap* aMap) const;
  void ExternalizeL(RWriteStream& aStream) const;
  void SetOriginalSizeInTwips(TSize aSize);
  void GetOriginalSizeInTwips(TSize& aSize) const;
protected:
  CFbsBitmap* iBitmap;
  TSize iSize;
  };
```

The constructor, CEditorPicture() takes a bitmap and its size, and assigns them to the local variables, iBitmap and iSize, respectively.

LineBreakPossible() returns a Boolean value to determine if a line break is possible before or after the picture. It defaults to ETrue, allowing line breaks, although this can be overwritten here.

ExternalizeL() sends the picture to a stream; this must be implemented in the derived class, however its implementation is not needed.

'Twips' are device-independent units (not pixels) that are defined as being 1/1440 of an inch. The Get and Set methods for the size in twips are used to return and assign the size of the bitmap (however we have already initialized this in the construction). For example, on a Nokia 7610, a 1000 × 1000 twip picture is approximately 70 × 70 pixels.

The Draw() function is practically the only part to which we need give any thought. It is a virtual function inherited from CPicture and must be implemented, even though we do not call it explicitly.

```
void CEditorPicture::Draw(CGraphicsContext& aGc,
                  const TPoint& aTopLeft,
                      const TRect& aRect,
              MGraphicsDeviceMap* aMap) const
  {
  TRect bitmapRect = Map->TwipsToPixels(TRect(TPoint(), iSize));
  bitmapRect.Move(aTopLeft);
  aGc.Reset();
  aGc.SetClippingRect(aRect);
  aGc.DrawBitmap(bitmapRect, iBitmap);
  }
```

The purpose of `Draw()` is to draw the area represented by the rectangle using the graphics context supplied. The graphics context is usually the screen, but it could be an off-screen bitmap or even a printer. It creates a `TRect`, `bitmapRect`, and assigns it the size of the bitmap. This is then moved to the position that was passed to `Draw()` through the framework. The graphics context, `gc`, is then cleared before drawing the bitmap to the screen. The amount of the bitmap to be drawn on screen is defined by `SetClippingRect()`.

This class now needs to be included into the rich-text editor class so that we can add a picture to our editor. A new method is needed to add the picture:

```
void CRTextEditor::InsertMyPictureL(CFbsBitmap* myBitmap)
  {
  CMyPicture* picture;
  picture = new(ELeave) CMyPicture(TSize(1000,1000), *myBitmap);
  CleanupStack::PushL(picture);
  TPictureHeader header;
  header.iPicture = TSwizzle<CPicture>(picture);
  CRichText* richText = RichText();
  TInt documentLength = richText->DocumentLength();
  richText->InsertL(documentLength, header);
  CleanupStack::Pop();
  }
```

First, we create an instance of the picture class which draws the image. This takes a size parameter and a pointer to the bitmap to draw. Note that the rich-text-editor class has ownership of the picture, so we must call `Pop()` on the cleanup stack once ownership has been transferred.

An interface to the picture is provided through `TPictureHeader` which is used to hold the type, size and stream ID of the picture. We can use its public member variable `iPicture` to store a pointer to the picture which can be added to the editor, in the same way we would add text using `InsertL()`. `iPicture` is a 'swizzle' storing either the ID of the stream in which the picture is stored or a pointer to the internalized picture. `TSwizzle` is a template class used to define the type of object that the swizzle represents. The `TPictureHeader` can now be inserted into the rich-text editor using `InsertL()`. Finally, the picture is popped from the cleanup stack.

4.5   Bitmap Images

An S60 phone uses the Symbian OS image conversion library (ICL) to support many image formats such as Jpeg and Gif, but within an application a standard Symbian bitmap file is usually used for icons and simple graphics. One or more bitmaps may be packaged as a multiple bitmap file (.mbm) which is built as part of the application, providing easy access to the images.

During the build an .mbg file is generated, which holds enumerated values for each image that can be used within the program. There are a couple of different ways to generate the .mbm file: either by defining it in the project's .mmp file or by generating it using a command-line tool to define the number of bitmaps and the names of the files to generate. Our preference is to use the traditional approach of the .mmp as it is included in the correct directory, with the correct name, from the start. The generated .mbm file should have been created in the emulator's z:\ directory, but it is worth checking that it is in the correct directory.

Defining the .mbm file is simple. Consider the code below:

```
START BITMAP    menuicons.mbm
HEADER
TARGETPATH      \system\apps\cookbook
SOURCEPATH      ..\bitmaps
SOURCE C12      icon1.bmp
SOURCE C12      icon1_mask.bmp
SOURCE C12      icon2.bmp
SOURCE C12      icon2.bmp_mask.bmp
SOURCE C8       last.bmp
END
```

START BITMAP defines the name of the .mbm file to be generated. TARGETPATH and SOURCEPATH define where the .mbm file is to be saved and where to find the bitmaps, respectively. Each SOURCE line defines a bitmap and C12 defines it as having 12 colors. The last.bmp file is a 1-pixel dummy image. It is handy when all the images need to be displayed on screen as it allows us to loop through the enumerations, using the last bitmap as a stop point.

As for creating the bitmaps and their masks, this is up to you. Some bitmaps do not require masks. For example, a full-screen title page on start-up does not need a mask as it fills the entire screen, however smaller, more intricate images require masking to prevent a background color being shown around the edges.

There are many different ways of manipulating graphics within a program, from drawing simple text on the screen, using the Draw() method, to drawing full screen bitmaps or icons with masks. We noted that rich-text editors allow pictures to be inserted.

The Draw() method handles the drawing of bitmaps, in the same way as described in Section 4.4. To manipulate graphics with the Draw() method, create a variable with a handle to the system graphics context.

The CFbsBitmap class allows the loading, drawing and manipulation of bitmaps. The Load() method takes the file name and the name of the bitmap. The name is enumerated in the generated .mbg file (remember to include it in the .cpp file). KMbmFileName contains the full path and file name for the bitmap:

```
_LIT(KMbmFileName, "c:\\system\\apps\\cookbook\\StartUp.mbm");
```

Note that, while working on the emulator, different folders may be used to store the .mbm file. This may require you to copy the .mbm file into the current emulator's SDK folder so that the images can be displayed on screen.

Firstly, we need to create a new instance of the bitmap using

```
CFbsBitmap* iBitmap;
iBitmap = new(ELeave) CFbsBitmap;
```

We now have a CFbsBitmap object which we can manipulate. However, iBitmap currently does not hold a bitmap image, so we need to load one. The Load() method takes two parameters: the full path and file name where the .mbm file is stored (KMbmFilename) and the bitmap to load. The bitmap to load is denoted by an enumeration in the .mbg file, which should be included in the source file. On completion of Load(), an integer value is returned. If this is KErrNone, the load has been successful and the bitmap can be drawn to screen using DrawBitmap(), otherwise it is likely that the compiler cannot navigate to the bitmap and you should check your file and path names.

```
TInt err = iBitmap->Load(KMbmFilename, EBitmapOne);
  if (err == KErrNone)
```

```
{
gc.DrawBitmap(aRect, iBitmap);
}
```

Bitmaps can be resized and altered once loaded in the program. The following code returns the current size of the bitmap:

```
TSize aSize = iBitmap->SizeInPixels();
```

We cannot manipulate the `TSize` object either by directly changing its height and width values through the public member variables `iHeight` and `iWidth` or by using `SetSize()`. Once the new size has been determined, the bitmap can be resized using `Resize()`.

```
if (KErrNone == iBitmap->Resize(aSize))
```

Saving the bitmap is a trivial process made easy by the `Save()` method. To save a bitmap, call `Save(KMbmFileName)` using the full path name and bitmap name. It replaces any existing bitmap with this name.

Drawing large bitmaps to screen is all well and good but if a small bitmap is needed in an area that includes other bitmaps or controls, will the images overlap? To make this a little easier to understand, look at Figure 4.10a. The rectangle outline marks the area that will be drawn on the screen; if this was drawn on a colored background, a white outline would be present.

Masking allows certain sections of an image to be displayed rather than the whole rectangle. Creating a mask is simple. The area that is to be visible should be filled in with a single block color (black is common). The image should be saved as a monochrome bitmap as shown in Figure 4.10b.

To draw a masked bitmap, both the bitmap and its mask need to be loaded as `CFbsBitmaps`. `BitBltMasked` is used to draw the masked bitmap. It takes a number of parameters:

- `TPoint` – position of the top left corner of the bitmap
- `CFbsBitmap*` – the bitmap

Figure 4.10 a. Bitmap image b. Bitmap mask

- `TRect` – how much of the bitmap is to be drawn (if a full screen bitmap is to be displayed, use `aRect` that is passed to `Draw()`).

- `CFbsBitmap*` – the bitmap mask

- `TBool` – determines the mask color: `EFalse` indicates that the masked section is Black and `ETrue` if it is white.

```
TInt err = iBitmap->Load(KMbmFilename, EMbmIconsSelect);
if (err == KErrNone)
  {
  CFbsBitmap* maskBitmap = new(ELeave) CFbsBitmap();
  CleanupStack::PushL(maskBitmap);
  User::LeaveIfError(maskBitmap->Load(KMbmFilename,
                        EMbmIconsSelect_mask));
  gc.BitBltMasked(selectionPosition, iBitmap, aRect, maskBitmap, EFalse);
  CleanupStack::PopAndDestroy();
  }
```

4.6 Observer Mixin Classes

In the previous section, we have considered the display of bitmap images. The standard image format supported by Symbian is bitmap images stored in the proprietary multiple bitmap format. It is often necessary to store images in alternative formats, for example as a compressed Jpeg image format to save file size or to provide compatibility with other applications. Image conversion is carried out using an asynchronous object. In order to carry messages back to the main application when the asynchronous task is completed, we must use a mixin class.

Mixin classes are intended to be inherited along with a concrete class. Generally, mixins consist of virtual functions that must be implemented by the developer. The mixin class provides a mechanism for requiring the implementation of specific functions. In the case of asynchronous objects, the mixin class is usually given a name that ends with the word `Observer` or `Handler`, indicating that the class provides functions that are watching for a particular event and can broadcast the changes, for example, an asynchronous event.

In this example, we look at the `CMdaImageFileToBitmapUtility` class which is provided to convert image files into bitmaps in memory. There are other related classes, not least of which is the `CMdaImageBitmapToFileUtility`. Note that this class is deprecated from Symbian OS v7.0 to be replaced with the `CImageEncoder` class, which performs in a similar manner but allows for image conversion tasks to be carried out in their own threads.

In order for this example to work, two libraries must be included into the .mmp file: MediaClientImage.lib provides the functionality for the utility class and fbscli.lib is necessary for the bitmap object itself. You need to create a basic GUI application, stripped down to a minimal application.

The mixin class that is necessary for providing the callback functions is called MMdaImageUtilObserver and it should be inherited by the container class. This requires the implementation of three functions:

```
void MiuoConvertComplete(TInt aError);
void MiuoCreateComplete(TInt aError);
void MiuoOpenComplete(TInt aError);
```

The names are fairly straightforward to understand: Miuo stands for MDA image utility observer and the three functions are called when the Convert, Create, and Open operations are completed, respectively. In fact, there are no Create functions for file to bitmap conversion and so an empty implementation is all that is required for the MiuoCreateComplete() method.

Finally, we need to add member variables to the class: a pointer to a CMdaImageFileToBitmapUtility object; a pointer to a CFbsBitmap object; and two Boolean variables to flag up whether or not the image has been loaded and if there was any error loading the bitmap. The modified class declaration is shown below:

```
class CBitmapConversionExampleContainer : public CCoeControl,
                                    public MMdaImageUtilObserver
  {
 public:
   void ConstructL(const TRect& aRect);
   ~CBitmapConversionExampleContainer();
 private:
   void SizeChanged();
   void Draw(const TRect& aRect) const;
   void MiuoConvertComplete(TInt aError);
   void MiuoCreateComplete(TInt aError);
   void MiuoOpenComplete(TInt aError);
 private:
   CMdaImageFileToBitmapUtility* iBitmapUtility;
   CFbsBitmap* iBitmap;
   TBool iBitmapLoaded;
   TBool iBitmapError;
  };
```

The implementation is relatively straightforward. First, we need to provide a path to a Jpeg image:

```
_LIT(KImageLocation, "c:\\symbian\\images\\sunset.jpg");
```

Note that this path is relative to the phone's C drive, not the computer's C drive. In the second-phase constructor, we must initialize the Boolean flag to false to tell the application that the image is not yet loaded, create a new instance of the bitmap class and a new instance of the bitmap conversion utility, passing the location of the container class as a reference to the mixin observer instance, that is, telling the utility object where to find the callback methods.

Finally, we start the first of the asynchronous operations by calling the OpenL() method of the utility class. For images, such as Jpegs, that store an image-type identifier within the file, only the image file name is necessary as the utility class detects the correct codec type. When OpenL() completes, the mixin observer's callback method, MiuoOpen-Complete(), is called.

```
void CBitmapConversionExampleContainer::ConstructL(const TRect& aRect)
    {
    CreateWindowL();
    SetRect(aRect);
    ActivateL();
    iBitmapLoaded = EFalse;
    iBitmapError = EFalse;
    iBitmap = new(ELeave) CFbsBitmap;
    iBitmapUtility = CMdaImageFileToBitmapUtility::NewL(*this);
    iBitmapUtility->OpenL(KImageLocation);
    }
```

The callback method checks to see if there were any errors, in which case the IBitmapError flag is set to ETrue, otherwise a new bitmap is created.

The FrameInfo() method of the utility class is used to retrieve the image file parameters, returning a TFrameInfo object. If the bitmap is created successfully, ConvertL() is called (note that, since MiuoOpen-Complete() is a non-leaving function, any errors must be trapped here) and passes a pointer to the target bitmap:

```
void CBitmapConversionExampleContainer::MiuoOpenComplete(TInt aError)
    {
    if (aError == KErrNone)
```

```
    {
    TFrameInfo frameInfo;
    iBitmapUtility->FrameInfo(0, frameInfo);
    Tint err = iBitmap->Create(frameInfo.iOverallSizeInPixels, EColor64K);
    if (err != KErrNone)
        {
        Tint error;
        TRAP(error, iBitmapUtility->ConvertL(*iBitmap));
        if (error != KErrNone)
            {
            iBitmapLoaded = EFalse;
            iBitmapError = ETrue;
            }
        }
    else
        {
        iBitmapLoaded = EFalse;
        iBitmapError = ETrue;
        }
    }
else
    {
    iBitmapError = ETrue;
    }
}
```

When `ConvertL()` completes, it calls the `MiuoConvertComplete()` method. If there are no errors, then the Boolean flag is set to true, and the `DrawNow()` method is called to refresh the screen:

```
void CBitmapConversionExampleContainer::MiuoConvertComplete(TInt aError)
    {
    if (aError != KErrNone)
        {
        iBitmapLoaded = EFalse;
        iBitmapError = ETrue;
        }
    else
        {
        iBitmapLoaded = ETrue;
        iBitmapError = EFalse;
        DrawNow();
        }
    }
```

Finally, the `Draw()` method is where we draw the image to the screen. If there has been no error in loading the image or the image has not been loaded yet (for example, when the application first opens), then the screen is cleared. For simplicity, if there is an error, the screen remains blank,

Figure 4.11   Displayed Jpeg image

although one might wish to post an error message. If all goes well, the image is displayed (stretched or shrunk to fill the screen):

```
void CBitmapConversionExampleContainer::Draw(const TRect& aRect) const
  {
  CWindowGc& gc = SystemGc();
  if (iBitmapError)
    {
    ; // display error message here
    }
  else if (iBitmapLoaded)
    gc.DrawBitmap(aRect, iBitmap);
  else
    gc.Clear();
  }
```

The final result is shown in Figure 4.11.

4.7   Handling User Input

There are a number of ways a user can interact with a mobile phone. Figure 4.12 shows some of the possible input methods.

The obvious inputs are through the keys on the phone, which are referred to as key presses. These can be broken down into three sub-sections: the keypad (which holds 0–9, * and #), the soft keys and the

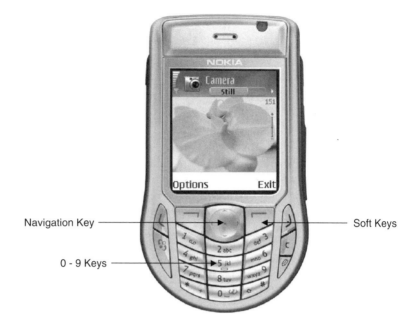

Figure 4.12   User input

navigation key. The keypad can be used for numeric and text input. The soft keys can be used for opening menus, selecting menu options and exiting applications. The navigation key allows the cursor to be moved and a click on it acts like a selection or OK press.

If we think a little more widely, there are other ways a user can enter information into the phone. A mobile phone is designed for telephony and, hence, speech is the main input. Recent developments are seeing new speech-activated applications, which are sure to be popular. Infrared and Bluetooth technologies allow input and output from the mobile device.

In this section, we look at basic user input (the interesting Bluetooth development is discussed in Chapter 7).

Key Presses

To get the chance to handle key presses, we need to derive a class from `CoeControl`, which provides a virtual method, `OfferKeyEventL()`. This should be implemented to match handled key presses and is called by the framework when an event occurs. You must inherit the class from `CoeControl` and define the `OfferKeyEventL()` method.

```
#include <coecntrl.h>
class CKeyPressContainer : public CCoeControl, MCoeControlObserver
  {
  ...
  TKeyResponse OfferKeyEventL(const TKeyEvent& aKeyEvent,
                                   TEventCode aType);

  ...
  }
```

When this method is called by the framework, it can either process the event or ignore it. For each instance, the framework can be informed of what is happening by returning a `TkeyResponse`: `EKeyWasNotConsumed` if the event was ignored and `EKeyWasConsumed` if action was taken. This allows other controls to handle the event, or not if the event was consumed. When a key event occurs, the `OfferKeyEventL()` methods of all of the controls on the stack are called.

The first check determines the type of key event: key up, key down or standard key press. The code below looks only at the standard key presses. `EKeyWasNotConsumed` is returned if the event is not the type we are concerned with.

```
TKeyResponse CKeyPressContainer::OfferKeyEventL(
  const TKeyEvent& aKeyEvent, TEventCode aType)
  {
  if (aType != EEventKey)
    return EKeyWasNotConsumed;
  else
    {
    if (aKeyEvent.iCode == '5')
      {
      ...
      return EKeyWasConsumed;
      }
    }
  }
```

The second check is for the event itself. `TKeyEvent` is a structure with four fields:

- `iCode` contains the character code of the key press. The code above checks this part of the structure to determine if the number 5 was pressed

- iModifiers (defined in TEventModifier) defines the state of the modifier keys and pointing device

- iRepeats counts the auto repeats but is rarely used

- iScanCode (defined in TstdScanCode) defines the scan codes of keys.

It may be necessary to generate an event, for instance when an application starts up. The following code creates an instance of the TKeyEventStructure and assign its fields to imitate an event. Offer-KeyEventL() is called with the event we have just generated and the key code EEventKey.

```
TKeyEvent myEvent;
myEvent.iCode = EEventKeyDown;
myEvent.iModifiers = EAllModifiers;
myEvent.iRepeats = 0;
myEvent.iScanCode = EAllModifiers;
OfferKeyEventL(myEvent, EEventKey);
```

Other key press events can be caught using the same method, for example, the following code checks for the right navigation key to be pressed:

```
if (aType == EEventKeyDown)
  {
  switch (aKeyEvent.iScanCode)
    {
    case EStdKeyRightArrow:
      if (iSelected == KNoOfIcons)
        {
        ...
        }
    }
  }
```

Menu Input

The HandleCommandL() method deals with menu selections and other commands defined in the resource file. It is a virtual function, defined in CEikAppUi and called by ProcessCommandL() in the framework. The usual place for implementing HandleCommandL() is in the AppUi (which inherits the method from CEikAppUi).

The easiest way of implementing the `HandleCommandL()` method is by using a `switch` statement. `HandleCommandL(Tint aCommand)` receives an integer parameter referring to the number of the resource that caused the event. This can be used to control the switch, as follows:

```
void CKeyPressAppUi::HandleCommandL(TInt aCommand)
  {
  switch (aCommand)
    {
    case EEikCmdExit:
      {
      Exit();
      break;
      }
    case EAknSoftkeyBack:
      {
      ActivateLocalViewL(KMainViewId);
      break;
      }
    case EStartGame:
      {
      iContainer->StartGame();
      break;
      }
    }
  }
```

There should always be an option to exit from the application, either through a softkey event or a menu option. This should use the standard `EEikCmdExit` and call `Exit()`.

The Back option is useful when designing view-switching applications. The reserved keyword `EAknSoftkeyBack` is used for a softkey labeled 'Back' and generates this event when pressed.

4.8 Putting It Into Practice: Creating a GUI-based Card Game

We are now going to continue the development of the card-game application from Chapter 3. Having gained the knowledge required for creating a GUI, we can enhance our game so that we don't simply use textual names and number keys but also card images and menu items.

First, we create a new application, called `CardGame`, which has `Application`, `Document`, `AppUi` and `Container` classes. Two menu options should be defined, called Deal and Shuffle. Neither option does anything for the moment so they contain just the keyword break. CardGame also needs a Draw function that, for now at least, simply clears the screen. Finally, we modify the ModeSelected enumeration to have three states (EModeNoneSelected, EModePlaying and EModePaused) and add a method called Mode() that returns the current mode.

Displaying the Cards

In order to display a bitmap, we need to include a variable in our program that stores the bitmap. The variable is a CFbsBitmap type, which (after a quick reference to the SDK) requires the inclusion of the fbs.h library and compilation against the fbscli.lib library (add them to the .mmp file and reload the project). This bitmap is added to the Container class as shown:

```
class CBasicGUIContainer : public CCoeControl
  {
public:
  CBasicGUIContainer();
  void ConstructL(const TRect& aRect, CBasicGUIAppUi* iAppUi);
  ~CBasicGUIContainer();
private:
  // From CoeControl
  void Draw(const TRect& aRect) const;
  // Member variables
  TModeSelected iMode;
  CFbsBitmap* iBitmap;
  CBasicGUIAppUi* iAppUi;
  TInt iBitmapError;
  };
```

Since we have created a pointer to our bitmap object, we must initialize the bitmap in the second-phase constructor, ConstructL(), and tidy up in the destructor:

```
void CBasicGUIContainer::ConstructL(const TRect& aRect,
                              CBasicGUIAppUi* aAppUi)
  {
  iBitmap = new(ELeave) CFbsBitmap;
  User::LeaveIfError(iBitmap->Load(KCardsFile, 0));
  iAppUi = aAppUi;
  CreateWindowL();
  SetRect(aRect);
```

```
ActivateL();
}

CBasicGUIContainer::~CBasicGUIContainer()
{
delete iBitmap;
}
```

A pointer to the `AppUi` is passed to `ConstructL()` allowing us to call methods from the `AppUi` which we need later when drawing the bitmap. The bitmap is loaded using `Load()`. `KCardsFile` is a literal string defining the path and name of the `cards.mbm` file and the 0 parameter represents the bitmap number of the `.mbm` file to load.

If the load is unsuccessful, then there is not much point in carrying on the application, as the player needs to see the cards to play the game. The application may as well leave so we use `User::LeaveIfError()`, which leaves if an error occurs.

We display the image in `Draw()`:

```
void CBasicGUIContainer::Draw(const TRect&/* aRect*/) const
{
CWindowGc& gc = SystemGc();
TRect rect = Rect();
gc.Clear(rect);
rect.Resize(-130, -90);
rect.Move(0, 25);
gc.DrawBitmap(rect, iBitmap);
}
```

Firstly we create a rectangular area to draw the card. `Rect()` returns the control area, of which we can alter the size using `Resize()` and move the position using `Move()`. The bitmap is then displayed on screen using `DrawBitmap()` in the area and position defined by `rect`.

When you have tested and run the previous code – in other words, once you have properly tested the exception handling – you should place the `cards.mbm` file (a copy of which you can get from the accompanying website ***http://developer.symbian.com/main/academy/press/books/s60p***) in the Epoc32 emulator directory for the project. Note that this is a useful place to store image files whilst developing and testing an application, but images in released applications should be saved into and retrieved from the application directory. The `cards.mbm` file contains 53 bitmap images for 52 cards: ace to king in each of the four suits, hearts,

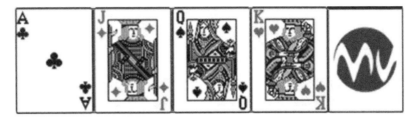

Figure 4.13   Example images from `cards.mbm`

clubs, diamonds and spades, and a card back. An example of these is shown in Figure 4.13.

Linking in the Cards Class

We are now ready to link in the cards class. Copy the header file into the source directory and the include directory. We use a deck of cards in the `AppUi` class.

Include the `cards.h` file into the header file of the `Container` and add a pointer to a deck of cards into the `Container` class as below:

```
CCards * iDeckOfCards;
```

The deck needs to be instantiated. We can add a new method, `StartGame()`, to initialize the card game:

```
void CBasicGUIAppUi::StartGame()
  {
  iPlayerWins = iPhoneWins = 0;
  iDeckOfCards = CCards::NewL(2);
  iDeckOfCards->Shuffle();
  }
```

Here we see the addition of two new variables, `iPlayerWins` and `iPhoneWins`, which are integer values used to hold the score. We then create a new deck which consists of two packs of cards and shuffle the deck. Run the program and confirm that it still works as before.

Letting the GUI Control the Deck

Now we need to add a couple of functions to allow the GUI to control the deck by adding accessor functions to the Deal and Shuffle methods:

```
void CBasicGUIAppUi::ShuffleDeck()
  {
  iDeckOfCards->Shuffle();
  iGameMode = EModeNoneSelected;
  }
void CBasicGUIAppUi::DealFromDeck()
  {
  //Deals two cards to the player and the phone
  iPlayerHand[0] = iDeckOfCards->Deal();
  iPlayerHand[1] = iDeckOfCards->Deal();
  iPhoneHand[0] = iDeckOfCards->Deal();
  iPhoneHand[1] = iDeckOfCards->Deal();
  iNumPlayerCards = iNumPhoneCards = 2;
  }
```

DealFromDeck() deals four cards, two for the player's hand and two for the phone's hand. These are stored in integer arrays which should be defined in the class declaration along with the card counts, iNumPlayerCards and iNumPhoneCards. KNoOfCards is defined in a global header file and has the value of 5, as that is the maximum amount of cards that is allowed in the game.

```
TInt iPlayerHand[KNoOfCards];
TInt iPhoneHand[KNoOfCards];
TInt iNumPlayerCards;
TInt iNumPhoneCards;
```

We can now edit the GUI command handler to use the Deal-FromDeck() and ShuffleDeck() functions:

```
void CBasicGUIAppUi::HandleCommandL(TInt aCommand)
  {
  switch (aCommand)
    {
    case EAknSoftkeyBack:
    case EEikCmdExit:
      {
      Exit();
      break;
      }
    case EMyAppCmdDeal:
      {
      DealFromDeck();
      break;
      }
    case EMyAppCmdShuffle:
      {
```

```
    ShuffleDeck();
    break;
    }
  default:
    break;
  }
}
```

To display the cards dealt, we need a method of passing the value of the cards we want to the Draw() function. A 'get' function to return the cards should be added to the AppUi which is called from Draw().

```
void CBasicGUIAppUi::GetCards(TInt* aPlayersCards, TInt* aPhonesCards)
  {
  for(TInt i = 0; i < iNumPlayerCards; i++)
    aPlayersCards[i] = iPlayerHand[i];
  for(TInt j = 0; j < iNumPhoneCards; j++)
    aPhonesCards[j] = iPhoneHand[j];
  }
```

GetCards() has two parameters, pointers to the phone's and player's cards which are defined as local variables in Draw():

```
TInt playersHand[KNoOfCards];
TInt phonesHand[KNoOfCards];
iAppUi->GetCards(playersHand, phonesHand);
```

Finally, modify the bitmap loader so that the drawn card is displayed:

```
TInt err = iBitmap->Load(KCardsFile, playersHand[i]);
```

Testing the code through the menu is a little tedious and it is worth modifying the application so that the '1' key can be used to deal cards and the '2' key to shuffle:

```
TKeyResponse CBasicGUIAppUi::HandleKeyEventL(const TKeyEvent& aKeyEvent,
                                             TEventCode aType)
  {
  if (aType==EEventKey)
    {
    switch (aKeyEvent.iCode)
      {
      case '1':
```

```
        {
        DealFromDeck();
        iAppContainer->DrawNow();
        return EKeyWasConsumed;
        }
    case '2':
        {
        ShuffleDeck();
        iAppContainer->DrawNow();
        return EKeyWasConsumed;
        }
    }
  }
return EKeyWasNotConsumed;
}
```

Test and verify the operation of your program.

5

Storing Data

Introduction

Now that we can create basic GUI-based applications, we turn our attention to the information that is presented to the user and how it is created or consumed within our applications. Whether your mobile application is a game or a payment system, it requires the control and manipulation of information of some sort. In Symbian OS, we define the information required by our application as resources.

In the first section of this chapter, we define how to use resource files to create an efficient and flexible methodology for changing and utilizing the resources we need. The next section deals with the presentation of information to the users through dialogs, which can be used to prompt users to carry out an action or to inform them if the application is performing a particular task. This could mean selecting a particular menu option or informing the user that the application is sending an SMS message or connecting to the Internet. Following this, we consider forms, which are effectively dialogs that allow us to present information in a defined structure that is easy for the user to understand. Forms are normally associated with the user entering or altering information such as addresses, and we provide examples for this purpose.

As in Chapter 4, we are not concerned in this book about the methodologies available to come up with these designs (although we always recommend that you consult suitable sources on the subject) but rather we provide the means of implementation. Storing and retrieving information is most often associated with files that form the repository of information. In the penultimate section, we show how Symbian OS handles these practices. Finally, we put these skills into practice for our card game by enabling users to save their names and high scores.

5.1   Resource File Header

A resource script (.rss) defines the behavior of the system in terms of its resources. A resource can be defined as a user-visible element, such as a form or a dialog. Using a resource file has a number of advantages, such as the ability to load resources when they are needed, thus decreasing code size and increasing efficiency. It is also quicker and easier to alter layouts of menus and other elements by rearranging them in the resource file (there is no need to alter source code).

A compiled .rss file produces an .rsg file that contains the resource IDs, which the executable program will use. The .rsg file must be included into the source file (.cpp) in which the resource is to be used.

There are a number of project wizards that can be used to create a template project. A template project creates a template resource file that includes all the initial resource data. The resource file can be categorized into two sections: a header and a main body. The header follows a standard structure that satisfies the Symbian OS resource-loading framework and the body section defines the content of the resource file.

A resource starts with the keyword NAME followed by a four-letter ID which represents the name of the resource file. This name is unique to this resource within the application and is used if more than one resource file is included.

```
NAME    AWIZ
```

Include Files

Include files should follow the resource NAME. These are defined as #include statements, followed by the name of the file to include. If the file name is enclosed in " " signs, it generally implies that the file is owned by the project and has been created by you, while < > signs are typically used to include compiled files provided by the operating system.

```
#include <eikon.rh>
```

```
#include "cookbook.hrh"
#include "cookbook.loc"
#include <avkon.rsg>
#include <avkon.rh>
#include <avkon.mbg>
#include <avkon.loc>
```

In the first line of the code above, `Eikon.rh` defines resource structures, such as the `DIALOG` resource. The following two lines are user include files. The `.hrh` file holds user enumerations which can be used as unique menu option IDs or control IDs. For example:

```
enum TCardGameMenu
  {
  EStartGame = 0x1000,
  EStopGame,
  EPauseGame
  };
```

An enumeration (enum) is a set of integer values with meaningful names; the names are used rather than the number which increases readability of the code. Note that the start of the enumerations is at 0×1000. This prevents any overlapping with Avkon enumerations.

The `.loc` file holds user localized strings such as:

```
#define my_app_delete "Delete Item"
```

This string can be used within the resource file and globally within the application. Localized strings are separated from the main application resources in order to ease translation of application resources. Locating the strings within a separate file makes it much easier for non-technical people to translate your application into other languages.

`Avkon.rsg` holds the compiled Avkon resource file. It defines standard menu panes, control buttons and other pre-compiled resources that can be utilized in the application. We see examples of these in the following sections.

`Avkon.rh` contains the resource structure definitions for Avkon – in the same way as `Eikon.rh` defines basic resource structures, `Avkon.rh` supplements them with additional Avkon-specific definitions.

`Avkon.mbg` contains a list of identifiers that may be used to refer to images within resources.

Resource Signature

The resource signature is required by the framework, but its contents are not used, so it should be left blank:

```
RESOURCE RSS_SIGNATURE { }
```

A document name is required by the framework after the resource signature. This is a `TBuf` resource that defines the default document name for the application. It is wise to keep this the same as the application name. In this example, the application is called `CookBook`:

```
RESOURCE TBUF { buf = "CookBook"; }
```

`EIK_APP_INFO` Resource

The final part of the header is the definition of the `EIK_APP_INFO` resource. This is the standard resource that the application user interface will use. Not all of the fields are required; in fact there are only two main fields in the structure that are commonly used: `menubar` and `CBA`.

- `Menubar` defines the menu structure to use; it is handled by `HandleCommandL()` in the `AppUi`. We take a closer look at the menu structure in the next section.

- `CBA` is an abbreviation for Control Button Array, in other words, the name for the left and right softkey buttons. Predefined softkey names are stored in `avkon.hrh`, but there is a resource to define custom softkeys. Again, we will look at this later.

- `Hotkeys` are basically keyboard shortcuts. Key combinations can be defined to invoke particular commands. They are not widely used in S60.

- `Toolbar` has the same functionality as `CBA`. It was implemented in S60 1st Edition and quickly removed in S60 2nd Edition.

- `Toolband` is the horizontal tool bar at the top of the screen. It is currently not used in S60.

- `Status_pane` provides information on the current phone status, such as signal strength and battery level. Its default value is 0, which creates a default status pane.

For example:

```
RESOURCE EIK_APP_INFO
  {
  hotkeys = r_cookbook_hotkeys;
  menubar = r_cookbook_menubar;
  cba = R_AVKON_SOFTKEYS_OPTIONS_EXIT;
  }
```

Defining Specific Resources

The main body of the resource file is more interesting as this is where your application's resources are defined.

Menus, CBA buttons, strings, dialogs and lists are just some of the elements that can be defined in a resource entry. Each of these elements is defined in the same way, using the keyword RESOURCE followed by a structure name. For example, the following code defines a dialog resource:

```
RESOURCE DIALOG r_my_dialog
```

The following sections look more closely at specific resources.

5.2   Menus

Menus are accessed by pressing a softkey on an S60 mobile phone. As a rule of thumb, the left softkey should be used for positive actions, such as displaying the menu, and the right softkey should be used for negative actions, such as returning to a previous view or exiting.

A menu displays a list of options that the user can scroll through and select using the navigation key. Menus can be static or dynamic, allowing the user to see only the commands relevant at that time. Figure 5.1 shows some example menus.

The MENU_BAR Resource

We start by defining a MENU_BAR resource in the resource file. The structure for the menu bar resource is defined in uikon.rh (which is included in Eikon.rh). It has one afield, titles, which defines a number of MENU_TITLE resources.

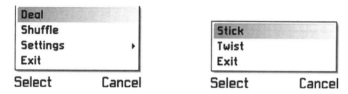

Figure 5.1 Example menus

```
RESOURCE MENU_BAR r_cardgame_menubar
  {
  titles =
    {
    MENU_TITLE { menu_pane = r_cardgame_menupane; }
    };
  }
```

r_cardgame_menubar is the name of the MENU_BAR resource. Once compiled, it appears as a #define in the .rsg file. The MENU_TITLE resource then provides a link to a menu pane where the items for the menu are defined.

As a general rule of thumb, resource entry types and resource compiler keywords are entered in capital letters, e.g. RESOURCE MENU_BAR in the above example. The resource entries that you create should generally be written in lower case, though this is purely optional. Resource fields, i.e. members of resource entries, such as titles and menu_pane should be written in lower case.

Other optional fields in the MENU_TITLE structure are:

- txt gives a title to appear in the menu bar

- flags defaults to zero; ETitleDimmed hides the title

- bmpfile takes the full filename of an .mbm file that holds icons for the menu title

- bmpid is the ID of the bitmap to use from the bmpfile

- bmpmask is the ID of the corresponding bitmap mask.

The MENU_PANE Resource

The MENU_PANE resource has one field and an array of items. Each item is a MENU_ITEM resource, which has the following structure:

- command – an integer value that identifies the menu item; it should be unique to this menu pane. It is advisable to store all these IDs together as enumerated types, so that they can be used in the event handler later on. Typically these are stored within your application's `.hrh` file

- cascade – links the menu option to a submenu, as shown in Figure 5.2, of type MENU_PANE

- flags – defines the display of the menu, such as dimming items or spacing. These flags are:

  ○ EEikMenuItemDimmed – dims the menu item

  ○ EEikMenuItemSeparatorAfter – a separator appears after the menu item

  ○ EEikMenuItemCheckBox – sets the menu item to a check box

  ○ EEikMenuItemRadioStart – sets the menu item to the first position in a radio button

  ○ EEikMenuItemRadioMiddle – sets the menu item to the middle position in a radio button

  ○ EEikMenuItemRadioEnd – sets the menu item to the end position in a radio button

  ○ EEikMenuItemSymbolOn – displays a symbol if the menu item is a check box or a radio button

  ○ EEikMenuItemSymbolIndeterminate – no symbol is displayed if the menu item is a check box or a radio button

- txt – defines the name to appear on the menu item

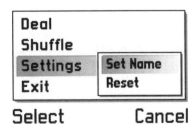

Figure 5.2 Submenu

- `extratxt` – in Western locales, this displays text in a lighter colored font to the right of the menu item.

- `bmpfile`, `bmpid` and `bmpmask` define the location, ID and mask ID of a bitmap to be used next to the menu item.

```
RESOURCE MENU_PANE r_cardgame_menupane
  {
  items =
    {
    MENU_ITEM {command = EMyAppCmdDeal; txt = deal_txt;},
    MENU_ITEM {command = EMyAppCmdShuffle; txt = shuffle_txt;},
    MENU_ITEM {command = EMyAppCmdStick; txt = stick_txt;},
    MENU_ITEM {command = EMyAppCmdTwist; txt = twist_txt;},
    MENU_ITEM
      {
      command = EMyAppCmdSettings;
      txt = settings_txt;
      cascade = r_basicgui_settings_menu;
      },
    MENU_ITEM {command = EAknCmdExit; txt = "Exit";}
    };
  }
```

Please note how the resource is structured using a comma after each line, but not on the last item. When working with RESOURCE array entries, then a comma should be used to separate each entry within the resource array. Additionally, the array itself should contain a closing semi-colon after the last closing brace. For example, `items` in the above code includes a trailing semi-colon after the closing brace.

Using the Menu Resource

Once the menu resource is defined, and the IDs for each of the menu items are enumerated, the menu can be handled in the application user interface. Basic applications will start by handling menu commands in the `AppUi` that is inherited from `CAknAppUI`. If view architecture is used, the class will be inherited from `CAknView` (see Chapter 6). Both of these classes inherit the `HandleCommandL()` method which allows menu events to be captured and handled. Dialog-derived classes implement similar functionality by use of the `ProcessCommandL()` method.

`HandleCommandL()` is called by the framework on receipt of an event. It receives an integer parameter which relates to the command ID of the menu option selected. The command ID is the same as the value you associated with the `command` field of the resource.

The most elegant way to deal with events is by using a `switch` statement. If a small menu is implemented, a number of `if` statements could be used instead of a `switch`.

```
void CBasicGUIAppUi::HandleCommandL(TInt aCommand)
  {
  switch (aCommand)
    {
    case EAknSoftkeyBack:
    case EEikCmdExit:
      {
      iAppContainer->SaveDataL();
      Exit();
      break;
      }
    case EMyAppCmdDeal:
      {
      iAppContainer->DealFromDeck();
      break;
      }
    case EMyAppCmdShuffle:
      {
      iAppContainer->ShuffleDeck();
      break;
      }
    default:
      break;
    }
  }
```

The `switch` statement improves code readability, making it easy to locate menu items. Each menu item can be handled here. For example, selecting 'Deal' from the menu (`EMyAppCmdDeal`) calls `Deal-FromDeck()`, a method in the container class.

Note that you must use `break` in each `case` field, otherwise all of the code after the `break` is executed as well.

Softkey events can also be defined here. The softkey Back command (`EAknSoftkeyBack`) is generally used in view-architecture applications to return to a previous screen. `EEikCmdExit` can catch an Exit key press, which in turn can call `Exit()`.

5.3   CBA Buttons

CBA buttons define the labels for the left and right softkeys. There are a number of pre-defined softkeys in `avkon.hrh`, see Table 5.1 for a full list.

Table 5.1 Softkey Definitions

Left Softkey	Right Softkey	Definition
–	–	R_AVKON_SOFTKEYS_EMPTY
–	–	R_AVKON_SOFTKEYS_EMPTY_WITH_IDS
OK	–	R_AVKON_SOFTKEYS_OK_EMPTY
SELECT	CANCEL	R_AVKON_SOFTKEYS_SELECT_CANCEL
OK	CANCEL	R_AVKON_SOFTKEYS_OK_CANCEL
OK	DETAILS	R_AVKON_SOFTKEYS_OK_DETAILS
CALL	CANCEL	R_AVKON_SOFTKEYS_CALL_CANCEL
OPTIONS	BACK	R_AVKON_SOFTKEYS_OPTIONS_BACK
OPTIONS	DONE	R_AVKON_SOFTKEYS_OPTIONS_DONE
OPTIONS	CANCEL	R_AVKON_SOFTKEYS_OPTIONS_CANCEL
OPTIONS	EXIT	R_AVKON_SOFTKEYS_OPTIONS_EXIT
OK	BACK	R_AVKON_SOFTKEYS_OK_BACK
–	CANCEL	R_AVKON_SOFTKEYS_CANCEL
–	BACK	R_AVKON_SOFTKEYS_BACK
–	CLOSE	R_AVKON_SOFTKEYS_CLOSE
DONE	BACK	R_AVKON_SOFTKEYS_DONE_BACK
DONE	CANCEL	R_AVKON_SOFTKEYS_DONE_CANCEL
SELECT	BACK	R_AVKON_SOFTKEYS_SELECT_BACK
MARK	BACK	R_AVKON_SOFTKEYS_MARK_BACK
UNMARK	BACK	R_AVKON_SOFTKEYS_UNMARK_BACK

(*continued overleaf*)

Table 5.1 (*continued*)

Left Softkey	Right Softkey	Definition
YES	NO	R_AVKON_SOFTKEYS_YES_NO
UNLOCK	–	R_AVKON_SOFTKEYS_UNLOCK_EMPTY
SAVE	BACK	R_AVKON_SOFTKEYS_SAVE_BACK
SHOW	CANCEL	R_AVKON_SOFTKEYS_SHOW_CANCEL
SHOW	EXIT	R_AVKON_SOFTKEYS_SHOW_EXIT
ANSWER	EXIT	R_AVKON_SOFTKEYS_ANSWER_EXIT
–	EXIT	R_AVKON_SOFTKEYS_EXIT
READ	EXIT	R_AVKON_SOFTKEYS_READ_EXIT
LISTEN	EXIT	R_AVKON_SOFTKEYS_LISTEN_EXIT
SEARCH	BACK	R_AVKON_SOFTKEYS_SEARCH_BACK
AGAIN	QUIT	R_AVKON_SOFTKEYS_AGAIN_QUIT
–	QUIT	R_AVKON_SOFTKEYS_QUIT
INSERT	BACK	R_AVKON_SOFTKEYS_INSERT_BACK

It is useful to customize applications by defining specific softkeys using the CBA resource structure. It contains a `buttons` field that takes two `CBA_BUTTON` definitions. The `CBA_BUTTON` structure takes an ID for the button and a text-based name. The ID can be used to refer to the button in your code, as we show later. The following code illustrates the definition of custom softkeys:

```
RESOURCE CBA r_blackjack_gameplay_buttons
  {
  buttons =
    {
    CBA_BUTTON
      {
      id = EAknSoftkeyPause;
```

```
    txt = "Pause";
    },
  CBA_BUTTON
    {
    id = EAknSoftkeyBack;
    txt = "Back";
    }
  };
}
```

As stated earlier, it is advisable to keep the left softkey for positive actions and the right softkey for negative actions, as this format is used in most applications and allows the user to adapt more quickly to the application. Also, if only one softkey is needed, the text string in the resource can be left blank, but it should still define an ID.

5.4   Changing the Application Title

To change the title of the application, locate the `name_caption.rss` file. This file should have been declared in the project file (`.mmp`) alongside the main resource file.

The file contains a `CAPTION_DATA` resource structure that takes two text items: a caption and a short caption.

- `caption` is the name of the application that will be seen during execution.

- `shortcaption` is the name of the application in menu view.

The names may be defined here in this structure:

```
RESOURCE CAPTION_DATA
  {
  caption = "Card Game";
  shortcaption = "Cards";
  }
```

Alternatively, you may define the names in a localization file (`.loc`) elsewhere in the project:

```
RESOURCE CAPTION_DATA
  {
  caption = qtn_app_caption_string;
  shortcaption = qtn_app_short_caption_string;
  }
```

5.5 Dialogs

Dialogs are used in most applications to notify users of changes to the system or to obtain information from a user. They are also useful in debugging when tracking sections of code. A dialog can appear in many formats: for instance, a standard dialog allows the user to input information; other dialogs inform the user of an event, such as a warning note.

Standard Dialog

Standard dialogs prompt the user to input data. The left and right softkeys are used to confirm and cancel the action, respectively (see Figure 5.3).

The easiest way to create a standard dialog is by defining it in the resource file as a RESOURCE DIALOG. You can customize the dialog by setting the number of lines, the control type and labels. There is also the option to add icons and set flags to control the use of the dialog. The different flags can be found in avkon.hrh and the pre-defined buttons can be found in avkon.rsg.

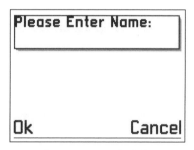

Figure 5.3   Simple dialog

The following code example creates a dialog with one EDWIN control line. It may be useful to add another line that has a LABEL control to indicate to the user what they need to enter.

```
RESOURCE DIALOG r_setname_dialog
  {
  flags = EEikDialogFlagNoDrag | EEikDialogFlagCbaButtons |
                                  EEikDialogFlagWait;
  buttons = R_AVKON_SOFTKEYS_OK_CANCEL;
  items =
    {
    DLG_LINE
      {
      id = ESetNameEditor;
```

```
  type = EEikCtEdwin;
  control = EDWIN
    {
    maxlength = KMaxNameLength;
    width = KMaxNameLength;
    };
  }
};
}
```

The DIALOG structure uses a number of fields, such as flags, buttons and items. These are the minimum required to define the dialog. There are, however, other fields to define icons and tooltips (as we have seen in the menu).

- flags define the behavior of the dialog in general:
  - EEikDialogFlagNoDrag allows no dragging
  - EEikFlagCbaButtons allows the use of softkeys
  - EEikDialogFlagWait means that the program does not execute the next line (after launching the dialog) until the dialog has been dismissed
- buttons define the softkeys to use (see Section 5.3)
- items are the lines in the dialog, defined as a DLG_LINE structure. As a minimum, each line should take the following fields:
  - id – used to reference the dialog. There are predefined IDs that can be used or you can create a new ID (in which case you should enumerate it, for example, in your application's .hrh file)
  - type – defines the type of control, where EAknCtQuery (from avkon.hrh) uses a query-style control and EEikCtEdwin (from uikon.hrh) uses an editor-based control. There are many standard types provided by the framework, defined in avkon.hrh and uikon.hrh
  - control – is specific to the type of control specified in the type field. Common control resource structures are defined in avkon.rh, eikon.rh and uikon.rh.

Now the dialog resource is defined, a class can be derived from CAknDialog, the S60 dialog base class. This class includes the virtual methods PreLayoutDynInitL(), OkToExitL() and RunDlgLD().

`PreLayoutDynInitL()` is used for initialization, for example, preparing the dialog controls with initial values for different fields. `RunDlgLD()` and any other methods that run a dialog should be defined as 'static'. This allows the method to be run without creating an instance of the class.

```
class CSetNameDialog : public CAknDialog
  {
public:
  static TInt RunDlgLD(TDes& aName);
protected:
  TBool OkToExitL(TInt aButtonId);
  void PreLayoutDynInitL();
private:  // Constructor
  inline CSetNameDialog(TDes& aName) : iName(aName) { }
private:  // data
  TDes& iName;
  };
```

The constructor, `CSetNameDialog()` takes the descriptor that initializes the dialog, stored in `iName`.

```
TInt CSetNameDialog::RunDlgLD(TDes& aName)
  {
  CSetNameDialog* nameDialog = new(ELeave) CSetNameDialog(aName);
  return nameDialog->ExecuteLD(R_SETNAME_DIALOG);
  }
```

In the example above, the `RunDlgLD()` method creates a new instance of the dialog object (in this example, the dialog is a text query defined in `AknDialog.h`). The parameter `aName` is modified by the dialog and is passed to the constructor for initialization. `ExecuteLD()` is then called to display the dialog. Since we specified `EEikDialogFlag-Wait` as one of the flag bitmask values in the dialog resource definition, the `ExecuteLD()` line does not return until the dialog is dismissed from the screen.

If the Cancel button is pressed, `ExecuteLD()` returns zero which is returned by `RunDlgLD()` to the calling function. The `OkToExitL()` method is called when any softkey event occurs apart from Cancel. This callback presents an opportunity to validate and save data, for example, to update `iName` with the data that the user entered at run time.

It is worth mentioning again that the trailing 'D' in the `ExecuteLD()` method name indicates that the function call deletes the dialog object.

This means that there is no need to explicitly call delete on the `NameDi-alog` pointer after `ExecuteLD()` returns.

```
TBool CSetNameDialog::OkToExitL(TInt aButtonId)
  {
  if (EAknSoftkeyOk == aButtonId)
    {
    CEikEdwin* editor;
    editor = static_cast<CEikEdwin*>(Control(ESetnameEditor));
    if (editor)
      editor->GetText(iName);
    }
    return ETrue;
  }
```

`OkToExitL()` is called by the framework when any softkey other than Cancel is pressed. In our example, we first check if the OK button was pressed; if so, we use the `Control()` method to obtain a `CCoeControl` pointer that corresponds to a specific dialog line ID. In the resource definition for the dialog, we defined a line `ID = ESet-nameEditor` for our `CEikEdwin` editor control. Therefore, we use `Control(ESetnameEditor)` to obtain a pointer to this control, which we then cast to the concrete `CEikEdwin` type. This allows us to access the text from the dialog using `GetText()` and the result is stored in our data member, `iName` (which is the initializing reference that was passed upon dialog construction). The function returns `ETrue`, which allows the dialog to exit.

Dialogs can be initialized in the resource or at run time using `PreLay-outDynInitL()`, which is called prior to displaying the dialog and can be use to initialize dialog lines. The following example will initialize a label with `KLabelText`, a `_LIT` macro string, in the dialog.

```
_LIT(KLabelText, "Label Text");
void CSetNameDialog::PreLayoutDynInitL()
  {
  CEikLabel* label = static_cast<CEikLabel*> (Control(ELabelDialog));
  if(label)
    {
    label->SetTextL(KLabelText);
    }
  }
```

A handle to the `ELabelDialog` control is obtained using `Con-trol()`. `SetTextL()` can then be called to dynamically set the text of the dialog.

To call the dialog from a container class, create a descriptor with initial data. In the following code, a TBuf descriptor, item, has been used. It will be displayed in the edit box when the resource first loads. As the method is static, it can be called directly by using the class name and a double colon to reference the method.

```
_LIT(KEditorPrompt, "Type Name Here");
TBuf<KMaxItemLength> item(KEditorPrompt);
TInt okPressed = CSetNameDialog::RunDlgLD(item);
```

Remember to include the header file for the dialog class in the .cpp file that is calling the dialog. The example above defines the prompts inside the code itself. However, a more practical solution would define all text strings inside the resource file and would then read the prompts by resource ID. This makes it easier to translate the application.

Note Dialog

A note dialog is a pop-up message that informs the user of an event that has occurred. For instance, if memory is running low on the phone, a warning note appears. A note contains text and can also contain an icon. It can sound an audible tone on activation. The note destroys itself after a period of time. Notes do not require user input, however, if the user causes a key press event, then it cancels the note. As user input is not required, a note does not display softkey labels (the wait note is an exception to this: it displays a Cancel right softkey).

A number of types of note exist, such as information notes, confirmation notes and warning notes. The note dialog's class structure is shown in Figure 5.4.

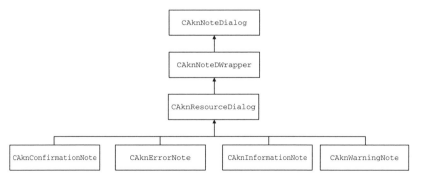

Figure 5.4 Note dialog class hierarchy

Figure 5.5 Information note

Each of the note dialogs needs to link against `avkon.lib`, `eikcdlg.lib` and `eikctl.lib` and to include `aknnotewappers.h`.

Information Note

Information notes (see Figure 5.5) are used to inform the user of a change to the application and may indicate minor errors, such as duplication information. The notes can also be useful in debugging, for example, informing the programmer 'I am here!' in sections of code.

The note classes with which we need to familiarize ourselves are `CAknInformationNote`, `CAknConfirmationNote`, `CAknWarning Note`, `CAknErrorNote` and `CAknGlobalNote`. Luckily for us, the method of construction for different types of note is the same and only the class name needs to be changed.

```
_LIT(KHelloWorldText, "Hello World");
CAknConfirmationNote * note = new(ELeave) CAknConfirmationNote();
note->ExecuteLD(KHelloWorldText);
```

A literal string, `KHelloWorldText` is used to define the text in the note. The note is then instantiated using the standard Symbian OS memory allocation idiom, a call to the leaving variant of operator `new()`. `ExecuteLD()` runs the note, displaying it on the screen. Again, notice the 'D' appended to `ExecuteLD()` which we have seen previously. This informs us that the note destroys itself, so we do not need to explicitly delete the `note` object.

Notes can be customized either using a resource definition, where icons and static elements can be added, or using methods from `CAkn-NoteDialog` to dynamically alter the appearance of the note (an example of this is provided in the Wait Note section).

```
RESOURCE DIALOG r_my_confirmation_note
  {
```

```
flags = EAknErrorNoteFlags;
items =
  {
  DLG_LINE
    {
    type = EAknCtNote;
    id = EConfirmationNote;
    control = AVKON_NOTE
      {
      layout = EGeneralLayout;
      singular_label = qtn_akntanote_error_singular;
      plural_label = qtn_akntanote_error_plural;
      imagefile = qtn_akntanote_icon_mbm_dir;
      imageid = EMbmAkntanoteiconAkntanoteerroricon;
      imagemask = 0xffff;
      };
    }
  };
}
```

By now we should be familiar with the structure of a dialog resource; we can see the use of flags and items which we have seen in previous resources. However, a new control, AVKON_NOTE, is introduced, which defines the note dialog.

The layout field defines how the note will appear. Avkon.hrh defines layouts such as EGeneralLayout. The label fields, singular_label and plural_label, are used to define single and plural text, respectively, for the note.

Imagefile, imageid and imagemask are used to define an image for the note. Imagefile is the .mbm file where the image is stored, imageid is the image to use, which is defined in the corresponding .mbg file and finally a mask can be used if necessary.

To create and execute the note, you should create a new class that derives from CAknNoteDialog.

```
CAknNoteDialog* note = new(ELeave) CAknNoteDialog
            (CAknNoteDialog::EConfirmationTone,
                CAknNoteDialog::EShortTimeout);
note->PrepareLC(R_MY_ CONFIRMATION_ NOTE);
note->SetTextPluralityL(ETrue);
note->RunLD();
```

The CAknNoteDialog constructor takes two parameters, the tone to play and the timeout period for the note. PrepareLC() takes the resource id of the note. The resource definition of the note allows us to

Figure 5.6   Wait note

dynamically change the text by using either single or plural fields. Set-
TextPluralityL(ETrue) is called to ensure that the plural_label
is used. Finally, RunLD() executes the resource and deletes the note
object once the note is dismissed.

Wait Note

If a process takes a noticeable time to complete, a wait note, as illustrated
in Figure 5.6, is a good way of informing the user that the program is still
executing (and has not crashed). This is a deterrent, keeping the impatient
user from pressing keys. It should, however, be utilized sparingly; instead,
more effort should be spent improving code efficiency to prevent the need
for a wait note.

To implement the wait note, a RESOURCE of type DIALOG needs to be
defined in the resource file. We need to set one flag, EAknWaitNote-
Flags, to enable the animations. Following this, the lines of the dialog
can be set under the items field. Only one line should be needed as this
can define text, a static bitmap image and an animation.

```
RESOURCE DIALOG r_wait_note
  {
  flags = EAknWaitNoteFlags;
  items =
    {
    DLG_LINE
      {
      type = EAknCtNote;
      id = EWaitNoteID;
      control = AVKON_NOTE
        {
        layout = EWaitLayout;
        singular_label = "Please Wait";
        imagefile = "z:\\system\\data\\avkon.mbm";
        imageid = EMbmAvkonQgn_note_erased;
        imagemask = EMbmAvkonQgn_note_erased_mask;
        animation = R_QGN_GRAF_WAIT_BAR_ANIM;
        };
      }
```

```
  };
}
```

An image file can be used; you can create your own .mbm file, as described in Chapter 4. avkon.mbm contains pre-defined system bitmaps that can be reused. This requires the inclusion of avkon.mbg in the resource file that holds the IDs of the bitmaps. The imageid and imagemask fields can then access the enumerated bitmap files in the avkon.mbg.

The animation field in the code above is set to the standard animation, R_QGN_RAF_WAIT_BAR_ANIM. To experiment with other animations, right-click on R_QGN_RAF_WAIT_BAR_ANIM and Go to macro definition. This opens avkon.rsg, where other animations are defined and can be used (avkon.mbg). You can also alter the layout and images by using the same technique. The best way to learn which one is best suited to your application is to experiment with them all.

Note that while altering the resource file, the emulator must be closed; otherwise an error will appear: 'Symbian Resource – cannot open...'.

There are a couple of techniques you can use to implement a wait note. The first involves creating a class derived from MAknBackground-Process and implementing the note inside an active object, where the active note wrapper object, CAknWaitNoteWrapper, allows processes to occur in the background. The second method is much simpler and only requires creating an instance of the CAknWaitNote and calling its ExecuteLD() method. The second method is quick and easy and is discussed here.

First, define an instance of CAknWaitDialog* iWaitDialog in the class declaration. In the .cpp file, add #include <aknwaitdia-log.h>. At the code location where the wait note should be displayed, create the new instance of the wait note where the constructor parameters are a pointer to itself and a Boolean value that determines whether to display the dialog immediately. SetTextL() is used to set the text for the wait note. The dialog is executed using ExecuteLD(), which returns an integer value that can be used to determine which key has been pressed.

```
_LIT(KWaitConnection, "Please wait");
if(iWaitDialog)
  delete iWaitDialog;
iWaitDialog = NULL;
iWaitDialog = new(ELeave) CAknWaitDialog(NULL, ETrue);
```

```
iWaitDialog->SetTextL(KWaitConnection);
TInt retVal = iWaitDialog->ExecuteLD(R_INTERNET_WAITDIALOG);
iWaitDialog = NULL;
if (retVal != EAknSoftkeyDone)
  {
  // User has cancelled this connection process
```

To stop the dialog, call the `ProcessFinishedL()` method:

```
if(iWaitDialog)
  {
  iWaitDialog->ProcessFinishedL();
  iWaitDialog = NULL;
  }
```

A more advanced version of the wait dialog is a progress dialog. This has the same functionality as the wait dialog with the added extra of a progress bar. In the inheritance hierarchy, the `CAknWaitDialog` object derives from the `CAknProgressDialog` object. This means that `CAknWaitDialog` inherits some functionality from the progress dialog. However, it is worth pointing out that calling `CAknWaitDialog::GetProgressInfo()` is not supported and results in your code being panicked.

Query Dialog

A query dialog (see Figure 5.7) prompts the user to answer a question. The query may be a simple yes or no answer, but can also be more complex, offering a list with options for a user to select one or more before continuing. Designing an application using state diagrams allows you to determine where the queries will go.

The resource below shows the definition of a query. It is almost identical to the standard query, but `EGeneralQueryFlags` is set and

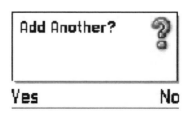

Figure 5.7 Query dialog

the type of dialog is set to EAknCtQuery. You can reuse the pre-defined Avkon button structures or you can define your own.

```
RESOURCE DIALOG r_yesno_confirmation_query
  {
  flags=EGeneralQueryFlags;
  buttons = R_AVKON_SOFTKEYS_YES_NO;
  items =
    {
    DLG_LINE
      {
      type = EAknCtQuery;
      id = EQueryAddAnother;
      control = AVKON_CONFIRMATION_QUERY
        {
        layout = EConfirmationQueryLayout;
        label = "Add Another?";
        bmpfile = qtn_akntaquery_mbm_file_path;
        bmpid = EMbmAvkonQgn_note_query;
        bmpmask = EMbmAvkonQgn_note_query_mask;
        animation = R_QGN_NOTE_WARNING_ANIM;
        };
      }
    };
  }
```

Remember that it is advisable to follow S60 conventions by assigning a positive action to the left softkey and a negative action to the right softkey. In the example above, we have added an icon to the query, to indicate what the query is asking for.

Now the query is defined in the resource script file, it is possible to create an instance of a CAknQueryDialog object to execute the resource. The query can be run using the ExecuteLD() method and passing it the name of the query resource. This returns a Boolean value, either ETrue if Yes was selected or EFalse if No was selected.

```
TBool CAddItem::AddAnotherL()
  {
  CAknQueryDialog* anotherItemQuery = CAknQueryDialog::NewL();
  if (anotherItemQuery->ExecuteLD(R_YESNO_CONFIRMATION_QUERY))
    {
    return ETrue;
    }
  return EFalse;
  }
```

Data Query Dialog

A data query dialog (see Figure 5.8) asks for input from the user. It has the functionality of a standard dialog, with the layout of a query.

The data query dialog is handled in the same way as the other dialogs we have looked at. First we create a resource and set all the appropriate fields:

```
RESOURCE DIALOG name_dialog
  {
  flags = EGeneralQueryFlags | EEikDialogFlagNotifyEsc;
  buttons = R_AVKON_SOFTKEYS_OK_CANCEL;
  items =
    {
    DLG_LINE
      {
      type = EAknCtQuery;
      id = EGeneralQuery;
      control = AVKON_DATA_QUERY
        {
        layout = EDataLayout;
        label = "Enter Name";
        control = EDWIN
          {
          maxlength = 40;
          };
        };
      }
    };
  }
```

EGeneralQueryFlags is a combination of defined flags to make the dialog wait for input, prevent it being dragged and ensuring it has no title bar or CBA buttons. This is defined in avkon.hrh but links to other flags that are defined in uikon.hrh.

The EEikDialogFlagNotifyEsc flag will set the dialog framework to call OkToExitL when the Cancel button is pressed (recall that the

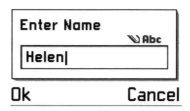

Figure 5.8 Data query dialog

standard behavior is not to call OkToExitL() when the dialog is cancelled). Other flags like these are defined in uikon.hrh. The buttons field describes the softkey buttons to use for the dialog.

Notice that there is only one DLG_LINE defined, yet we have a label and edit section on the dialog. If a standard dialog were to be implemented, both the label and the edit box would require a separate line. However, a data query dialog provides a label field as part of a dialog, so there is no need to specify separate lines.

The dialog is executed using the RunDlgLD() method as before. This time we can pass a descriptor to the dialog, for a default input.

```
LIT(KPrompt, "Add Name Here");
TBuf<KMaxItemLength> name(KPrompt);
TInt okPressed = CAddItem::RunDlgLD(name);
```

Multipage Dialog

Breaking down information into smaller sections often makes it easier for the user to digest. A multipage dialog is split over different screens and uses the navigation bar to display a tab describing each page, as shown in Figure 5.9. Each page of the dialog is accessed by pressing the navigation key left and right. If the dialog resource defines the pages field, these events are handled by the framework and therefore the developer does not have to handle the key events explicitly.

To define a multipage dialog, create a new dialog resource in the .rss file. The fields of interest are the dialog flags, buttons and pages. The pages field links the dialog to an array of pages. The ARRAY resource structure can be defined as:

```
RESOURCE ARRAY page_array
  {
  items =
    {
    PAGE
      {
      Text = "Page 1";
      Lines = page_1_lines;
      },
    PAGE
      {
      Text = "Page 2";
      Lines = page_2_lines;
      }
    };
  }
```

Figure 5.9 Multipage dialog showing a. page tabs b. the text-input identifier

The above code defines two pages. The `text` field defines the name of the page that will appear in the navigation tab and the `lines` field assigns the definition of the characteristics of each page. These can be defined in the same way as a standard dialog.

Note that the only difference between defining single and multipage dialogs is `avkon` flags.

If an Edwin editor is used, it will show the text-input 'abc' identifier in the navigation bar rather than the name of the page tabs (see Figure 5.9b). This is due to the Edwin control having higher priority. To solve this, set `avkon_flags` to `EAknEditorFlagNoEditIndicators`.

5.6   Forms

Forms are another type of dialog that allows the user to enter different types of data. Forms have two modes: in edit mode, the user has read–write access, and in view mode, the user has read-only access. Each section of the form may have different controls, for example a 'Name' field may use an Edwin control allowing the user to type their name, whereas a 'Game Level' field may allow only values in a range, for example, 1 to 10, therefore a slider control may be appropriate since it allows the user to choose a number in the specified range. A form may also have pop-up fields making it easier for the user to read the information.

Like all dialogs, a form is created from a resource. Each field of the form is known as a `DLG_LINE`. It contains certain attributes that define the type of resource, the maximum length and labels as well as other options. Before defining the intricacies of the form, it is necessary to consider the basic elements of any resource, such as the softkeys, flags and buttons. A form may have a single page or multiple pages, which is again defined in the resource. These decisions should be made during the design phase of the project.

As with the resource structures that have already been discussed, we start in the resource file. First, create a dialog with `flags` and `buttons` fields. The `form` field holds the actual form resource.

```
RESOURCE DIALOG r_direction_form_dialog
  {
  flags = EEikDialogFlagNoDrag | EEikDialogFlagFillAppClientRect |
                  EEikDialogFlagNoTitleBar | EEikDialogFlagWait |
                                          EEikDialogFlagCbaButtons;
  buttons = R_AVKON_SOFTKEYS_OK_CANCEL;
  form = r_direction_form;
  }
```

One of the benefits of using a resource to define a form is the ease of formatting. Each line can define its own format which can be clearly seen in the resource. The FORM resource also allows addition of icons, prompts, and input types. With the ability to add lots of information to the resource at this point, it may look a little daunting at first.

```
RESOURCE FORM r_direction_form
  {
  flags = EEikFormEditModeOnly | EEikFormUseDoubleSpacedFormat;
  items =
    {
    DLG_LINE
      {
      type = EEikCtEdwin;
      prompt = "Direction";
      id = ERecipeFormDirection;
      control = EDWIN
        {
        width = 20;
        maxlength = KTextEntryMaxLength;
        lines = 2;
        };
      },
    DLG_LINE
      {
      type = EEikCtEdwin;
      prompt = "Duration (minutes) :";
      id = ERecipeFormDuration;
      control = EDWIN
        {
        flags = EEikEdwinNoHorizScrolling | EEikEdwinResizable;
        width = 20;
        lines = 1;
```

```
    maxlength = KTextEntryMaxLength;
    numeric_keymap = EAknEditorPlainNumberModeKeymap;
    allowed_input_modes = EAknEditorNumericInputMode;
    default_input_mode = EAknEditorNumericInputMode;
    };
  }
};
}
```

The resource defines two dialog lines, both Edwin controls, where the first line takes text input and the second takes numeric input, by defining the `allowed_input_modes` (there is also a `number_editor` that can be used to take integer values).

`Prompt` is a text label that precedes each dialog line. The position of the label depends upon the number of lines contained within the dialog. For a single line, the label appears to the left of the dialog, for two or more lines, the label will appear above the dialog. A selection of forms is illustrated in Figure 5.10.

Each `DLG_LINE` should be specified as one type of control. The available editor controls are listed in Table 5.2.

Each dialog line has the same basic layout: `type`, `prompt`, `id`, `flags` and `control` fields. It is possible to specify an icon using the `bmpid`, `bmpmask` and `bmpfile` fields or use the `avkon` pre-defined bitmaps. Be sure to include `EEikFormShowBitmaps` in the `flags` field.

```
bmpfile = "Z:\\System\\Data\\avkon.mbm";
bmpid = EMbmAvkonQgn_prop_nrtyp_phone;
bmpmask = EMbmAvkonQgn_prop_nrtyp_phone_mask;
```

The `control` field should be used to implement a structure that corresponds to the type of editor that has been selected. For example, if your line contains an `EEikCtEdwin` control type, then you should

Figure 5.10 Forms

Table 5.2 Editor Control Definitions

Description	Type	Control
Text editor	EEikCtEdwin	EDWIN
Numeric editor	EEikCtNumberEditor	NUMBER_EDITOR
Date editor	EEikCtDateEditor	DATE_EDITOR
Time editor	EEikCtTimeEditor	TIME_EDITOR
Duration editor	EEikCtDurationEditor	DURATION_EDITOR
Password editor	EEikCtSecretEd	SECRETED
Slider	EAknCtSlider	SLIDER

implement the `EDWIN` resource structure as the corresponding control field.

To create a form, start by adding `#include <aknform.h>` at the top of your file and then create a new class that derives from `CAknForm`. You will notice the derived function names are the same as the dialog classes.

```
class CMyForm : public CAknForm
  {
public:
  static CMyForm* NewL(TFormData* aFormData);
  TBool OkToExitL(TInt aButtonId);
  ~CMyForm();
protected:
  void DynInitMenuPaneL(TInt aResourceId, CEikMenuPane* aMenuPane);
  void PreLayoutDynInitL();
private:
  inline CMyForm(TFormData* aData): iData(aData) {}
  TFormData* iData;
  };
```

We are going to need somewhere to store the form data. This could be locally in variables or in a file. In this instance, a structure is used for convenience. This can be defined in the form header file:

```
struct TFormData
  {
  TBuf<KTextEntryMaxLength> iTextEntry;
```

```
TBuf<KTextEntryMaxLength> iDescriptionEntry;
};
```

Again, `PreLayoutDynInitL()` is called before the form is displayed. This callback can be used to seed the fields displayed within the form with their initial values.

As forms have their own menu options it is usually necessary to include a `DynInitMenuPaneL()` implementation, which allows options to be 'dimmed' when they are inappropriate for the currently highlighted form line. If extra menu options are required, a resource for a new menu pane should be defined in the resource file. To handle the menu options, the virtual method `ProcessCommandL()` needs to be overridden. For more information on dynamic menus, see Chapter 6.

```
void CMyForm::DynInitMenuPaneL(TInt aResourceId,
                     CEikMenuPane* aMenuPane)
  {
  CAknForm::DynInitMenuPaneL(aResourceId,aMenuPane);
  }
```

On construction of the class, a record structure should be passed allowing the data to be saved. This can be manipulated in other objects as long as the lifetime of the structure is maintained beyond the lifetime of the dialog. The saving of form information can be manipulated in the `SaveFormDataL()` method, which is called when the Save menu options are selected. You can also save data in the `OkToExitL()` callback, which is called before the form is closed, and eliminate the Save option from the menu.

```
TBool CMyForm::OkToExitL(TInt aButtonId)
  {
  if (aButtonId == EAknSoftkeyOk)
    {
    CEikEdwin* editor = static_cast <CEikEdwin*>
                        (Control(EFormName));
    if (editor)
      editor->GetText(iData->iTextEntry);
    editor = static_cast <CEikEdwin*> (Control
                        (EFormDescription));
    if (editor)
      editor->GetText(iData->iDescriptionEntry);
    }
  return ETrue;
  }
```

`aButtonId` holds the ID of the softkey that the user pressed. If OK was pressed, the data needs to be saved, and possibly validated, here. `Control()` uses the ID of the specified dialog line in the form, to access that control. Since the form contained editor controls, this is then cast to an Edwin editor object, `CEikEdwin`, allowing the text from the dialog to be accessed using `GetText()`. The result is stored in `iData`, which is part of the structure that was passed to the `CMyForm` constructor. The same technique is used to receive the description.

To use the form from the container class, we first need to create a structure to allow the form data to be saved. An instance of the form is then created using its `NewL()` constructor. The form is run using `ExecuteLD()`, passing the method the form resource ID which can be found in your application `.rsg` file.

```
_LIT(KInitialValue, "Initialize");
TFormData formData;
formData.iTextEntry = KInitialValue;
CMyForm* form = CMyForm::NewL(&formData);
TBool canceled = form->ExecuteLD(R_BASIC_FORM_DIALOG);
```

The form appears in its own window, with its own menu structure. Pressing Save returns control back to the container window.

5.7 Files, Streams and Stores

A common requirement of application development is the ability to save data. Symbian OS offers, amongst other methods, files, streams and stores. A stream allows reading and writing of data through a stream object. A store is a collection of streams and a file is where the actual data is stored. The following sections detail the use of files, streams and stores. The use of the `RFile`, the lowest level file abstraction object, enables the manual manipulation of files. However, Symbian OS streams make data manipulation much easier as they provide direct support for basic built-in persistence as well as supporting more complicated object persistence via C++ templates. Since streams sit above the underlying raw file, working with streams makes implementation more straightforward and makes the code easier to read and maintain. For this reason, `RFile` is not discussed here and the preferred method of streams is highlighted. However, you can consult the SDK documentation for more details.

File Server

The `RFs` class provides a session to the file server so that the program can manipulate objects in the file system. A session to the file server is required for any operation performed at the file-system level, such as adding files or moving and renaming directories.

As with all standard Symbian OS server objects, a connection to the file server is initiated by calling `RFs::Connect()`. When the session is no longer required, it may be closed by calling `RFs::Close()`.

```
RFs fsSession;
const TInt err = fsSession.Connect();
User::LeaveIfError(err);
CleanupClosePushL(fsSession);
```

It is worth mentioning that all applications already have a file server session provided for them by the application framework. The pre-initialized (i.e. connected) `RFs` object can be obtained at any time in the application by calling `CCoeEnv::FsSession()`. For example, if a file server connection is required at the level of `CAknAppUi`, `iCoeEnv ->FsSession()` can be used to obtain the `RFs` object. Alternatively, if the object in question has no immediate `iCoeEnv` pointer to refer to, `CCoeEnv::Static()->FsSession()` can be used instead, though it is slightly slower due to a thread-local-storage lookup.

Care should be taken to ensure that any explicitly opened file server connection is closed. The CONE Framework takes care of closing its own file server session, so the developer need not be concerned with this unless a session is created within the developer's own code.

Note that if you are using the file server APIs, then you must link your project against `efsrv.lib` in the `.mmp` file and include `f32file.h` in the `.cpp` or `.h` file.

To create a new directory, use `MkDir()` with the path of the new directory. The new directory should be a child of a parent directory and its name should be unique within its parent. The path name should use a final backslash '\' which tells the file server this is a directory and not a file. The `MkDirAll()` method permits an application to create an entire directory tree with a single call. For example, the following code creates the entire directory tree specified within the `KDirectoryPath` literal constant:

```
_LIT(KDirectoryPath, "C:\\System\\Apps\\MyApp\\Data\\");
```

```
RFs& fsSession = iCoeEnv->FsSession();
const TInt error = fsSession.MkDirAll(KDirectoryPath);
User::LeaveIfError(error);
```

If the creation is successful, MkDir() and MkDirAll() return KErrNone. A common error that may be returned is KErrAlreadyExists, which occurs when the directory that you attempted to create already exists. Likewise, should the directory not exist, KErrNotFound is returned. KErrNotReady is returned if the directory is on removable media that is not present.

Delete() deletes a single file provided there is write access to the file system and the file is not open (and, therefore, in use) by other clients of the file server. KErrNone is returned if successful.

Rename() renames a file or a directory. It takes two parameters, the name to be changed and a new name, both in the form of descriptors. This method can also be used to move files and directories, if the second parameter provides a new path, as long as it is on the same drive. As usual, KErrNone is returned if the rename was successful.

Streams

The ability to read and write to the file can be obtained by manipulating RReadStream and RWriteStream, respectively. These require the inclusion of two header files, s32std.h and s32file.h, and the project needs to be linked against estor.lib. The code below shows how to connect to the file server and set up a read stream.

```
User::LeaveIfError(fsSession.Connect());
CleanupClosePushL(fsSession);
RFileReadStream readStream;
TInt error = readStream.Open(fsSession, KParentFileName, EFileRead);
if (KErrNone==error)
```

This sets the read stream to open a filename, KParentFileName (a _LIT string), in read-only mode. On return of Open(), an error value is checked to determine if the method was successful.

Data can then be read into variables using a number of methods, such as ReadUint16L() or the >> operators. Generally, the methods are used for reading integer values and the >> for streaming descriptors or other more complex objects.

```
TInt playerWins = readStream.ReadUint16L();
```

Integers can be read in 8, 16, 32 and 64 bits, signed or unsigned:

- `ReadInt8L()` streams an 8-bit signed integer
- `ReadInt16L()` streams an 16-bit signed integer
- `ReadInt32L()` streams an 32-bit signed integer
- `ReadUInt8L()` streams an 8-bit unsigned integer
- `ReadUInt16L()` streams an 16-bit unsigned integer
- `ReadUInt32L()` streams an 32-bit unsigned integer
- `ReadReal32L()` reads a 32-bit floating-point number
- `ReadReal64L()` reads a 64-bit floating-point number

Note that you need to remember to push the read stream onto the cleanup stack before calling any functions that may leave, thus allowing the stream to be closed if a leave occurs. This, of course, requires a relevant `Pop()` to ensure the cleanup stack does not become unbalanced.

`RFileWriteStream` uses a similar approach to `RFileReadStream`, except that it is used to write data. An existing file can be opened using the method `Open()`. Files can also be created and replaced, for example:

```
writeStream.ReplaceL(fsSession, KParentFileName, EFileWrite);
```

This deletes any existing file with `KParentFileName` and creates a new empty file.

Before writing any data, use `PushL()` to put the write stream on the cleanup stack. Data can then be written using methods such as `WriteInt32L()` and the << operators to stream descriptors to the file.

```
writeStream.PushL();
writeStream << iPlayerName;
writeStream.WriteUint32L(iPlayerWins);
```

When all data is written, the stream needs to be closed. Before that, the write stream object needs to be removed from the cleanup stack. `CommitL()` ensures all buffered data is written to the file.

```
writeStream.CommitL();
writeStream.Pop();
writeStream.Close();
```

Alternatively, this can be more simply written as:

```
writeStream.CommitL();
writeStream.PopAndDestroy();
```

The `CommitL()` call ensures that all data is persisted and the `PopAnd-Destroy()` call to the cleanup stack ensures that the stack is balanced and that the stream is closed.

An alternative, and more efficient, method can be achieved by using `CleanupClosePushL()`. This method still pushes a pointer to the stack but also checks for stack imbalance which is performed automatically by `EUSER`. This can prevent difficult problems later on where the wrong object is popped and destroyed by accident.

```
writeStream.CleanupClosePushL();
...
CleanupStack::PopandDestroy(&writeStream);
```

Stores

A store is a collection of related streams, which are used to implement persistent objects.

The API provides a number of different types of stores, each derived from the base store, `CStreamStore`. The most commonly used types are permanent, embedded, direct and secure. The most common use for stores is a relational database, so the rest of this chapter uses a database example.

Direct File Store

A direct file store is used for creating a primary copy of data as streams within this type of store cannot be altered, replaced or deleted once they have been committed. Usually the file store is created when the application is opened, and committed when the application is closed or in response to a 'save' menu command. As it is not possible to modify the store, the entire set of data needs to be loaded into an internal data structure, altered and then the whole store saved again.

To create a new direct file store, ensure `s32file.h` is included and the project is linked against `estor.lib`.

```
void CMyContainer::CreateStoreL()
  {
  CFileStore* store = CDirectFileStore::CreateLC(iFs, FileName,
                                                       EFileWrite);
  store->SetTypeL(TUidType(store->Layout()));
  CleanupStack::Pop(store);
  iStore = store;
  }
```

The store is created using the `CreateLC()` method and has the following parameters: a session to the file server, the name of the store and the access mode. Once the store is created, `SetTypeL()` is used to define whether the store is direct or permanent. This is determined by specifying the UID of the store layout. `CreateLC()` pushes the object on to the cleanup stack, so that the store resources will be cleaned up should a leave occur.

The store is now ready for use, so we can create a stream to output data:

```
RStoreWriteStream stream;
TStreamId id = stream.CreateLC(*iStore);
```

`CreateLC()` returns an ID for the stream object; this is required to uniquely identify the stream within the store. A stream dictionary allows the streams and their IDs to be mapped together. This can be implemented by creating an instance of `CStreamDictionary` and assigning an ID:

```
const TUid KUidAssociatedWithMyStream = { 0x12345678 };
iRootDictionary = CStreamDictionary::NewL();
iRootDictionary ->AssignL(KUidAssociatedWithMyStream, id);
```

where `id` is the identifier of the stream that was returned when the stream was created. In the above example, an association is made between the stream's ID and a known UID. This permits the developer to look up the ID of the stream later on, based upon the known UID. This will make it easier to locate the stream when the store is reopened, for example, when the application is next started.

All of the streams that have been created can now be written to the dictionary. However, there is still one more thing to consider: the dictionary that was created earlier contains the associated IDs of the streams that we have created. Unless this is saved to the store, these IDs

and their associated UIDs are lost and we are unable to locate the streams
when we come to open the store. Therefore, we create another stream in
which we store the dictionary itself:

```
RStoreWriteStream rootStream;
const TStreamId rootStreamId = rootStream.CreateLC(*iStore);
rootStream << *iRootDictionary;
rootStream.CommitL();
CleanupStack::PopAndDestroy(&rootStream);
iStore->SetRootL(rootStreamId);
iStore->CommitL();
```

We first create a new stream. We then use the << operators to
externalize the stream dictionary (iRootDictionary) to the stream.
The chevron operators call the templated ExternalizeL() function
within the CStreamDictionary object. This ensures that the stream
dictionary's contents are saved. The stream is then committed and closed.
Following this, the root stream is set within the store.

The CFileStore base class, CPersistentStore, implements the
SetRootL() and Root() methods that allow a special stream identifier
to be associated with the store. Unlike the other streams, where we used
a stream dictionary in order to ensure we didn't 'lose' their identifiers,
the root stream ID is maintained internally by the store itself. By ensuring
that rootStreamId is set as the root stream, we can locate the same
root stream by calling Root() when we come to re-read the store data.

Reading data back from the store is essentially the reverse procedure of
the way the store and streams were created. This time, we open the store
in Read access mode. We can obtain the root stream ID from the store by
calling Root(). Since we now know the root stream ID, we can create a
read-stream object that allows us to internalize the stream's data – in this
case, this is the stream dictionary. The dictionary object itself should first
be created and then the root data from the store can be streamed into the
dictionary.

```
RStoreReadStream rootStream;
rootStream.OpenLC(*store, store->Root());
rootStream >> *dictionary;
```

The dictionary can then be used to look up the stream ID that
corresponds to our known UID. This is achieved using the At() method.

```
TStreamId id = dictionary->At(KUidAssociatedWithMyStream);
```

The stream itself can then be read using the >> operator.

```
RStoreReadStream stream;
stream.OpenLC(*store, id);
stream >> item;
```

Permanent File Store

Permanent file stores are mainly used for storing databases, as the store allows modification of the stream data, without having to re-create the entire store contents. If we consider the functionality of a database, after it has been created, records are loaded in one at a time and viewed or modified. Entries can also be deleted and new records may be added. Once the database contents have been entered, the whole database is rarely replaced and is considered permanent. This is the layout and functionality that a permanent file store provides.

There are a number of issues to consider. When modifying part of the stream, its length must not change and overwrite any other part of the data or it will cause a leave. Luckily, CPermanentFileStore provides all the functionality to create a permanent file store, and in turn a database.

We do not go into great detail here about creating a database, just creating a permanent file store. A good example of creating databases can be downloaded through the Forum Nokia web site.

Before creating the store, it may be necessary to check if the store already exists or is open. If so, the ReplaceL() method can be used to overwrite it:

```
iFileStore = CPermanentFileStore::ReplaceL(iFsSession, aNewDatabase,
                                EFileRead | EFileWrite);
iFileStore->SetTypeL(iFileStore->Layout());
TStreamId id = iRecipesDb.CreateL(iFileStore);
iFileStore->SetRootL(id);
iFileStore->CommitL();
```

CFileStore* iFileStore is the store, pre-defined in the class declaration. A new store is created using a session to the file server, the name of the store aNewDatabase, and the mode in which to access the store, in this case, read and write.

The type of file store is set using Layout(). CreateL() uses the file store to create the new database, iRecipesDb, which returns the stream

ID. This is used as the root stream ID which is set using `SetRootL()`. `CommitL()` defines the completion of the database.

Once created, the store is initialized and ready for use. To open it manually (i.e. if the database is already created), first check if the database exists. If so, `OpenL()` can be used to open the store in read/write mode.

```
iFileStore = CPermanentFileStore::OpenL(iFsSession,
          aExistingDBFile, EFileRead|EFileWrite);
iFileStore->SetTypeL(iFileStore->Layout());
iRecipesDb.OpenL(iFileStore, iFileStore->Root());
```

An instance of `RDbStoreDatabase`, `iRecipesDb`, is created which provides the implementation of the `DBMS API`. This is opened using `OpenL()` which takes two parameters: the store that contains the database and the root stream id of the database. `OpenL()` leaves with `KErrArgument` if the stream id does not identify the database.

We are assuming that the database has previously been created using `CreateL()`, which returns the stream id. This id is passed to `OpenL()` to open the database.

A database is made up of a table, or number of tables, which also need to be created before the database can be opened. A table consists of columns which are used to hold the fields of data. Here is a brief example of a basic table. We do not go into great detail as we are more concerned with how the permanent file stores work and not the database itself.

To create the columns we need to use the `CDbColSet` class which manages the column definitions that describe the table. You can create an empty column set using the Symbian OS standard construction idiom, that is, a call to a static `NewL()` method.

```
CDbColSet* columns = CDbColSet::NewL();
```

Each column needs to be defined in terms of its attributes using `TDbCol`. Its constructor's parameters are

- `const TDesC&` – the column name
- `TDbColType` – the column type (see the SDK help for a list of types)
- `TInt` – the maximum length; this is an optional field and is only required if the column type is a descriptor.

```
TDbCol IDCol(KRecipesIDCol, EDbColUint8);
```

We can define the column outside the constructor using the public member variables, `iAttributes`, `iMaxLength`, `iName` and `iType`. For example, the following code sets the column to automatically increment for each new field:

```
IDCol.iAttributes = IDCol.EAutoIncrement;
```

Once the columns are defined, we can add them to the table using `AddL()` using the column name as the parameter.

```
columns->AddL(IDCol);
```

When all the columns have been added to the table, the table can be created using `CreateTable()`, which takes a pointer to the `CDbColSet` and returns `KErrNone`, if successful, or one of a number of system-wide error codes or DBMS error codes.

```
TInt errorcode = iRecipesDb.CreateTable(KRecipesTable, *columns);
```

The columns are no longer needed once added to the table, so they should be cleaned up to release resources:

```
columns->Clear();
delete columns;
```

Once the tables have been defined and added to the database, we can add the data. You must create a literal string to define an SQL statement. A view is defined to store the results of the query, which is prepared using `Prepare()` and executed using `EvaluateAll()`.

```
LIT(KQueryString, "SELECT * FROM table ORDER BY id, name");
RDbView view;
User::LeaveIfError(view.Prepare(iRecipesDb, TDbQuery(KQueryString,
                                          EDbCompareFolded)));
User::LeaveIfError(view.EvaluateAll());
```

The view generates rowsets from the SQL query. These results are now available to be modified:

```
view.InsertL();
view.SetColL(2, aTitle);
```

```
RDbColWriteStream writeStream;
writeStream.OpenLC(view, 3);
writeStream.WriteL(aDescription);
writeStream.CommitL();
CleanupStack::Pop(&writeStream);
writeStream.Close();
view.PutL();
view.Close();
return KErrNone;
```

In the code above, `InsertL()` adds a new row so that we can add data. `SetColL()` takes the column number to write to and the data that we are writing. For example, `view.SetColL(2, aTitle)` writes a title descriptor into column 2. Another approach to adding data is to use a stream, which is required for storing binary data. The stream is opened using `OpenLC()` which takes the current row in the rowset and puts a pointer to the column onto the cleanup stack. Data can be written to the stream using `WriteL()`. Once finished, the write stream is popped from the cleanup stack.

`View.PutL()` completes the insertion and the view can now be closed using `Close()`. Notice that column 1 has not been added here, this is because its attributes have been set to auto-increment.

Deleting the file store is usually performed in the destructor. The keyword 'delete' is used to destroy the store.

5.8   Putting It Into Practice: Saving Your Name and High Score

We are going to finish this chapter by using what we have learnt to add menus and settings to our card game. In this tutorial we add a settings menu that allows users to supply their name and save/reset settings in a file.

Adding a Settings Menu

If we are to take our application further, we need to add a settings menu. This menu will give users the ability to change their name and reset the scores. It also provides an example of how we can use cascading menus to create more complex menu structures.

We must first add another option, Settings, to the Options menu. We use the `cascade` structure member to tell the UI framework that there is a submenu, in this case, the Settings submenu. This new submenu contains the Set Name and Reset options, which are defined in the `.rss` file, as below, with enumerations in the `.hrh` file and text labels in the `.loc` file:

```
RESOURCE MENU_PANE r_basicgui_menu
  {
  items =
    {
    MENU_ITEM {command = EMyAppCmdDeal; txt = qtn_appl_deal;},
    MENU_ITEM {command = EMyAppCmdShuffle; txt = qtn_appl_shuffle;},
    MENU_ITEM {command = EMyAppCmdStick; txt = qtn_appl_stick;},
    MENU_ITEM {command = EMyAppCmdTwist; txt = qtn_appl_twist;},
    MENU_ITEM {command = EMyAppCmdSettings; txt = qtn_appl_settings;
                          cascade = r_basicgui_settings_menu;},
    MENU_ITEM {command = EAknCmdExit; txt = qtn_options_exit;}
    };
  }
RESOURCE MENU_PANE r_basicgui_settings_menu
  {
  items =
    {
    MENU_ITEM {command = EMyAppCmdSettingsSetName;
                txt = qtn_appl_settings_setname;},
    MENU_ITEM {command = EMyAppCmdSettingsReset;
                 txt = qtn_appl_settings_reset;}
    };
  }
```

Run the application and you will see the new menu and submenu appear, although if you select the Set Name or Reset options, nothing will happen, because we haven't handled the commands yet.

The Reset operation is simple: create a reset function in the Container to set the `iPlayerWins` and `iPhoneWins` variables to 0 and call this function from the `AppUi` when the Reset option is selected. Finally, set the Settings menu so that it is hidden when the `EModePlaying` flag is set (i.e. it is not available during the game).

Adding a Dialog

The last thing we have left to implement is the Set Name handler. This is a little more complicated, since we have to open a dialog for the user to enter their name.

A dialog is created by defining a dialog resource and then creating a class to handle the resulting data (i.e. validating, saving and reloading the data).

We start again in the `.rss` resource file and define a simple dialog resource:

```
RESOURCE DIALOG r_basicgui_setname_dialog
  {
  flags = EEikDialogFlagNoDrag | EEikDialogFlagCbaButtons |
                                   EEikDialogFlagWait;
  buttons = R_AVKON_SOFTKEYS_OK_CANCEL;
  items =
    {
    DLG_LINE
      {
      id = EMyAppCmdSetnameEditor;
      type = EEikCtEdwin;
      control = EDWIN
        {
        maxlength = KMaxSetNameLength;
        };
      }
    };
  }
```

The resource starts with its definition as a dialog resource. The dialog resource structure includes provision for setting flags: `EEik-DialogFlagNoDrag` sets the dialog such that it cannot be dragged; `EEikDialogFlagCbaButtons` enables the use of softkey buttons, defined in the next line as OK and CANCEL; and `EEikDialogFlag-Wait` sets the dialog to wait for input. The Edwin (text editor) dialog line can be given a maximum length, which is defined in the `.hrh` file (so that the same constant can be used in the main application and if changes are necessary, they only need to be made in one place).

In the `.hrh` file, we need to add enumerations for `EMyAppCmd-SetNameDialog` and `EMyAppCmdSetNameEditor` and define the `KMaxSetNameLength` constant (we've chosen a value of 20).

In the code below, we write a dialog class. For simplicity's sake, we create a new header and source file for our dialog class: `setname.h` and `setname.cpp` (these can be created in the include and source directories, respectively). Note that you must remember to add the `.cpp` file to the `.mmp` file, before reloading the project.

```
#ifndef SETNAME_DIALOG_H
#define SETNAME_DIALOG_H
#include <akndialog.h>  // CAknDialog
class CSetNameDialog : public CAknDialog
  {
```

```
public:
  static TBool RunDlgLD(TDes& aPlayerName);
protected:
  TBool OkToExitL(TInt aButtonId); // from CAknDialog
  void PreLayoutDynInitL(); // from CEikDialog
private:
  inline CSetNameDialog(TDes& aPlayerName) :
                iPlayerName(aPlayerName) {};
  TDes& iPlayerName;
  };
#endif
```

The class inherits from the `CAknDialog` class (note that this makes the code specific to S60 phones; it would need to be redesigned for a UIQ phone). The class requires the following functions:

- `RunDlgLD()`, which controls the first- and second-phase construction and ensures that the dialog is deleted once it is finished with (due to the 'D' suffix)

- `OkToExitL()` (inherited from the `CEikDialog` class), which is used to save data before the dialog closes

- `PreLayoutDynInitL()`, which is inherited from the UI framework-agnostic `CEikDialog` class and is called before the dialog is displayed, allowing dynamic initialization.

The standard C++ constructor simply places the input descriptor into a data member variable, `iPlayerName`, and so is fully declared in the header file. It is this descriptor that ultimately holds the name that the user enters using the dialog.

The implementation of `RunDlgLD()` is fairly straightforward: creating an instance of the dialog and then calling the framework `ExecuteLD()` method which shows the dialog. We pass the resource definition of our settings dialog, R_BASIC_SETNAME_DIALOG, so that the framework knows how to lay out the dialog controls. Again, this is defined in the `.rsg` file so we must ensure we include that into the `.cpp` file:

```
TBool CSetNameDialog::RunDlgLD(TDes& aPlayerName)
  {
  // C++ first-phase construction
  CSetNameDialog* playerNameDialog = new(ELeave)
                CSetNameDialog(aPlayerName);
  // Second-phase construction
  return playerNameDialog->ExecuteLD(R_BASICGUI_SETNAME_DIALOG);
  }
```

As per previous examples, calling `ExecuteLD()` shows the dialog and, when it is dismissed, takes care of deleting the memory associated with `playerNameDialog`.

The `OkToExitL()` and `PreLayoutDynInitL()` functions are only a little more complicated. In `OkToExitL()`, we need to save the input text and, in `PreLayoutInitL()`, we need to load the text from the application. These both follow a similar path.

As with earlier examples, we perform a static cast to obtain a concrete text-editor control pointer and either get or set the text:

```
TBool CSetNameDialog::OkToExitL(TInt aButtonId)
  {
  if (aButtonId == EAknSoftkeyOk)
    {
    CEikEdwin* editor = static_cast<CEikEdwin*>(ControlOrNull
                             (EMyAppCmdSetnameEditor));
    if (editor)
      editor->GetText(iPlayerName);
    }
  return ETrue;
  }
void CSetNameDialog::PreLayoutDynInitL()
  {
  CEikEdwin* editor = static_cast<CEikEdwin*>(ControlOrNull
                           (EMyAppCmdSetnameEditor));
  if (editor)
    {
    editor->SetTextL(&iPlayerName);
    }
  }
```

In `PreLayoutDynInitL()`, we seed the dialog with the player name based upon any existing contents of the `iPlayerName` data member. For the dialog class to compile, you need to add the following include statements and link against `eikdlg.lib`:

```
#include "SetNameDialog.h"
#include <avkon.hrh> // EAknSoftkeyOk
#include <eikedwin.h> // CEikEdwin
#include <eiklabel.h> // CEikLabel
#include <stringloader.h> // StringLoader
#include <basicgui.rsg> // resource definitions
#include "basicgui.hrh" // dialog lines
```

Finally, we need to call the dialog from the `AppUi`. We create a function, `LaunchSettingNameDialogL()`, in the Container class to handle the dialog control:

```
case EMyAppCmdSettingsSetName:
  {
  iAppContainer->LaunchSettingNameDialogL();
  break;
  }
```

In the Container header, we need to create a prototype for the `Launch-SettingNameDialogL()` function and a `TBuf<KMaxSetNameLength>` variable called `iPlayerName`, which requires the `.hrh` file to be included (for the constant definition).

In the implementation, we need to create the function as follows:

```
void CMyAppContainer::LaunchSettingNameDialogL()
  {
  CSetNameDialog::RunDlgLD(iPlayerName);
  DrawDeferred();
  }
```

Note that calling a leaving function makes this function capable of leaving in turn. Once we have obtained a new player name (using our new dialog), we ensure that the player's name is reflected in the UI by redrawing our container control, using a call to `CCoeControl::DrawDeferred()`.

Finally, we need to display the name on the screen, by modifying the `Draw()` method to use the new name:

```
_LIT(KStatsFormat, "%S: %d   Phone: %d");
TBuf<45> stats;
stats.Format(KStatsFormat, &iPlayerName, iPlayerWins, iPhoneWins);
```

Note that it is rather elegant to initialize the variable `iPlayerName` to 'Player', so that a name appears from the start.

We've covered a lot of information in a short space of time, so make sure that the application compiles (watch out for the position of the semicolons in the dialog resource) and check that you can add the player's name.

Saving Settings

We have now included customizable content and our final task is to create a persistent connection for this content, using a local file. Before we can use the file functions, we need to include the `f32file.h` header file and compile against `efsrv.lib`.

We also use streams, which make life a little easier, although they require the inclusion of another two header files, `s32std.h` and `s32file.h`, and have to be linked against `estor.lib`.

First we need to create a connection to the file server. This is done by creating a variable, `iFs`, of type `RFs`, which is defined in the `AppUi` class. Next, we need to create a new function called `SaveDataL()`, as follows:

```
void CBasicGUIAppUi::SaveDataL()
  {
  RFileWriteStream writeStream;
  TInt error = writeStream.Replace(iFs, KGameSave, EFileWrite);
  if (KErrNone==error)
    {
    // The following lines may leave so push
    // the writeStream onto the cleanup stack
    writeStream.CleanupClosePushL();
    writeStream << iPlayerName;
    writeStream << iPlayerEmail;
    writeStream.WriteInt32L(iPlayerWins);
    writeStream.WriteInt32L(iPhoneWins);
    writeStream.CommitL();
    CleanupStack::PopAndDestroy(&writeStream);
    writeStream.Close();
    }
  }
```

This function declares an `RFileWriteStream` variable, which is used to replace any previous instance of the same file by calling `Replace()`. The `Replace()` method requires a connection to the file server (see how to connect to it in the next fragment of code), the name and path of the file to save (`KGameSave`) and the mode in which we are accessing the file. The return value from `Replace()` is checked against `KErrNone` to make sure no problems occurred when opening the file, for example, insufficient disk space. Once the file is open, the stream needs to be pushed onto the cleanup stack in case of a leave.

The player's details, `iPlayerName` and `iPlayerEmail`, can be written to the file using the templated `<<` operator. Integer values, such as `iPlayerWins`, use the `WriteInt32L()` method. When we are finished writing to the file, we commit the changes before popping the stream from the cleanup stack and closing it.

Now that the data has been saved to file, we need to read it at the start of the application. We shall create a new method, `StartGameL()`, which is called from `ConstructL()`. This method allows us to set the initial game states, create new decks of cards and read in player information from the file we previously saved.

```
void CBasicGUIAppUi::StartGameL()
  {
  iGameMode = EModeNoneSelected;
  iPlayerWins = iPhoneWins = 0;
  iDeckOfCards = CCards::NewL(2);
  iDeckOfCards->Shuffle();
  User::LeaveIfError(iFs.Connect());
  RFileReadStream readStream;
  TInt error = readStream.Open(iFs, KGameSave, EFileRead);
  if (KErrNone==error)
    {
    readStream.PushL();
    //inBuf is created to initially read in the iPlayerName
    HBufC* inBuf = HBufC::NewL(readStream, KMaxSetNameLength);
    iPlayerName.Copy(*inBuf);
    delete inBuf;
    inBuf = HBufC::NewL(readStream, KMaxSetNameEmailLength);
    iPlayerEmail.Copy(*inBuf);
    delete inBuf;
    //read in previously saved scores
    iPlayerWins = readStream.ReadInt32L();
    iPhoneWins  = readStream.ReadInt32L();
    readStream.Pop(); //pops the read stream off the cleanup stack
    readStream.Close();
    }
  else //use defaults
    iPlayerName.Append(KPlayerName);
  }
```

After initializing game states we need to connect to the file server using `Connect()`; similarly, we require a `Close()`, which we can handle in the destructor.

Note that to read in the player's name we need to use a constant heap buffer, with reads from the stream for a specific length of data (when the << operator was used to write to the file, a value preceded the descriptor with its length). A further variable sets the maximum length of the buffer to be read – in this case the maximum length we have allowed for the player's name. Reading the integers back in is self-explanatory.

Finally, we need to call the `SaveDataL()` function from the command handler of the `AppUi`:

```
case EAknSoftkeyBack:
case EEikCmdExit:
    {
    iAppContainer->SaveDataL();
    Exit();
    break;
    }
```

Test and run the application – we can now save settings.

6

Complex Interfaces

Introduction

In Chapter 4, we introduced the importance of the user interface and provided some simple methods for enhancing applications. One of the great features of Symbian OS over other environments is that we can produce very effective structures for presenting our application to the user, thus enhancing its usability.

We can consider usability as the degree to which the design of a particular user interface makes the experience of the user effective, efficient and satisfying. In this chapter, we start with a discussion of the most powerful method for enhancing your user interface: multiple views. A view can be considered as the display on the screen and Symbian OS has an ability to switch between different views, depending on the user input. This allows us to produce very effective ways of presenting information to the user.

After that, we explore dynamic menus, in which we adapt the menu choices displayed to the user depending on the operating point of the user within the overall program. This enables us to present to the user only the amount of information that is strictly necessary.

Then we turn our attention to efficient use of graphics. In any program, and games in particular, most of the computational effort is spent in putting pixels onto the screen. One of the most powerful techniques is that of double buffering.

We put some of these techniques into practice for our card game. Finally, we take you through the process of getting the application onto a phone, which is always a deeply rewarding experience, especially if this is your first application.

6.1 Multiple View Applications

In its simplest form, a view is a screen within a program. There may be a number of screens, or states, that a single program may initiate and handle during execution. For example, an application may have a start screen, a main menu screen and an exit screen. More complex applications may introduce a new screen for each menu option they have, so one can imagine how difficult it could be to structure a program. Luckily, the S60 view architecture provides a number of methods for switching between views.

The ability to display a number of different views (or states) in an application can add a much more professional appearance to it as well as improve code readability. It can, for instance, be used to improve readability by breaking down information into smaller chunks and encapsulating each view in a class, eliminating the need to handle lots of `if` and `switch` statements. The main advantage of views is in the reusability of your code, as the view is encapsulated in its own class. This allows views to be placed into other applications relatively easily. Some examples of view switching that you have probably seen on your S60 phone are the messaging and calendar applications.

To grasp the concept of views, simply imagine a menu-driven system that loads a different screen depending on which menu item is selected. If each screen has different functionality, it would be difficult to contain all this information in one view class (it would also be unreadable and difficult to debug). One solution is to separate each of the different screen functionalities into separate classes. This is more readable, but how is it handled? To save the user a lot of time and effort, view switching was invented.

The view architecture allows an application to register views and switch between them, with one view running at a time. This requires the use of unique identifiers (UIDs) with each view requiring its own UID. The first view ID should be assigned to 1, as 0 is not a valid view ID. This UID can be stored in a number of different ways, either as `#defines` in a global header file or as enumerations. As long as each view has a different UID and a consistent approach is utilized, there should be no problems.

```
const TUid KMainViewId = { 1 };
```

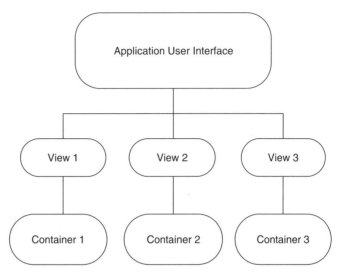

Figure 6.1   Multiple views architecture

The way an application is structured using views depends on the developer. A common approach allows each view class to be initiated in the application user interface and this user interface class is the main event handler. Control can be passed down to specific view classes that own a container, which is where the functionality of the view is implemented (see Figure 6.1).

Where the handling of the view switching occurs often depends on the differences between applications. For example, if one view leads to another in the same order every time (for example, the main screen is always loaded after the startup screen), then it is logical to handle the switch locally. This is implemented within the View class by calling `ActivateLocalViewL(newViewId)`, which is provided by the `CAknViewAppUi` class found in `aknViewAppUi.h`. The method works by calling `DoActivateL()` in the new view class, which constructs any new objects.

Once a new view is constructed, the previous view can be disregarded so `ActivateLocalViewL()` calls the `DoDeactiveL()` method for the old view. This handles any object cleanup that belongs to the class. The view class is likely to own a container class which should be cleaned up here. The switch is now complete.

Switching locally avoids going back up any unnecessary class levels and puts fewer function calls onto the stack. It may be more secure to keep the handle local as this reduces the risk of misuse. On the other hand, if an application can switch to and from views randomly (say through the use of a menu), then it is more readable to have all the view switching in the same place, making it easier to track. All the view switching can be handled in the main `AppUi`. This requires calling the `HandleCommandL()` method of the `AppUi` and passing it the view to switch to. A pointer to the `AppUi` is provided by `AppUi()`.

```
AppUi()->HandleCommandL(aViewSwitch);
```

Now that we know the basic idea, we shall consider a simple step-by-step example of view switching. A state diagram is an easy way to model view switching, as each state can map to a view (see Figure 6.2).

Figure 6.2 shows an application with three states: waiting for a key press, adding a name and displaying a name. The actions that cause transitions between the states are shown on the arrows. The waiting state can be interpreted as a main screen, with menu options or list options that allow adding and displaying of a name.

We start by defining a unique identifier (UID) for each view. If the same UID is used for more than one view, the program will crash without an error message. A good place to store the UIDs is in a global file; we call it `uids.h` and save it to the include directory.

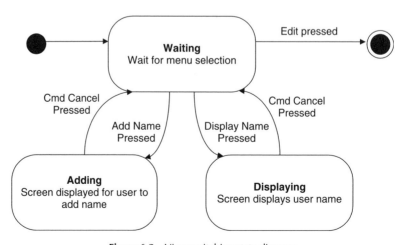

Figure 6.2   View-switching state diagram

```
#ifndef __UIDS_H__
#define __UIDS_H__
const TUid KAppUid = {0x0d139d3d};
const TUid KMainViewId = { 1 };
const TUid KAddViewId = { 2 };
const TUid KDisplayViewId = { 3 };
#endif  //_UIDS_H__
```

KAppUid is the ID of the entire application, which can be found in the project file (.mmp). Three view Ids are then defined: a main view, an add view and a display view. These IDs map to the states in Figure 6.2.

The next task is quite time-consuming, but easy to do. In this example, we create three views. Each view requires a view handle and a container class. The corresponding header files are also needed to define each of the classes. Therefore, for three views, 12 new files need to be created.

MainContainer.cpp	MainContainer.h
MainView.cpp	MainView.h
AddContainer.cpp	AddContainer.h
AddView.cpp	AddView.h
DisplayContainer.cpp	DisplayContainer.h
DisplayView.cpp	DisplayView.h

The source files are saved to the source directory and added to the .mmp file so that they can be used in the project. The header files are saved to the include folder, so that they can be included in other classes.

We can now look at defining the classes. Each view class is structured in the same manner, as they all perform the switch in the same way; the only difference is the functionality of its container class. The CAknView class provides a number of virtual functions that need to be implemented to perform the switch.

Id() returns the UID for the view that was defined in globals.h. Id() is accessed by the view-switching framework to determine the view to switch to, so this is the only point where we need to consider making the view unique.

```
TUid CMainView::Id() const
  {
  return KMainViewId;
  }
```

DoActivateL() is called by the framework when Activate-LocalViewL() is called by the user to switch to another view. Its responsibility is for creating the new container class (the new screen). The three parameters that are passed to DoActivateL() are the ID of the previous view, the ID of a message and a message. These parameters are rarely needed or used, since we do not need IDs to construct a new class. Later on, we see an example of using the descriptor message to pass data between views.

```
void CMainView::DoActivateL(const TVwsViewId& /*aPrevViewId*/,
  TUid /*aCustomMessageId*/, const TDesC8& /*aCustomMessage*/)
  {
  if (!iContainer)
    {
    iContainer = new(ELeave) CMainContainer();
    iContainer->SetMopParent(this);
    iRect = AppUi()->ClientRect();
    iContainer->ConstructL(iRect);
    AppUi()->AddToStackL( *this, iContainer );
    }
  }
```

iContainer is an instance of the container class which defines what that particular view does. SetMopParent(this) sets the enclosing parent class, denoted by this. The next two lines of code describe the construction of the container class. First, we need an area of screen that the view can access. In this instance, we allow the ClientRect() area, which is stored in a TRect called iRect. Full-screen applications require ApplicationRect() (a more detailed discussion is provided in Chapter 4). ConstructL() is called to construct the container class and uses iRect to set the area of screen to which it has access. Finally, a pointer to the view class and container class is added to the control stack allowing it to receive keyboard events.

DoActivateL() has a corresponding DoDeactivateL() method which cleans up anything DoActivateL() has created. As we have created an instance of the container class, it must be taken off the stack and deleted. However, if the view becomes more complicated it can make sense to construct the container only once. It is wise to zero-initialize the pointer to the container so validation can be performed to check if it exists.

```
void CMainView::DoDeactivate()
  {
  if ( iContainer )
```

```
    {
  AppUi()->RemoveFromStack( iContainer );
    }
delete iContainer;
iContainer = NULL;
  }
```

These are the main functions that are required to create a view. Of course there needs to be a form of construction for the view class. The view actually needs an `AVKON_VIEW` resource. This allows each view to have its own menu structure and CBA buttons.

```
RESOURCE AVKON_VIEW r_main_view
  {
menubar = r_main_menu;
cba = R_AVKON_SOFTKEYS_OPTIONS_EXIT;
  }
```

The `AVKON_VIEW` resource comprises up to three fields:

- `menubar` defines the menu to be used
- `cba` defines the buttons to use. There are a number of predefined buttons in `avkon.hrh`, such as `R_AVKON_SOFTKEYS_OPTIONS_EXIT`, which declares the left softkey as 'Options' and the right softkey as 'Exit'. For more information, see Section 5.3.
- `hotkeys` defines any keyboard shortcuts when running the application in the emulator or on a mobile device with a keyboard.

If no resource is defined, the view uses the main application's menu and buttons.

To construct the view resource, we call `BaseConstruct(TInt)`, which is also defined in `CAknView`. This takes an integer value that refers to the view resource to construct. Once compiled, the resource number appears in the `.rsg` file, which can be included and utilized.

```
BaseConstructL( R_MAIN _VIEW );
```

If no resource is used, `BaseConstructL()` should be called instead, to use the main application's resource structure.

Now the application loads one view, which is not much more than a standard single-view application at this time. However, we now get to the interesting part that enables us to switch to other views.

Just like a standard application, each view has its own menu system and its own event handler that provides a place for handling the switch. For example, in Figure 6.2 we need to get from the waiting state to the add state. We can interpret our waiting state as the main screen, with a menu option for adding a name. So we need to handle a menu event for Add name to activate an Add name view. For example, when Add Name is selected on the menu, it should activate `AddNameView`.

The following code gives us a generic view handler, which we have seen in previous sections. When Exit is selected on the menu, it calls `User::Exit(0)` to clean up all its resources and kill any child threads. It takes an integer value, a reason code, to explain the exit (0 is a standard exit).

```
void CMainView::HandleCommandL(TInt aCommand)
  {
  switch ( aCommand )
    {
    case EAknSoftkeyExit:
      {
      User::Exit(0);
      }
    case EAddNameView:
      {
      AppUi()->ActivateLocalViewL(KAddNameViewId);
      break;
      }
    default:
      AppUi()->HandleCommandL(aCommand);
      break;
    }
  }
```

If `EAddNameView` is selected on the menu, `ActivateLocal-ViewL()` is called. This uses the UID of the new view and handles the switch. The framework calls `DoActivateL()` of the new view, followed by `DoDeactivateL()` of the previous view to clean up any resources.

However, it may be more readable to handle all the switching in the main event handler in the `AppUi`. This requires the use of `AppUi()`, a pointer to the `AppUi` to call the `HandleCommandL()`, which can be seen as the 'default' action. Placing all the view switching together in the `AppUi` is easier to trace in debugging, and makes alterations easier to track down.

The container class can now be implemented, just like a single-view container class (such as `helloworld.cpp`). A pointer to the view can be passed down to the container class if it contains controls whose actions within the container cause a view switch. For example, a listbox event that is generated in the container may need to activate a new view. This requires calling the `HandleCommandL()` method of the view, which may in turn pass the handle up another level to the `AppUi`.

First, rewrite the container constructor to take a pointer to the view, and assign it to a local pointer, `iView`, which is stored in the container class.

```
CMainContainer::CMainContainer(CMainView* aView) : iView(aView)
```

Then, when creating the container within the view, pass a pointer of the view (`this`).

```
iContainer = new(ELeave) CMainContainer(this);
```

When an event occurs that requires a switch, simply use

```
iView->HandleCommandL(EAddNameView);
```

where `EAddNameView` is the name of a command in the event handler. This calls the `HandleCommandL()` of the view class from inside the container class.

Now we are able to create new views and switch between them. But what happens if the result of one view determines the state of the next? For example, the main view may contain a listbox where each item in the list represents a different file. Thus, the item selected determines which file is opened in the next view. Data sharing between views can be tricky, although it can be accomplished in a number of different ways, such as a global data store, file stores or, if manipulated carefully, passed straight from one view to another.

Global data stores are quick and easy solutions, but not necessarily the most efficient because they require more memory to store the duplicate data and more function calls are required to access the data. File stores are another option but also increase application size and users have to be careful when connecting and closing file stores, which are often temperamental when left open.

The current method for switching between views uses `ActivateLo-calViewL(TUid aId)`, which takes the UID of the view to switch to. However, there is an overloaded version of this method that also takes a `const TDesC&` message and an ID for the message. This is quite useful in a situation which only requires a file name to be passed between the views. The code below shows how this method can be manipulated:

```
HBufC8* aMess = HBufC8::NewL(KMaxItemLength);
aMess->Des().Append(KFileName);
TDesC8& aMessage = *aMess;
AppUi()->ActivateLocalViewL(KDisplayViewId, KDisplayViewId, aMessage);
```

`KFileName` is a `_LIT` descriptor holding the name of the file, which is used to create a new `HBufC8` (a heap-based descriptor). `aMessage` is a pointer to the descriptor, which can be passed to the new view through the `ActivateLocalViewL()` method. The receiving `DoActivateL()` method in the child's view can store the data from the message and pass it to the child's container constructor. The child container is then able to access the correct file name.

6.2 Dynamic Menus

In Chapter 5, we discussed how to generate our own menus and handle their items accordingly. We can extend the menu capabilities by introducing a dynamic element, i.e. making the menu appear to change over the lifetime of a program, depending on the state of the system.

A dynamic menu is defined in the resource file, the same as a static menu. Submenus may also be dynamic and are defined in the same way. The only feature that changes is an addition of a new method, which is called when a menu event is generated.

`DynInitMenuPaneL()` is a virtual method from the mixin class, `MEikMenuObserver`. It can be written to initialize the menu dynamically. The method is not called directly by the program, but by the `Uikon` framework on receipt of the menu event, before the menu is displayed. It receives two parameters: an ID for the resource activated and the menu pane from which it was activated. It is advisable to check the correct menu is being accessed before performing any actions. This can be done by comparing the Resource ID with the menu pane that should be accessed.

```
void CDisplayView::DynInitMenuPaneL(TInt aResourceId,
                                    CEikMenuPane* aMenuPane)
  {
  if (aResourceId != R_VIEW_MENUPANE)
    {
    return;
    }
```

The process of hiding menu options can be somewhat confusing at first. The following line of code makes the `EMyAppCmdDeal` menu item visible:

```
aMenuPane->SetItemDimmed(EMyAppCmdDeal, EFalse);
```

The name of the `SetItemDimmed()` method is not up to date. In earlier versions of Symbian OS, the menu item would be grayed out (dimmed), so that the user could still see the option but could not select it. However, in S60 SDK V6.1 and higher versions, rather than the item appearing dimmed, it disappears instead. Thus, setting the value to `ETrue` causes the item to disappear and setting it to `EFalse` causes the item to appear.

A good technique for structuring the `DynInitMenuPaneL()` method is first to dim all the menu options. Then you can use system states (enumerations are a good way of implementing this) to check the current states and alter the dimmed items accordingly.

6.3 Advanced Graphics

One of the problems often faced when dealing with graphics is the problem of flicker. This is caused by repeated calls to draw graphics to individual parts of the screen. Symbian OS goes some way towards solving this problem by buffering graphics calls so that a number of updates are made to the screen at once.

A more elegant solution is to use an off-screen buffer. Using this technique, a bitmap image is created with the same dimensions as the visible screen. Graphics intended for the screen are drawn first to the off-screen buffer and then, when the changes have been completed, the bitmap is sent to the physical screen in one go. In this way, the whole screen is updated at once.

In this section, we demonstrate the use of an off-screen buffer through the creation of a bespoke menu class. The technique is most widely used in the programming of graphically intensive applications, such as games.

Our bespoke menu class provides an object which can be included into any project, with a dynamic number of options. As the user scrolls through the options, the current selection is highlighted and a second line of text appears in an expanded selection area (see a screenshot from the emulator in Figure 6.3). When an option is selected the command is passed back to the AppUI class to be handled. The class is easily customizable and could be extended to offer color choices, icons, etc.

The menu class, CMenu, inherits from CBase and is constructed using a static NewL() method and standard two-phase construction. Five public methods are provided to use and operate the menu:

- AddMenuOptionL() is used to add new options to the menu (this example doesn't provide a RemoveMenuOptionL() method, although it would be relatively straightforward)

- BackBuffer() returns a pointer to the screen buffer

- MoveUp() and MoveDown() move the cursor position

- Select() is called when one of the menu options is selected by the user.

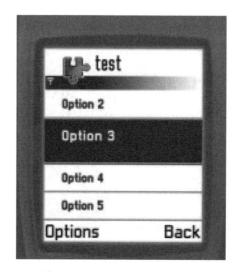

Figure 6.3   Dynamic menu screen

An additional private method, `PrepareMenu()`, updates the screen buffer before it is drawn to screen.

A number of private member variables are added to the class to manage the menu operations:

- `iSelected` is the currently selected item
- `iFirst` is the first menu item which is visible on the screen
- `iNumItemsVisible` stores the number of items that can be seen on screen at once
- `iNumItems` is the total number of items in the menu.

Further to these variables, there are a number of variables to manage the screen buffer:

- `iRect` stores the size of the screen
- `iBitmap` is the off-screen buffer
- `iFbsDevice` provides a device interface for drawing into `iBitmap`
- `iFbsGc` is the graphics context for the graphics device, providing drawing functions to the off-screen buffer.

Finally, three dynamic arrays are used to store the `CommandID` and the two lines of text for each label. We have also created a simple wrapper class, `CLabel`, for the text labels; this provides a structure which can be expanded in the future to incorporate more complex label types if necessary.

The class declaration is shown below:

```
#ifndef __MENU_H__
#define __MENU_H__
#include <e32base.h>
#include <fbs.h>
#include <bitdev.h>
#define KSelectedHeight 50
#define KNormalHeight   30
#define KMaxLabelLength 30
class CMenu : public CBase
  {
  public:
    static CMenu* NewL(TRect aRect);
    ~CMenu();
    void AddMenuOptionL(TBuf<KMaxLabelLength> aMainLabel,
      TBuf<KMaxLabelLength> aMinorLabel, TInt aCommandId);
```

```
  CFbsBitmap* BackBuffer();
  void MoveUp();
  void MoveDown();
  void Select();
private:
  class CLabel : public CBase
    {
    public:
      TBuf<KMaxLabelLength> iLabel;
    };
  CMenu(TRect aRect);
  void ConstructL();
  void PrepareMenu();
  TInt iSelected;
  TInt iFirst;
  TInt iNumItemsVisible;
  TInt iNumItems;
  TRect iRect;
  CFbsBitmap* iBitmap;
  CFbsBitmapDevice* iFbsDevice;
  CFbsBitGc* iFbsGc;
  CArrayFixFlat<TInt>* iCommandIds;
  RPointerArray<CLabel>* iMainLabels;
  RPointerArray<CLabel>* iMinorLabels;
  };
#endif // MENU_H
```

The project must be linked against two libraries: `bitgdi.lib` (for `CFbsBitmapDevice` and `CFbsBitGc`) and `fbscli.lib` (for `CFbs-Bitmap`). The implementation of the menu is pretty straightforward. The most complex part is the initial construction of the class.

The first-phase constructor sets the menu size and calculates the number of menu items that are visible on screen:

```
CMenu::CMenu(TRect aRect) : iRect(aRect)
  {
  iNumItemsVisible = 1 + (iRect.Height() - KSelectedHeight) /
                                              KNormalHeight;
  iNumItems = 0;
  }
```

The second-phase constructor creates a new bitmap the size of the menu rectangle and with 256 colors (it is good practice to create the bitmap in the same color depth as the device, otherwise the phone must convert the bitmap when it is drawn to screen). A new bitmap device is then created, with a reference to the screen buffer, and a graphics context is created for this device. Finally, the dynamic arrays are initialized. The `iCommandIds` array has a granularity of 4. This means that memory is set aside for four items at a time. This type of array would be inefficient if the menu items were to fluctuate, but the assumption is that the number of menu options would only vary occasionally:

```
void CMenu::ConstructL()
  {
  iBitmap = new(ELeave) CFbsBitmap;
  User::LeaveIfError(iBitmap->Create(iRect.Size(), EColor256));
  iFbsDevice = CFbsBitmapDevice::NewL(iBitmap);
  User::LeaveIfError(iFbsDevice->CreateContext(iFbsGc));
  iCommandIds = new(ELeave)  CArrayFixFlat<Tint>(4);
  iMainLabels = new(ELeave)  RPointerArray();
  iMinorLabels = new(ELeave) RPointerArray();
  }
```

The destructor is fairly straightforward, although the arrays need to be reset before destruction:

```
CMenu::~CMenu()
  {
  delete iBitmap;
  delete iFbsDevice;
  delete iFbsGc;
  if (iCommandIds)
    {
    iCommandIds->Reset();
    delete iCommandIds;
    }
  if (iMainLabels)
    {
    iMainLabels->ResetAndDestroy();
    delete iMainLabels;
    }
  if (iMinorLabels)
    {
    iMinorLabels->ResetAndDestroy();
    delete iMinorLabels;
    }
  }
```

The menu function calls the `PrepareMenu()` method, and then returns a pointer to the off-screen buffer:

```
CFbsBitmap* CMenu::BackBuffer()
  {
  PrepareMenu();
```

```
return iBitmap;
}
```

The `MoveUp()` function simply decrements the cursor position (if the cursor is not already in the topmost position) and checks to see if the new selection is off the screen, in which case the first visible item variable is also decremented:

```
void CMenu::MoveUp()
{
  if (iSelected>0)
    iSelected--;
  if (iSelected<iFirst && iFirst>0)
    iFirst--;
}
```

Similarly, the `MoveDown()` function increments the cursor position if more options are available. Again, if the new option is not currently visible on the screen, then the first item counter is incremented:

```
void CMenu::MoveDown()
{
  if (iSelected<iNumItems-1)
    iSelected++;
  if (iSelected-iFirst>=iNumItemsVisible)
    iFirst = iSelected - iNumItemsVisible + 1;
}
```

The select method passes the relevant command ID back to the `HandleCommandL()` method of the `AppUI` class. These commands should be enumerated in the `.hrh` resource header file and then handled in the `AppUI` class. The `AppUi` is accessed via a static pointer to the `Eikon` environment (in a more sophisticated application, it would be simpler to have a pointer to the `AppUi` but this method of accessing can be useful, particularly when debugging applications):

```
void CMenu::Select()
{
  CEikonEnv::Static()->EikAppUi()->HandleCommandL(iCommandIds->
                                          At(iSelected));
}
```

`PrepareMenu()` is the longest of the functions, but is not particularly complicated. First, the brush and pen are set to white with a solid brush and the bitmap is cleared. The pen and brush are then set to dark blue, ready for writing the menu text or drawing the menu highlight. There are two versions of the implementation: the first is used if there are fewer items to be displayed than the maximum number that could be displayed and the second if there are more items available. Each item is then drawn onto the screen, with the currently selected item drawn with both lines of text, a blue background, white text for the first line and light blue text for the second line. A line is drawn after each menu item and a local variable, y, is used to keep track of the current drawing position on the off-screen buffer:

```
void CMenu::PrepareMenu()
  {
  iFbsGc->SetBrushColor(KRgbWhite);
  iFbsGc->SetPenColor(KRgbWhite);
  iFbsGc->SetBrushStyle(CGraphicsContext::ESolidBrush);
  iFbsGc->Clear();
  iFbsGc->SetPenColor(KRgbDarkBlue);
  iFbsGc->SetBrushColor(KRgbDarkBlue);
  TInt i;
  TInt y = 0;
  TInt width = iRect.Width();
  if (iNumItems<=iNumItemsVisible)
    {
    for (i=0; i<iNumItems; i++)
      {
      if (i==iSelected)
        {
        iFbsGc->DrawRect(TRect(0,y+2,width,y+KSelectedHeight-1));
        iFbsGc->SetPenColor(KRgbWhite);
        iFbsGc->UseFont(CEikonEnv::Static()->NormalFont());
        iFbsGc->DrawText((iMainLabels->At(i)->iLabel,TPoint(20,y+25));
        iFbsGc->SetPenColor(KRgbBlue);
        iFbsGc->UseFont(CEikonEnv::Static()->LegendFont());
        iFbsGc->DrawText((iMinorLabels->At(i))->iLabel,TPoint(20,y+40));
        iFbsGc->SetPenColor(KRgbDarkBlue);
        y+=KSelectedHeight;
        }
      else
        {
        iFbsGc->UseFont(CEikonEnv::Static()->LegendFont());
        iFbsGc->DrawText((iMainLabels->At(i))->iLabel,TPoint(20,y+20));
        y+=KNormalHeight;
        }
      iFbsGc->DrawLine(TPoint(0,y),TPoint(width,y));
      }
    }
  else
```

```
   {
   for (i=iFirst; i<iFirst+iNumItemsVisible; i++)
     {
     if (i==iSelected)
       {
       iFbsGc->DrawRect(TRect(0,y+2,width,y+KSelectedHeight-1));
       iFbsGc->SetPenColor(KRgbWhite);
       iFbsGc->UseFont(CEikonEnv::Static()->NormalFont());
       iFbsGc->DrawText((iMainLabels->At(i))->iLabel,TPoint(20,y+25));
       iFbsGc->SetPenColor(KRgbBlue);
       iFbsGc->UseFont(CEikonEnv::Static()->LegendFont());
       iFbsGc->DrawText((iMinorLabels->At(i))->iLabel,TPoint(20,y+40));
       iFbsGc->SetPenColor(KRgbDarkBlue);
       y+=KSelectedHeight;
       }
     else
       {
       iFbsGc->UseFont(CEikonEnv::Static()->LegendFont());
       iFbsGc->DrawText((iMainLabels->At(i))->iLabel,TPoint(20,y+20));
       y+=KNormalHeight;
       }
     iFbsGc->DrawLine(TPoint(0,y),TPoint(width,y));
     }
   }
 }
```

Finally, the `AddMenuOption()` method adds a new menu item to the end of the menu, taking two text labels and a command ID. These are appended to the relevant dynamic arrays and the item count incremented:

```
void CMenu::AddMenuOptionL(TBuf<KMaxLabelLength> aMainLabel,
       TBuf<KMaxLabelLength> aMinorLabel, TInt aCommandId)
 {
 iCommandIds->AppendL(aCommandId);
 CLabel* label1 = new(ELeave) CLabel();
 CleanupStack->PushL(label1);
 label->iLabel.Format(aMainLabel);
 iMainLabels->Append(label1);
 CleanupStack::Pop(label1);
 CLabel* label2 = new(ELeave) CLabel();
 CleanupStack->PushL(label2);
 label->iLabel.Format(aMinorLabel);
 iMinorLabels->Append(label2);
 CleanupStack::Pop(label2);
 iNumItems++;
 }
```

In order to use the menu, an instance of the class must be created. For this example, the menu is owned by the container and created in its second-phase constructor. Some generic menu items have also been added at this point:

```
_LIT(KOption1, "Option 1"
_LIT(KDescription1, "Description 1")
_LIT(KOption2, "Option 2"
_LIT(KDescription2, "Description 2")
_LIT(KOption3, "Option 1"
_LIT(KDescription3, "Description 3")
_LIT(KOption4, "Option 4"
_LIT(KDescription4, "Description 4")
_LIT(KOption5, "Option 5"
_LIT(KDescription5, "Description 5")
...
iMenu = CMenu::NewL(aRect);
iMenu->AddMenuOptionL(KOption1,KDescription1), EMyCmdMenuOption1);
iMenu->AddMenuOptionL(KOption2,KDescription2), EMyCmdMenuOption2);
iMenu->AddMenuOptionL(KOption3,KDescription3), EMyCmdMenuOption3);
iMenu->AddMenuOptionL(KOption4,KDescription4), EMyCmdMenuOption4);
iMenu->AddMenuOptionL(KOption5,KDescription5), EMyCmdMenuOption5);
```

The menu object is deleted in the container's destructor and the key interaction is handled in the container's `OfferKeyEventL()` method. If the Up key is pressed, then `MoveUp()` is called and the screen is refreshed; if the Down key is pressed, then `MoveDown()` is called. If the Enter or OK key is pressed then the `Select()` method is called, but the screen is not refreshed as this depends on how the command is handled:

```
TKeyResponse CMyAppContainer::OfferKeyEventL(const TKeyEvent& aKeyEvent,
                                             TEventCode aType)
  {
  if (aType==EEventKey)
    {
    switch (aKeyEvent.iCode)
      {
      case EKeyUpArrow:
        iMenu->MoveUp();
        UserDraw();
        return EKeyWasConsumed;
      case EKeyDownArrow:
        iMenu->MoveDown();
        UserDraw();
        return EKeyWasConsumed;
      case EKeyEnter:
      case EKeyOK:
        iMenu->Select();
        return EKeyWasConsumed;
      }
```

```
   }
 return EKeyWasNotConsumed;
 }
```

The `Draw()` function simply draws the off-screen bitmap to screen:

```
void CMyAppContainer::Draw(const TRect& aRect) const
 {
 CWindowGc& gc = SystemGc();
 gc.BitBlt(TPoint(0,0), iMenu->Menu());
 }
```

For the sake of demonstration, the `AppUi` handles the commands by popping up a simple message in the debugger:

```
void CBooktestAppUi::HandleCommandL(TInt aCommand)
 {
 switch ( aCommand )
   {
   case EAknSoftkeyBack:
   case EEikCmdExit:
     {
     Exit();
     break;
     }
   case EMyCmdMenuOption1:
     {
     iEikonEnv->InfoMsg(KOption1);
     break;
     }
   case EMyCmdMenuOption2:
     {
     iEikonEnv->InfoMsg(KOption2);
     break;
     }
   case EMyCmdMenuOption3:
     {
     iEikonEnv->InfoMsg(KOption3);
     break;
     }
   case EMyCmdMenuOption4:
     {
     iEikonEnv->InfoMsg(KOption4);
     break;
     }
   case EMyCmdMenuOption5:
     {
     iEikonEnv->InfoMsg(KOption5);
     break;
```

```
        }
     default:
        break;
     }
  }
```

At the end of all this, we have a relatively straightforward demonstration of the creation and use of an off-screen bitmap. This example provides a simple but flexible bespoke menu class, but also demonstrates the underlying principles required for any graphics-intensive application, such as an arcade-type game.

6.4   Putting It Into Practice: The Blackjack Game

In this section, we add dynamic menus and use game states to structure visual output in the Blackjack card game.

Dealing the Cards

Now we are starting to consider the logic of the game, we need to introduce states to keep track of whether the game is being played, has not started or is finished. We can define an enumeration to manage the states.

```
enum TModeSelected {EModeNoneSelected, EModePlaying, EModeEndGame};
```

This can be defined within the `AppUi` class declaration and an instance should be declared.

We can introduce a new method to initialize the cards and other variables in the class, which can also be used to reset values if a second game is played. Initializing the cards to a value of 52 results in the back of the cards being shown:

```
void CBasicGUIAppUi::Reset()
  {
  iPlayerWins = 0;
  iPhoneWins = 0;
  iNumPlayerCards = 2;
  iNumPhoneCards = 2;
  for(TInt i = 0; i < iNumPlayerCards; i++)
     iPlayerHand[i] = iPhoneHand[i] = 52;
```

```
iGameMode = EModeNoneSelected;
}
```

Next we need to modify `DealFromDeck()` to introduce the game
state:

```
void CBasicGUIContainer::DealFromDeck()
{
iPlayerHand[0] = iDeckOfCards->Deal();
iPlayerHand[1] = iDeckOfCards->Deal();
iComputerHand[0] = iDeckOfCards->Deal();
iComputerHand[1] = iDeckOfCards->Deal();
iNumPlayerCards = iNumPhoneCards = 2;
iGameMode = EGamePlaying;
}
```

Displaying the Game Screen

Now we have set up the basic initialization for the game, the next step is
to begin displaying the game's output to the screen.

We need to create different outputs depending on the selected game
states:

- `EModeNoneSelected` displays the starting point, with no cards dealt
  or selected

- `EModePlaying` displays the face of the cards drawn by the player
  and the back of the phone's cards

- `EModeEndGame` displays the final end point, with the card faces of
  both the player and the phone showing.

To start with, we handle the basic elements to appear on all of the
screens. We set up the graphics context, clear the screen, display a top
bar that indicates the number of wins by the player or the phone and set
up a rectangle in which to display the cards from the `.mbm` file:

```
void CBasicGUIContainer::Draw(const TRect&) const
{
// Setup gc and clear screen
CWindowGc& gc = SystemGc();
TRect rect = Rect();
gc.Clear(rect);

// Display game statistics
```

```
TBuf<30> stats;
stats.Format(_L("Player: %d    Phone: %d"), iAppUi->GetPlayerWins,
                                            iAppUi->GetPhoneWins);
gc.UseFont(iCoeEnv->NormalFont());
gc.DrawText(stats, TPoint(10,15));
// Set card shape rectangle
rect.Resize(-130,-90);
rect.Move(0,25);
}
```

The size and positioning of the objects in this example was determined by trial and error, although a more detailed design consideration could have speeded up the process. Note that we need two more local variables to record the number of wins by the player and the phone, which are returned from the `AppUi`.

```
inline TInt GetPlayerWins() {return iPlayerWins;}
inline TInt GetPhoneWins() {return iPhoneWins;}
```

When the game is not being played, the application displays basic instructions:

```
_LIT (KInstructions, "INSTRUCTIONS");
_LIT (KPreGame, "Pre-Game Press");
_LIT (KPreButtons, "1: Deal     2: Shuffle");
_LIT (KInGame, "In-Game");
_LIT (KInButtons, "1: Stick     2: Twist");
//Write Instructions to screen
if (iGameMode==EModeNoneSelected)
  {
  gc.DrawText(KInstructions, TPoint(20,50));
  gc.DrawText(KPreGame, TPoint(20,70));
  gc.DrawText(KPreButtons, TPoint(20,90));
  gc.DrawText(KInGame, TPoint(20,110));
  gc.DrawText(KInButtons, TPoint(20,130));
  }
```

Finally for now, we handle the playing state:

```
else if (iGameMode==EModePlaying)
  {
  TInt numPlayerCards = iAppUi->GetNumPlayerCards();
  iAppUi->GetCards(playersHand, phonesHand);
  // Display Player Cards
  for (i=0; i<numPlayerCards; i++)
    {
    iBitmap->Reset();
```

```
// Load the specified card
TInt err = iBitmap->Load(KCardsFile, playersHand[i]);
if (KErrNone == err)
    {
    rect.Move(KMoveCard,0);
    gc.DrawBitmap(rect, iBitmap);   //Draws the card to screen
    }
}
// Display the back of the phone's cards
rect.Move(-20*i+10,55);
for (i=0; i<2; i++)
    {
    iBitmap->Reset();
    TInt err = iBitmap->Load(KCardsFile,52);
    if (KErrNone==err)
        {
        rect.Move(KMoveCard,0);
        gc.DrawBitmap(rect, iBitmap);
        }
    }
}
```

Test and run the program – at this stage, you should see a simple output of two cards face up and two cards face down; the face-up cards change each time the cards are dealt. Note that we have left quite a few things for you to do yourself along the way in order for you to repeat the lessons previously learned and you may therefore need to apply some debugging.

Twist or Stick

In the user instructions, we stated that the function of the two keys would vary depending on the game state. Once the game is in play, the 1 and 2 keys allow the player to Stick (keep the current hand) or Twist (ask for another card) rather than Deal or Shuffle.

To do this, we need to modify the key-event handler to change the reaction to key presses depending on the game state:

```
TKeyResponse CBasicGUIAppUi::HandleKeyEventL(
 const TKeyEvent& aKeyEvent,TEventCode aType)
    {
    if (aType==EEventKey)
        {
        switch (aKeyEvent.iCode)
            {
            case '1':
                {
```

```
      if (iGameMode == EModePlaying)
        {
        Stick();
        }
      else
        {
        DealFromDeck();
        }
      iAppContainer->DrawNow();
      return EKeyWasConsumed;
      }
    case '2':
      {
      if (iGameMode == EModePlaying)
        {
        Twist();
        }
      else
        {
        ShuffleDeck();
        }
        iAppContainer->DrawNow();
        return EKeyWasConsumed;
      }
    }
  }
  return EKeyWasNotConsumed;
  }
void CBasicGUIAppUi::Stick()
  {
  iGameMode = EModeEndGame;
  }
void CBasicGUIAppUi::Twist()
  {
  if (iNumPlayerCards < KNoOfCards)
    iPlayerHand[iNumPlayerCards++] = iDeckOfCards->Deal();
  if (iNumPlayerCards >= KNoOfCards)
    Stick();
  iAppContainer->DrawNow();
  }
```

If there are fewer than five cards (KNoOfCards), we deal another card; otherwise we ignore the key press. If we add a fifth card to the player's hand, we make the player stick. If the player sticks, we set the game state to EndGame and determine who has won. We have also modified the Shuffle function to set the game mode to NoneSelected.

Finding the Winner

Before we can decide who has won, we need to work out the number of points in a hand. To do this, we need to create a function that takes a pointer to an array of `TInt` values (i.e. the player's or phone's hand of cards) and an integer to indicate how many cards are in the hand. The function then steps through each of the cards in the hand and adds the card values, marking aces with a value of 1. Finally, if there are any aces and the score is less than 12, an optional 10 can be added to make the ace worth 11.

```
TInt CBasicGUIAppUi::CardHandTotal(TInt* aCards, TInt aNum)
  {
  TInt i, value, playerScore = 0;
  TInt numAces = 0;
  for (i=0; i<aNum; i++)
    {
    value = aCards[i]%13;
    if (value==0)
      {
      numAces += 1; // but still count them (with a value of 1)
      }
    if (value<9)
      {
      playerScore+=value+1;
      }
    else
      {
      playerScore+=10;
      }
    }
    if (numAces && playerScore<12)
      {
      playerScore+=10;
      }
    return playerScore;
  }
```

We need to use this function in a number of places within our program, starting with the `Twist()` function – once the player has drawn cards worth more than 21, the hand is 'bust', and we call the `Stick()` function to end the player's turn:

```
void CBasicGUIAppUi::Twist()
  {
  //Deals one card
  if (iNumPlayerCards < KNoOfCards)
    {
    iPlayerHand[iNumPlayerCards++] = iDeckOfCards->Deal();
    }
  if (CardHandTotal(iPlayerHand, iNumPlayerCards) > KCardHandMax)
    {
    Stick();
```

```
    }
  iAppContainer->DrawNow();
  }
```

For now, we leave the phone with just two cards and make a decision on the winner based on that score.

In the `Stick()` function, we check to see who has won, before setting the game mode flag to display the information for the end of the game. The winner is determined in the following order:

1. if the player's hand exceeds 21, the phone wins

2. if the phone's hand exceeds 21, the player wins

3. if the player has a higher total than the phone, the player wins

4. if the phone has a score that is better than or equal to that of the player, then the phone wins.

```
void CBasicGUIAppUi::Stick()
  {
  TInt playerScore = CardHandTotal(iPlayerHand, iNumPlayerCards);
  //Calculate winner
  if (playerScore > KCardHandMax)  //if player's hand is bust
    iWinner = EFalse;
  else
    {
    // Phone logic
    while (iNumPhoneCards < KNoOfCards &&
           CardHandTotal(iPhoneHand, iNumPhoneCards) < KPhoneStick)
      iPhoneHand[iNumPhoneCards++] = iDeckOfCards->Deal();
    TInt phoneScore = CardHandTotal(iPhoneHand, iNumPhoneCards);
    if (phoneScore > KCardHandMax)  //if phone has gone bust
      iWinner = ETrue;
    else if (KNoOfCards == iNumPhoneCards)
      iWinner = EFalse;
    else if (KNoOfCards == iNumPlayerCards)
      iWinner = ETrue;
    else if (playerScore > phoneScore)
      iWinner = ETrue;
    else
      iWinner = EFalse;
    }
  if (iWinner)
    iPlayerWins++;
  else
    iPhoneWins++;

  iGameMode = EModeEndGame;
```

```
    //Update screen with winner information
    iAppContainer->DrawNow();
  }
```

Notice we have also added some simple artificial intelligence to control the logic for the phone's hand. It will only stick if its hand is greater than KPhoneStick (defined as 15 in the global header file).

The End Game Screen

When the game has ended, we display all the cards of both the player and the phone, plus a message to say who has won. This requires one final addition to the Draw() method:

```
else  //if game is over
  {
  // Display Player Cards
  TInt numPlayerCards = iAppUi->GetNumPlayerCards();
  iAppUi->GetCards(playersHand, phonesHand);
  for (i=0; i<numPlayerCards; i++)
    {
    iBitmap->Reset();
    TInt err = iBitmap->Load(KCardsFile, playersHand[i]);
    if (KErrNone==err)
      {
      rect.Move(KMoveCard,0);
      gc.DrawBitmap(rect, iBitmap);
      }
    }

    // Display Phone Cards
    rect.Move(-20*i+10,55);
    TInt numPhoneCards = iAppUi->GetNumPhoneCards();
    for (i=0; i<numPhoneCards; i++)
      {
      iBitmap->Reset();
      TInt err = iBitmap->Load(KCardsFile, phonesHand[i]);
      if (KErrNone==err)
        {
        rect.Move(KMoveCard,0);
        gc.DrawBitmap(rect, iBitmap);
        }
      }
    rect.SetRect(TPoint(15,110), TPoint(125,145));
    gc.Clear(rect);
    TBool iWinner = iAppUi->GetWinner();
    if (iWinner)  //player wins
      gc.DrawText(KPlayerWins, TPoint(20,130));
```

```
  else
    gc.DrawText(KPhoneWins, TPoint(20,130));
  }
}
```

Dynamic Menus

We have already handled the change in the operation of the 1 and 2 keys in different game modes but we have left the Options menu items as Deal and Shuffle.

As we have seen in this chapter, menus in Symbian are dynamic and can be changed over the lifetime of an application using the `DynInitMenuPaneL()` method which is inherited from the `MEik-MenuObserver` mixin class.

We add two new menu options to the `.rss` resource file:

```
//    r_basicgui_menu
RESOURCE MENU_PANE r_basicgui_menu
  {
  items =
    {
    MENU_ITEM { command = EMyAppCmdDeal; txt = qtn_appl_deal; },
    MENU_ITEM { command = EMyAppCmdShuffle; txt=qtn_appl_shuffle; },
    MENU_ITEM { command = EMyAppCmdStick; txt = qtn_appl_stick; },
    MENU_ITEM { command = EMyAppCmdTwist; txt = qtn_appl_twist; },
    MENU_ITEM { command = EAknCmdExit; txt = qtn_options_exit; }
    };
  }
```

This requires the enumeration of the commands in the `.hrh` file:

```
enum TBasicGUICommandIds
  {
  EMyAppCmdDeal = 0x600,
  EMyAppCmdShuffle,
  EMyAppCmdStick,
  EMyAppCmdTwist
  };
```

And, finally the location-dependent language file:

```
#define qtn_appl_stick "Stick"
#define qtn_appl_twist "Twist"
```

We also need to modify the event handler in the UI class:

```
void CBasicGUIAppUi::HandleCommandL(TInt aCommand)
  {
  switch ( aCommand )
    {
    case EAknSoftkeyBack:
    case EEikCmdExit:
      {
      SaveDataL();
      Exit();
      break;
      }
    case EBasicGuiCmdDeal:
      {
      DealFromDeck();
      break;
      }
    case EBasicGuiCmdShuffle:
      {
      ShuffleDeck();
      break;
      }
    case EBasicGuiCmdStick:
      {
      Stick();
      break;
      }
    case EBasicGuiCmdTwist:
      {
      Twist();
      break;
      }
    case EBasicGuiCmdSettingsReset:
      {
      Reset();
      break;
      }
    case EBasicGuiCmdSettingsSetName:
      {
      LaunchDialogL();
      break;
      }
    default:
      break;
    }
  }
```

At last we can deal with the dynamic menu. The method `DynInit-MenuPaneL()`, which is called just before the menu is displayed, is inherited by our UI class and can be overridden as follows:

```
void CBasicGUIAppUi::DynInitMenuPaneL(TInt aResourceId,
                           CEikMenuPane* aMenuPane)
  {
  if (aResourceId == R_BASICGUI_MENU)
  if (iAppContainer->Mode()==EModePlaying)
    {
    aMenuPane->SetItemDimmed(EMyAppCmdDeal,ETrue);
    aMenuPane->SetItemDimmed(EMyAppCmdShuffle,ETrue);
    aMenuPane->SetItemDimmed(EMyAppCmdStick,EFalse);
    aMenuPane->SetItemDimmed(EMyAppCmdTwist,EFalse);
    }
  else
    {
    aMenuPane->SetItemDimmed(EMyAppCmdDeal,EFalse);
    aMenuPane->SetItemDimmed(EMyAppCmdShuffle,EFalse);
    aMenuPane->SetItemDimmed(EMyAppCmdStick,ETrue);
    aMenuPane->SetItemDimmed(EMyAppCmdTwist,ETrue);
    }
  }
```

In the overridden function we check to see if we have the correct menu (all of the application's menus are dealt with in the same function), then we get our game mode from the container. If the game mode is `EModePlaying`, we display the Stick and Twist options (i.e. we set the dimmed status to `EFalse`, hiding the Deal and Shuffle options). Otherwise we hide the Stick and Twist options.

In fact, creating the dynamic menus is quite easy – except for one final thing – you also need to include the `eikmenup.h` file before the `SetItemDimmed()` functions will work.

6.5 Getting Your Application Onto a Phone

Before continuing, make sure the application has been tested using the debugger and that there are no apparent memory leaks. If the application does contain memory leaks, the small amount of memory on the phone will be eaten up quickly and you will have to restart the phone.

Once your application is compiled in debug mode, it needs to be compiled in release mode. For S60 applications we generally use the ARMI compiler. This generates a package file (`.pkg`) in the install directory. If you open the file, it looks something like this:

```
;
; Installation file for CardGame application
;
;Languages
```

```
&EN
; Language-specific vendor names
%{"Lancaster University"}
; Unique, global vendor name
:"Lancaster University"
; SymCom
;Use UID allocated to this app by Symbian.
;
; UID is the app's UID
;
#{"Cardgame"},(0x10274E6E),1,0,0;
;Supports S60 v 2.0
;This line indicates that this installation is for the S60 platform v2.0
;This line must appear _exactly_ as shown below in the sis file
;If this line is missing or incorrect, the sis file will not be able
;to be installed on S60 v2.0 platforms
[0x101F7961], 0, 0, 0, {"Series60ProductID"};
; Six files to install
;
"\epoc32\release\armv5\urel\Cardgame.exe"
-"!:\sys\bin\Cardgame.exe"
"\epoc32\data\z\private\10003a3f\apps\Cardgame_reg.RSC"
-"!:\private\10003a3f\import\apps\Cardgame_reg.RSC"
"\epoc32\data\z\resource\apps\Cardgame_loc.Rsc"
-"!:\Resource\apps\Cardgame_loc.Rsc"
"\epoc32\data\z\resource\apps\Cardgame.rsc"
-"!:\Resource\apps\Cardgame.rsc"
"\epoc32\data\z\resource\apps\Cardgame.mbm"
-"!:\Resource\apps\Cardgame.mbm"
"\epoc32\data\z\resource\apps\cards.mbm"
-"c:\Resource\apps\cards.mbm"
```

We are interested in the files that are to be installed. The first part of the line is the current directory and the second part is where they are to be installed on the phone. Check that the directories are correct. Often they are incorrect, so use a search to determine their paths. Notice that `Cardgame.rsc`, `Cardgame_reg.rsc` and `Cardgame_loc.rsc` are all in the same directory.

If the project contains any `.mbm` files, they can be included here in the same way as the project files. Sounds and other files that are to be loaded on the phone can be included here too.

The next step is to generate an installation file for the phone, called the SIS file. This can be done by opening a command prompt and navigating to the project's install directory:

```
makesis projectname.pkg
```

(where `projectname` is the name of your project). This should return with:

```
Processing projectname.pkg...
Created projectname.sis
```

The SIS file is located in the project's install directory. If an error occurred, a line number is returned to indicate the position of the error in the `.pkg` file. Use this to check the code at that line, as it is usually typing errors that cause the problem.

All that is left to do is to send the `.sis` file to the phone. Use a Bluetooth connection from the computer to the phone, right-click on the `.sis` file and 'Send to. . .' the phone. Once on the phone, the application can be installed by following the instructions on the screen.

If another version of the same application is to be downloaded, delete the `.sis` file from the Inbox. It is often useful to remove the application too, by going into Tools, App. Manager and deleting the application from there.

7

Communications

Introduction

At its heart, a mobile phone is a communications device that can be used almost anywhere. The fact that the mobile phone allows us to stay connected 'on the go' differentiates mobile-phone applications from PC-based applications. In this chapter, we provide examples of how to use the various communications technologies. Since communication processes are generally asynchronous, we start with a discussion of Active Objects, which provide cooperative multitasking capabilities in a single thread. We then consider the functionality required for a basic serial communications link. These subjects are followed by a brief overview of text messaging, which can be used within an application to produce effective although asynchronous connectivity. The next section describes sockets that provide the foundation for other data-transfer mechanisms and leads onto our final section about infrared and Bluetooth. In many ways, IrDA was the precursor to Bluetooth, which provides a greater range and removes the need that IrDA had for line-of-sight access. Bluetooth is of particular interest to games developers who wish to provide multiplayer functionality within the range of Bluetooth. Finally, we show how Bluetooth can be used to turn our card game into a multiplayer version.

7.1 Active Objects

Active objects are the Symbian OS solution to the problem of dealing with asynchronous tasks operating in parallel using only a single thread. Each application executes in its own thread. An active object is responsible for issuing requests and handling the completion of requests. Active objects are handled using the Active Scheduler, which is responsible for devising the order in which events are handled based on the priority of individual active objects (it should be noted that the Active Scheduler does not implement round-robin scheduling of requests at the same priority and so special attention should be given to the allocation of priorities to individual active objects). Each thread can have one active scheduler which may have one or more active objects.

The CActiveScheduler class implements the active scheduler. It controls the handling of asynchronous events (active objects), by ordering (scheduling) the active object requests. The scheduler loops through the list looking for active objects that have completed. If it finds an active object that has completed it calls RunL().

CActive implements the active object by encapsulating the issuing of a request to an asynchronous method and handling the completion of that request. Three virtual functions provided by CActive are implemented in the derived class:

- RunL() is called by the active scheduler on completion of a function that has been activated using SetActive(); the SetActive() function indicates that the active object has issued a request

- DoCancel() implements the cancellation of any outstanding requests

- RunError() handles leaves that occur in RunL(), giving the active object the chance to handle its own errors and perform any cleanup.

RunL() and DoCancel() must be implemented before the code can be compiled.

```
class CMyActiveObject : public CActive
  {
public: // Constructor & Destructor
  static CMyActiveObject * NewL();
  ~CMyActiveObject();
public: // from CActive
  void RunL();
  void DoCancel();
  TInt RunError(TInt aError);
private:
  CMyActiveObject();
  void ConstructL(); // 2nd-phase construction
  }
```

In the constructor, we can give the active object a priority and add it to the active scheduler:

```
CBluetoothClient::CBluetoothClient() :
  CActive(CActive::EPriorityStandard)
  {
  CActiveScheduler::Add(this);
  }
```

Active object priorities can be found in e32base.h. Implementing active-object-derived classes require you to link against euser.lib.

```
enum TPriority
  {
  EpriorityIdle      = -100,
  EpriorityLow       = -20,
  EpriorityStandard  = 0,
  EpriorityUserInput = 10,
  EpriorityHigh      = 20
  };
```

To start the active object we first call our asynchronous function, then SetActive().

```
iSendingSocket.Connect(iSocketAddress, iStatus);
SetActive();
```

In this example, Connect() is asynchronous and completes when it connects to a socket. Once it completes, the active scheduler calls RunL(). iStatus is a TRequestStatus variable, inherited from CActive, that is used to determine whether the request has been successful. The active scheduler also uses this variable to check whether the request has completed.

```
void CBluetoothClient::RunL()
  {
  if (iStatus == KErrNone)
    {
    //add implementation here
    }
  }
```

If RunL() leaves, it calls RunError() passing the error code from the resulting leave.

```
void CBluetoothClient::RunError(TInt aError)
  {
  //handle error here
  }
```

The active object must also implement `DoCancel()` to handle any outstanding requests.

```
void CBluetoothClient::DoCancel()
  {
  // check if socket is connected and disconnect if necessary
  }
```

`DoCancel()` is called by the `CActive`'s `Cancel()` and should handle the closure of the active object requests. The user should not call it directly as it is handled by the `CActive` framework, therefore `Cancel()` should be called to cancel the active object.

Once an active object is finished with, it can be removed from the active scheduler using `Deque()`. However the `CActive` destructor automatically calls `Deque()`, so it is not normally required.

7.2 Serial Communications

Symbian provides a set of APIs that use a client–server framework to provide serial-communications functionality. When creating a serial application, it is first necessary to create a session with the serial server (`RCommServ`). The server provides information about the protocols available on the device, for example `RS232` or `RFComm`, and provides port discovery methods.

Access to serial ports is performed through the `RComm` class. This allows developers to configure the port as well as to read and write to it. The operation of the port is defined by a configuration block, `TCommConfig`, which is currently a typedef reference to the `TCommConfigV01` class, defined in `d32comm.h`:

```
class TCommConfigV01
  {
public:
  TBps iRate;
  TDataBits iDataBits;
  TStopBits iStopBits;
```

```
TParity iParity;
TUint iHandshake;
TUint iParityError;
TUint iFifo;
TInt iSpecialRate;
TInt iTerminatorCount;
TText8 iTerminator[KConfigMaxTerminators];
TText8 iXonChar;
TText8 iXoffChar;
TText8 iParityErrorChar;
TSir iSIREnable;
TUint iSIRSettings;
};
```

The parameters should be familiar to anyone who has dealt with serial ports before. They allow the definition of the data rate, the number of data and parity bits, handshaking protocols, etc. The configuration block is used to set up the serial port before use.

The capability of the serial port is similarly defined by a capabilities block, TCommCaps. The capabilities block is used to inform the client as to whether a specific combination is possible before attempting to implement that particular configuration. The example below illustrates how to determine if a serial port is capable of a particular speed:

```
TCommCaps commPortCaps;
comport.Caps(commPortCaps);
if (commPortCaps().iRate & KCapsBps9600)
  ; // capable of serial transmission at 9600 bps
if (commPortCaps().iRate & KCapsData8)
  ; // capable of data transmission with 8 data bits
if (commPortCaps().iRate & KCapsStop1)
  ; // capable of serial transmission with 1 stop bit
if (commPortCaps().iRate & KCapsParityNone)
  ; // capable of serial transmission with no parity bits
```

Possible values for the transmission rate parameter are: 50, 75, 110, 150, 300, 600, 1200, 1800, 2400, 3600, 4800, 7200, 9600, 19 200, 38 400, 57 600, and 115 200 (bits per second). As an example, the code below determines if a speed of 38 400 bps is possible:

```
if (commPortCaps().iRate & KCapsBps38400)
```

Similarly, 5, 6, 7 or 8 data bits can be transmitted; there can be 1 or 2 stop bits; and the parity options are none, even, odd, mark and space.

The code example below demonstrates how the communications port configuration module can be used to configure a specific communications port (note that it is good practice to save the previous port configuration and restore the settings when the port is released). The `Config()` method returns the current configuration of the communications port; the rate, parity, and data bits parameters are then changed, and the port is reconfigured with the new settings:

```
TCommConfig commPortConf;
commPort.Config(commPortConf);
commPortConf().iRate = Ebps38400;
commPortConf().iParity = EParityOdd;
commPortConf().iDataBits = EData7;
TInt error = commPort.SetConfig(commPortConfig);
```

Data is read from the port using the `Read()` method from the `RComm` class. The `Read()` method is passed a reference to an 8-bit descriptor (`TDes8`) and any received data is written into this descriptor. The `Read()` method is asynchronous and so it is also passed a `TRequestStatus` object which is used to indicate when the operation is complete. The `Read()` method can be passed a specific number of characters to read, or a specific time interval after which the read operation times out (normally the `Read()` method completes when the buffer is full). If it is necessary to stop reading before the buffer is full, then `ReadCancel()` should be called to end the read. It is also possible to query the buffer to determine how many bytes are currently waiting by using the `QueryReceiveBuffer()` method.

Similarly, data is written as a stream of bytes and is passed to the `Write()` function as an 8-bit descriptor. As with the read operation, the write operation is asynchronous and so a reference is passed to a `TRequestStatus` object. The write operation ends when the last character has been written; when an optional time-out expires; when a specific number of characters is written; or when `WriteCancel()` is called.

7.3   Text Messaging

The messaging architecture provides a framework for sending and receiving messages via protocols such as SMS and MMS. The functionality for each messaging protocol is provided through a series of different types of Machine-To-Machine (MTM) module, some of which provide API functions for that protocol. The SMS-client MTM module, `CSmsClientMtm`, provides operations for sending and receiving text messages. The `CSmsSettings` class is used to store the settings for the SMS-client MTM module. Progress information is obtained through the `TSmsProgress` class.

The SMS message is constructed using two classes: `CMsvEntry` deals with the message server entry; `TMsvEntry` represents the message contents and is stored as part of the `CMsvEntry` object.

Sending an SMS requires a series of steps. First, a connection is made to the messaging server using the `CMsvSession` class. An asynchronous connection to the messaging server is created by calling the method `OpenAsyncL()`. `OpenAsyncL()` requires a reference to an object that derives from `MMsvSessionObserver`, which requires the implementation of a method called `HandleSessionEventL()`. This means that the `CMsvSession` object should be instantiated within a class derived from the `MMsvSessionObserver` mixin and opened as follows:

```
iMsvSession = CMsvSession::OpenAsyncL(*this);
```

The `HandleSessionEventL()` method is called with `EMsvServerReady`, after the session has opened, or with `EMsvServerFailedToStart`, if it failed to open.

Once the server session has been constructed, it is necessary to construct an SMS-client MTM object (`CSmsClientMtm`). Handles to MTM clients are obtained from an instance of the `CClientMtmRegistry` class:

```
iClientMtmRegistry = CClientMtmRegistry::NewL(*iMsvSession);
iSmsMtm = static_cast<CSmsClientMtm*>(iClientMtmRegistry->
                          NewMtmL(KUidMsgTypeSMS));
```

The new message entry is created using the `TMsvEntry` class:

```
TMsvEntry msvEntry;
msvEntry.SetInPreparation(ETrue);
msvEntry.iMtm = KUidMsgTypeSMS;
msvEntry.iType = KUidMsvMessageEntry;
msvEntry.iServiceId = iSmsMtmServiceId();
msvEntry.iDate.HomeTime();
```

The message is added to the message server by the `CreateL()`
method. This then sets a new ID (of type `TMsvId`) for the created
message, which we must switch to:

```
iSmsMtm->Entry()->CreateL(msvEntry);
iMessageId = msvEntry.Id();
iSmsMtm->SwitchCurrentEntryL(iMessageId);
```

The body can be edited through a `CRichText` editor reference that
is returned from the MTM's `Body()` method. The addressee is added by
calling `AddAddresseeL()`. The changes are set in the message server
by calling the `ChangeL()` method:

```
iSmsMtm->Entry().ChangeL(msvEntry);
```

Next, the service-center number should be added to the message entry.
In the following code example, the default service-center number is used
(note that in a released application you should include a check to ensure
that a default SMS service center has been defined in the phone):

```
iSmsMtm->SwitchCurrentEntryL(iMessageId);
iSmsMtmLoadMessageL();
CSmsSettings& smsSettings = iSmsMtm->ServiceSettings();
CSmsNumber * serviceCenter =
    &(smsSettings.SCAddress(smsSettings.DefaultSC()));
iSmsMtm->SetServiceCenterAddressL(serviceCenter->Address());
iSmsMtm->SaveMessageL();
```

We need to update the `InPreparation` flag to tell the system that
the message is complete and ready to be sent, again using `ChangeL()`
to commit the changes:

```
msvEntry.SetInPreparation = EFalse;
msvEntry.SetSendingState(KMsvSendStateWaiting);
iSmsMtm->Entry().ChangeL(msvEntry);
```

Finally, the message is sent using two class instances, `CMsvOp-
eration` (which provides an interface for controlling asynchronous
messaging commands) and `CMsvEntrySelection` (which encapsu-
lates an array of message entries):

```
iMsvEntrySelection->AppendL(iMessageId);
iMsvOperation = iSmsMtm->InvokeASyncFunctionL( ESmsMtmCommandScheduleCopy,
                                    *iMSvEntrySelection, NULL, iStatus);
```

The message server operation is an asynchronous operation that should be wrapped in an active object; the message-sending success or failure should be checked within the RunL() method.

7.4 Socket Communications

Sockets provide a simple mechanism for connecting Symbian OS applications to remote devices. Sockets are provided through a client–server architecture, with RSocketServ providing a connection to the server (note that this is a Symbian OS server providing API functionality for socket connections rather than the remote machine that handles actual socket connections). The RSocket class thus provides a subsession to the RSocketServ session. A third class, RHostResolver, implemented as a subsession of the RSocketServ session, is used to provide name-resolution services, for example, IP or Bluetooth name resolution.

A number of additional classes may be encountered in association with sockets, including TSockAddr, TNameEntry, and TProtocolDesc. These classes are used to store name and protocol information required for establishing and using socket connections.

There are a number of functions available for reading from a socket:

- Recv() and Read() are used to read complete chunks of data from an established connection; the functions return when the descriptor provided in the function call is full, when the connection is broken if a stream connection has been made, or when a datagram has been received

- RecvOneOrMore() waits for at least one byte of data from an established connection but returns as soon as any data is available, using the TSockXfrLength type to return the number of bytes read

- RecvFrom() retrieves data from a connectionless socket and so a source address is also received with the data identifying the source of the information.

Data is written to a connected socket using Send() and to a connectionless socket using SendTo(). CancelSend(), CancelRead()

and `CancelRecv()` can be used to cancel any outstanding read or write operations.

At the end of this chapter, we shall see an example of sockets in action, providing the data connection between Bluetooth devices.

7.5   Infrared Communications

Symbian OS supports communications over infrared using the IrDA standard. Device discovery is carried out to find devices in range, followed by a service request and the use of a data protocol which enables data transfer. IrDA provides for either a socket-based or a serial connection.

Infrared socket communications make use of the `RSocket` class, with an `RSocketServ` socket server session. Available socket types include `TinyTP`, for a reliable packet-based network transfer protocol (the preferred method), and `IrMUX`, which provides a datagram network transfer protocol (datagram protocols are generally considered less reliable). The `RHostResolver` provides name-resolution services and returns information in a `TIrdaSockAddr`, which provides information about a specific (i.e. discovered) IrDA device. An interface to network databases is provided through `RNetDatabase`, with queries structured using a `TIASQuery` object and entries registered using `TIASDatabaseEntry`.

Serial connections over IrDA are made through the use of the `RComm` and `RCommServ` client–server classes, using either the `IrCOMM` service to connect to other devices or the `IrLPT` service to connect to infrared printers.

Finally, `IrTranP` provides a mechanism for receiving pictures from infrared-capable digital cameras. `CTranpSession` provides an interface to the camera and the mixin class `MTranpNotification` is used to monitor the progress of picture transfer operations. Images are transferred using the Unified Picture format that is encapsulated in the `TTranpPicture` type, which provides a `SaveAsJpeg()` method for converting the image into a more recognizable format.

7.6   Bluetooth Communications

Bluetooth is a short-range wireless communications technology that maintains high levels of security and robustness and uses little power. It operates on a frequency between 2.4 and 2.485 GHz using a time-division duplex baseband signal although, from the programmer's perspective, it appears to provide a full-duplex connection path. Most mobile phones can operate Bluetooth communications over a range of 10 meters; however other Bluetooth devices may have a range of up to 100 meters.

S60 provides Bluetooth functionality through a number of socket and Bluetooth-specific APIs that access the Symbian OS Bluetooth stack (see the generic stack shown in Figure 7.1).

Of interest to us is the software layer:

- Service Discovery Protocol (SDP) allows client devices to discover services offered by server devices; SDP also provides the functionality for detecting when a Bluetooth service is no longer available

- Radio Frequency Communications (RFCOMM) provides emulation of serial ports over the L2CAP protocol

- Logical Link Control and Adaptation Protocol (L2CAP) provides connection-oriented and connectionless data services between devices.

We need to take a look at a number of processes that must be completed to obtain a Bluetooth connection: device discovery, service discovery and finally the connection. Section 7.7 provides an extensive

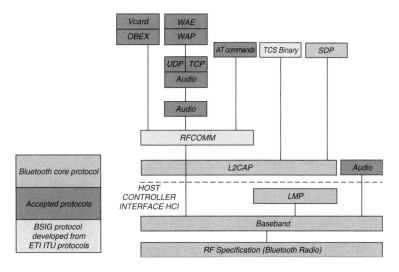

Figure 7.1   Bluetooth stack

example of how to produce a messaging application that uses Bluetooth technology.

7.7   Putting It Into Practice: A Bluetooth Messaging Application

In this final tutorial, we look at the design of a Bluetooth engine that can be incorporated into applications to provide connections between two local devices (i.e. to enable you to create two-player games). We have made this tutorial as simple and generic as possible so that you can incorporate the engine into a wide variety of applications. As you will discover, Bluetooth programming in Symbian OS is far from simple and so the key is to develop the application slowly, testing as often as possible. The engine implements a request–response protocol, and so your application should include a protocol for passing messages between connected devices.

There are three stages involved in Bluetooth communications: device discovery, service discovery, and the communications itself, in this case using a socket. The application therefore requires the creation of three main classes: CBTDeviceDiscovery, CBTServiceDiscovery and CBTMessager. The application uses a client–server approach, with the device initiating communications being the client and the device accepting the request being the server.

The CBTDeviceDiscovery class searches for devices within range of the client phone and the CBTServiceDiscovery class determines if any of the phones are running the required service (for the sake of simplicity, this example attempts to connect to the first device which supports the required service). The CBTMessager class creates a socket connection to the server.

State Machine Model

Bluetooth communications are controlled from the AppUI class using the following states (see Figure 7.2):

- EBTDormant: the application is waiting for the user or a client to request Bluetooth communications (the state when the application is created)

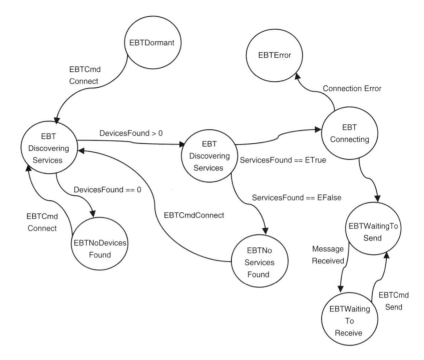

Figure 7.2   Bluetooth engine state-machine diagram

- `EBTDiscoveringDevices`: the application is searching for devices within range (when the user requests a connection)

- `EBTNoDevicesFound`: the application has found no devices (the user can restart the device-discovery process)

- `EBTDiscoveringServices`: the client is searching for the required service on each of the discovered devices

- `EBTNoServicesFound`: the client has not found the required service (the user can begin the device-discovery process again)

- `EBTConnecting`: the client has found the required service and is initiating a connection with the server

- `EBTWaitingToSend`: the client has established a connection with the server

- `EBTWaitingToReceive`: the server is connected

- `EBTError`: a fatal error has occurred; for simplicity, errors are reported here, although a full application may need to handle such errors more elegantly.

The application supports a simple turn-based half-duplex messaging protocol, with each application able to send messages to the other in turn; that is sufficient for creating a two-player card game.

Since we are building an engine for future use, for now the interface is kept very simple, with simple messages displayed on screen. These menu options would be integrated into the parent application, and the messages replaced with more meaningful responses within the application, for example, changes to the game state.

The following menu options are available in each state:

- `EBTDormant`: Connect, Exit

- `EBTDiscoveringDevices`: Exit

- `EBTDiscoveringServices`: Exit

- `EBTNoDevicesFound`: Connect, Exit

- `EBTNoServicesFound`: Connect, Exit

- `EBTConnecting`: Exit

- `EBTWaitingToSend`: Send, Exit;

- `EBTWaitingToReceive`: Exit

- `EBTError`: Exit

The following messages are displayed on the screen in each state:

- `EBTDormant`: Dormant

- `EBTDiscoveringDevices`: "Discovering devices. # found..."

- `EBTDiscoveringServices`: "Discovering services..."

- `EBTNoDevicesFound`: "No devices found."

- `EBTNoServicesFound`: "No compatible devices found."

- `EBTConnecting`: "Connecting to server..."

- `EBTWaitingToSend`: "Click Send to communicate."

- `EBTWaitingToReceive`: "Connected. Waiting for message."
- `EBTError`: "Communications error."

Creating a Basic Application Framework

We shall begin by creating a standard application framework which has `Application`, `Document`, `AppUi` and `Container` classes. We then need to create another three classes for the client, server and device discovery which can be named appropriately.

First, create a new project called `BTExample` and edit the container's `Draw()` method so that it clears the screen. Test your program to check that everything is working correctly. Next add the two new menu options, Send and Connect. For now, simply display an information message (`iEikonEnv->InfoMsg()`) when either of the menu options is selected.

Creating an Engine Class

The three worker classes for device discovery, service discovery, and Bluetooth connection can be combined into a single engine class that can easily be linked into different projects. Initially, we shall create a basic class that implements the engine and supports our state model. The class header defines an enumerated type `TBTState`, which has the state values listed above. The class also supports a standard two-phase constructor, implemented using the `NewL()` method:

```
enum TBTState {EBTDormant, EBTDiscoveringDevices, EBTNoDevicesFound,
        EBTDiscoveringServices, EBTNoServicesFound, EBTConnecting,
                EBTWaitingToSend, EBTWaitingToReceive, EBTError};
class CBTEngine : public CBase
  {
  public:
    static CBTEngine* NewL();
    ~CBTEngine();
    TBTState BTState() {return iState;}
  private:
    CBTEngine();
    void ConstructL();
    TBTState iState;
  };
```

You should be familiar enough now with creating Symbian classes to construct the corresponding `.cpp` file yourself and to create an instance of the engine within the `AppUi` class. Test it before continuing and ensure that there are no memory leaks.

Since the engine will operate asynchronously, we need to be able to inform the owner class when tasks have been completed (i.e. a state change has occurred) and so we need to create a callback class. This class is pretty straightforward, it is called `MBTEngineObserver` and it contains a single method called `HandleBTEngineStateChange()`:

```
class MBTEngineObserver
  {
  public:
    virtual void HandleBTEngineStateChange()=0;
  };
```

A pointer to the observer needs to be added to the Engine class, and the constructors updated to include a parameter providing a pointer to the observer:

```
static CBTEngine* NewL(MBTEngineObserver& aObserver);
CBTEngine(MBTEngineObserver& aObserver);
...
MBTEngineObserver& iBTEngineObserver;
```

Finally the `AppUi` needs to inherit from the `MBTEngineObserver` class and provide a pointer to itself when the Engine is constructed:

```
iBTEngine = CBTEngine::NewL(*this);
```

We can now update the Container class so that it contains a pointer to the Engine, and can update the Draw method in the Container class to give the appropriate display for each state:

```
_LIT(KBTDormantMessage, "Dormant.");
_LIT(KBTDiscoveringDevicesMessage, "Discovering devices...");
_LIT(KBTDiscoveringServicesMessage, "Discovering services...");
_LIT(KBTNoDevicesFoundMessage, "No devices found.");
_LIT(KBTNoServicesFoundMessage, "No services found.");
_LIT(KBTConnectingMessage, "Connecting to server...");
_LIT(KBTWaitingToSendMessage, "Click Send to Communicate.");
_LIT(KBTWaitingToReceiveMessage, "Connected. Waiting for message.");
_LIT(KBTErrorMessage, "Communications error.");
...
```

```
void CBTExampleContainer::Draw(const TRect& aRect) const
  {
  CWindowGc& gc = SystemGc();
  gc.Clear();
  gc.SetPenStyle(CGraphicsContext::ESolidPen);
  gc.SetPenColor(KRgbBlue);
  gc.UseFont(iCoeEnv->NormalFont());
  switch(iBTEngine->BTState())
    {
    case EBTDormant:
      gc.DrawText(KBTDormantMessage, TPoint(10,aRect.Height()/2));
      break;
    case EBTDiscoveringDevices:
      gc.DrawText(KBTDiscoveringDevicesMessage,
                  TPoint(10,aRect.Height()/2));
      break;
    case EBTNoDevicesFound:
      gc.DrawText(KBTNoDevicesFoundMessage,
               TPoint(10,aRect.Height()/2));
      break;
    case EBTDiscoveringServices:
      gc.DrawText(KBTDiscoveringServicesMessage,
                  TPoint(10,aRect.Height()/2));
      break;
    case EBTNoServicesFound:
      gc.DrawText(KBTNoServicesFoundMessage,
               TPoint(10,aRect.Height()/2));
      break;
    case EBTConnecting:
      gc.DrawText(KBTConnectingMessage,
          TPoint(10,aRect.Height()/2));
      break;
    case EBTWaitingToSend:
      gc.DrawText(KBTWaitingToSendMessage,
            TPoint(10,aRect.Height()/2));
      break;
    case EBTWaitingToReceive:
      gc.DrawText(KBTWaitingToReceiveMessage,
                TPoint(10,aRect.Height()/2));
      break;
    case EBTError:
      gc.DrawText(KBTErrorMessage, TPoint(10,aRect.Height()/2));
      break;
    }
  }
```

We can also implement the dynamic menus previously specified. This is achieved by modifying the `PreDynInitMenuPaneL()` method in the `AppUI` class, as shown:

```
void CBTExampleAppUi::DynInitMenuPaneL(TInt aResourceId,
                                CEikMenuPane* aMenuPane)
  {
  if (aResourceId==R_BTEXAMPLE_MENU)
    {
    switch(iBTEngine->BTState())
      {
      case EBTDormant:
      case EBTNoDevicesFound:
      case EBTNoServicesFound:
        aMenuPane->SetItemDimmed(EBTCmdConnect, EFalse);
        aMenuPane->SetItemDimmed(EBTCmdSend, ETrue);
        break;
      case EBTDiscoveringDevices:
      case EBTDiscoveringServices:
      case EBTConnecting:
      case EBTWaitingToReceive:
      case EBTError:
        aMenuPane->SetItemDimmed(EBTCmdConnect, ETrue);
        aMenuPane->SetItemDimmed(EBTCmdSend, ETrue);
        break;
      case EBTWaitingToSend:
        aMenuPane->SetItemDimmed(EBTCmdConnect, ETrue);
        aMenuPane->SetItemDimmed(EBTCmdSend, EFalse);
        break;
      }
    }
  }
```

Note that use of the CEikMenuPane requires the inclusion of eik-menup.h and linking against eikcoctl.lib.

We have now provided a simple framework for our Bluetooth Engine: a wrapper class with an observer that can be used to inform its owner of state changes. The hard work is about to begin, though, as we add in the Bluetooth functionality, so make sure that everything is still working before moving onto the next section.

Device Discovery Class

The next step is to add in the Bluetooth device-discovery class, CBTDeviceDiscovery, and provide a mechanism for discovering available Bluetooth devices.

This class handles the discovery of other Bluetooth devices and so works asynchronously, allowing the application to continue working whilst discovery is in progress. We create two new classes: a simple observer mixin class that handles any actions to be taken following the discovery of a Bluetooth device and the device-discovery class itself.

The observer mixin is fairly straightforward and provides a mechanism for informing the owner class that the discovery process is complete:

```
class MBTDeviceDiscoveryObserver
  {
  public:
    virtual void HandleBTDeviceDiscoveryCompleteL()=0;
  };
```

The `BTDeviceDiscovery` class inherits from `CActive`, allowing asynchronous operation. The basic class can be created using a standard two-phase constructor, initialized with a pointer to its parent:

```
class CBTDeviceDiscovery : public CActive
  {
  public:
    static CBTDeviceDiscovery* NewL(MBTDeviceDiscoveryObserver&
                                                    aObserver);
    ~CBTDeviceDiscovery();
  protected:
    void RunL();
    void DoCancel();
  private:
    CBTDeviceDiscovery(MBTDeviceDiscoveryObserver& aObserver);
    void ConstructL();
    MBTDeviceDiscoveryObserver& iBTDeviceDiscoveryObserver;
  };
```

Remember, however, that when constructing the class the active object's priority must be initialized and the active object should be cancelled in the destructor:

```
CBTDeviceDiscovery::CBTDeviceDiscovery(
    MBTDeviceDiscoveryObserver& aObserver) :
        CActive(CActive::EPriorityStandard),
      iBTDeviceDiscoveryObserver(aObserver)
  {
  CActiveScheduler::Add(this);
  }
...
CBTDeviceDiscovery::~CBTDeviceDiscovery()
  {
  Cancel();
  }
```

The class can now be incorporated into the Bluetooth Engine.

The `CBluetoothDeviceSearcher` class takes a reference parameter to the `MBluetoothObserver`, which is stored in a private data
variable. This is normally a reference to the parent class, which must
inherit from the mixin, and which provides an implementation for the
mixin's virtual function. Note that the active object is added to the active
scheduler and that it is cancelled when the object is destroyed, as in the
server class.

Before we can look for and discover Bluetooth devices, we need a data
structure to store information about any devices we discover. The next
step, therefore, is to create a structure which holds the device name, an
instance of the `THostName` declared in `es_sock.h`; the device address,
a `TBTDeviceAddr` object defined in the `bttypes.h` header; and the
RFCOMM service port, an unsigned integer. We must also link against
the `Bluetooth.lib` library. The structure, `TBTDeviceData`, is shown
below:

```
struct TBTDeviceData
  {
  THostName iDeviceName;
  TBTDevAddr iDeviceAddr;
  TUint iRfCommServicePort;
  };
```

We can now create an `RPointerArray` type definition for an array
of pointers to information about discovered devices:

```
typedef RPointerArray<TBTDeviceData> RBTDeviceDataArray;
```

Finally, we can create a pointer to the new `RBTDeviceDataArray`
type to our `BTDeviceDiscovery` class:

```
RBTDeviceDataArray* iDeviceDataList;
```

This is instantiated in the second-phase constructor and destroyed in
the destructor:

```
void CBTDeviceDiscovery::ConstructL()
  {
  iDeviceDataList = new (ELeave) RBTDeviceDataArray();
  }
...
CBTDeviceDiscovery::~CBTDeviceDiscovery()
```

```
{
Cancel();
if (iDeviceDataList)
  {
  iDeviceDataList->ResetAndDestroy();
  delete iDeviceDataList;
  }
}
```

Initiating Device Discovery

Now that we have an active object for dealing with asynchronous device requests, we need to initiate device discovery. In order to facilitate this, we shall add a new method to the `CBTDeviceDiscovery` class called `StartDeviceDiscoveryL()`. This method commences the search for Bluetooth devices within range of the client. It makes use of sockets to query devices and needs a reference to a socket server:

```
void StartDeviceDiscoveryL(RSocketServ& aSocketServ);
```

The socket server should be created in the Engine class:

```
RSocketServ iSocketServ;
```

This requires the inclusion of the `es_sock.h` header and the project should be linked against the `esock.lib` library. The socket server is initialized in the engine's `ConstructL()` method and closed in the engine's destructor:

```
User::LeaveIfError(iSocketServ.Connect());
...
iSocketServ.Close();
```

In order to discover devices, we need to add three new member variables to the `CBTDeviceDiscovery` class:

```
RHostResolver iHostResolver;
TInquirySockAddr iInquirySockAddr;
TNameEntry iNameEntry;
```

The RHostResolver class is used to translate host addresses (for example, Bluetooth addresses, DNS address, etc.); the TInquirySock-Addr class, which requires the inclusion of bt_sock.h, is used to store the socket address of the device we are talking to; and TNameEntry is used to store the name of the Bluetooth device.

The StartDeviceDiscoveryL() method resets the device datalist, cleaning up any existing records. Then it creates an instance of the protocol descriptor and uses the socket server of the Engine class to find the BTLinkManager protocol, before opening a connection to the host resolver instance:

```
void CBTDeviceDiscovery::StartDeviceDiscoveryL(RSocketServ& aSocketServ)
  {
  iDeviceDataList->ResetAndDestroy();
  TProtocolDesc protocolDesc;
  User::LeaveIfError(aSocketServ.FindProtocol(_L("BTLinkManager"),
                                              protocolDesc));
  User::LeaveIfError(iHostResolver.Open(aSocketServ,
      protocolDesc.iAddrFamily, protocolDesc.iProtocol));
  iInquirySockAddr.SetIAC(KGIAC);
  iInquirySockAddr.SetAction(KHostResInquiry |   KHostResName |
                                  KHostResIgnoreCache);
  iHostResolver.GetByAddress(iInquirySockAddr, iNameEntry,
                                      iStatus);
  SetActive();
  }
```

The SetIAC() method sets the inquiry access code, in this case to KGIAC (the general, unlimited, inquiry access code – the alternative is KLIAC for limited inquiry access code), and SetAction() sets the flags for resolving names and addresses. If KhostResName is the only flag set, then GetByAddress() looks up the name for the device specified through TBTSockAddr::SetBTAddr() and returns a TNameEntry with the original TInquirySockAddr and the hostname of the device. With only KHostResInquiry set, GetByAddress() performs an inquiry for devices using the specified IAC and returns one or more TNameEntry records with the device address and class of device fields filled in. If KhostResInquiry and KHostResName are both set, then GetByAddress() performs an inquiry for devices using the specified IAC and looks up the names of the returned devices, returning one or more TNameEntry records with the device address, class of device, and hostname fields filled in. If no flags are set, then KErrBadParams is returned.

We use the resolver to get the host name for the discovered device and set the active object as active, which tells the active scheduler that a request to the resolver is active. The request is marked as complete before the `RunL()` function is called or when the object is cancelled. The `RunL()` method completes the discovery process:

```
void CBTDeviceDiscovery::RunL()
  {
  if (iStatus != KErrNone)
    {
    iHostResolver.Close();
    iBTDeviceDiscoveryObserver->HandleBTDeviceDiscoveryCompleteL();
    }
  else
    {
    TBTDeviceData* deviceData = new (ELeave) TBTDeviceData;
    deviceData->iDeviceAddr =
        static_cast<TBTSockAddr>(iNameEntry().iAddr).BTAddr();
    deviceData->iDeviceName = iNameEntry().iName;
    iDeviceDataList->Append(deviceData);
    iHostResolver.Next(iNameEntry, iStatus);
    SetActive();
    }
  }
```

If the `iStatus` variable is not equal to `KErrNone`, then the discovery process is complete and we can close the `HostResolver` and invoke the `HandleBTDeviceDiscoveryCompleteL()` callback function. If, however, a device has been successfully found, then the device details are saved to an instance of the `TBTDeviceData` structure, and the pointer to it is appended to the device list, `iDeviceDataList`. Finally, we ask the `HostResolver` to look for the next device and reactivate the active scheduler.

If the process is cancelled, then the `DoCancel()` method cancels the active object and the `HostResolver`:

```
void CBTDeviceDiscovery::DoCancel()
  {
  Cancel();
  iHostResolver.Close();
  }
```

The device-discovery process can now be initiated from the `AppUi` class when the user selects the Connect menu command through a new method `DiscoverDevicesL()` which is added to the `BTEngine` class. The `HandleCommandL()` method in the `AppUi` class handles user commands and we can modify the Connect case:

```
case EBTCmdConnect:
  {
  iBTEngine->DiscoverDevicesL();
  break;
  }
```

`DiscoverDevicesL()` updates the engine state, calls the `StartDeviceDiscoveryL()` method, and then invokes the `HandleBTEngineStateChangeL()` method:

```
void CBTEngine::DiscoverDevicesL()
  {
  iState = EBTDiscoveringDevices;
  iBTDeviceDiscovery->StartDeviceDiscoveryL(iSocketServ);
  iBTEngineObserver->HandleBTEngineStateChange();
  }
```

When discovery is complete, the `HandleBTDeviceDiscoveryCompleteL()` method is invoked, and this, for now, changes the engine state and informs the `AppUi` class:

```
void CBTEngine::HandleBTDeviceDiscoveryCompleteL()
  {
  iState = EBTDiscoveringServices;
  iBTEngineObserver->HandleBTEngineStateChange();
  }
```

The application now allows the user to begin the device-discovery process, which changes the application state to `DiscoveringDevices`; on completion of the process, the application state changes to `DiscoveringServices`.

Note that now we are using the Bluetooth radio, you need to begin testing functionality directly on the phone (and to complete the tutorial you need at least two phones). If you are compiling for Symbian OS v9 or higher, the application must be given permission to access the Bluetooth services by providing the `LocalServices` capability (i.e. network services that do not typically incur a charge) in the MMP file:

```
CAPABILITY LocalServices
```

Advertising a Service

Now that we can detect other Bluetooth devices we need a means of checking each of these devices to find out which are running our specific application. The server will advertise the service for the client to detect.

The service discovery protocol (SDP) provides a simple mechanism for communicating between Bluetooth devices. The SDP uses a simple request–response model, which enables the client device to query the server. In this example, the client requests the service record from the server device. The service record contains all of the information about a specific service recorded in a series of service attributes (which consist of a 16-bit attribute ID and a variable-length attribute value). Once the application has finished searching for devices, it can search for suitable services.

Our services are advertised using a new class called `CBTServiceAdvertiser`. This is declared as follows:

```
#define KBTServiceUUID 0x1fa6
_LIT(KBTServiceName, "BTExample");
class CBTServiceAdvertiser : public CBase
  {
  public:
    static CBTServiceAdvertiser* NewL();
    ~CBTServiceAdvertiser();
    void StartAdvertisingL(TInt aChannel);
    void StopAdvertisingL();
  private:
    CBTServiceAdvertiser();
    void ConstructL();
    RSdp iSdp;
    RSdpDatabase iSdpDatabase;
    TSdpServRecordHandle iSdpServRecordHandle;
  };
```

The class requires the inclusion of `btsdp.h` to provide SDP functionality. The file contains a macro declaration for a constant `KBTServiceUUI`, which is used repeatedly to construct a 128-bit UUID for the Bluetooth service, and we also define a name for the service, in this case `BTExample`. Besides the usual two-phase construction, the class includes methods to start and stop advertising the service and references to the `RSdp` and `RSdpDatabase` classes which provide access to the SDP services.

The `StartAdvertisingL()` method is the more complex of the two methods to be implemented:

```
void CBTServiceAdvertiser::StartAdvertisingL(TInt aChannel)
  {
  User::LeaveIfError(iSdp.Connect());
  User::LeaveIfError(iSdpDatabase.Open(iSdp));
  iSdpDatabase.CreateServiceRecordL(TUUID(KBTServiceUUID, KBTServiceUUID,
              KBTServiceUUID, KBTServiceUUID), iSdpServRecordHandle);
  CSdpAttrValueDES* sdpAttrValueDescriptors =
          CSdpAttrValueDES::NewDESL(NULL);
  CleanupStack::PushL(sdpAttrValueDescriptors);
  TBuf8<1> channel;
  channel.Append((TChar)(aChannel%10));
  sdpAttrValueDescriptors->StartListL()
    ->BuildDESL()->StartListL()->BuildUUIDL(KL2CAP)->EndListL()
            ->BuildDESL()->StartListL()->BuildUUIDL(KRFCOMM)
                        ->BuildUintL(channel)->EndListL()
                                    ->EndListL();
  iSdpDatabase.UpdateAttributeL(iSdpServRecordHandle,
      KSdpAttrIdProtocolDescriptorList, *sdpAttrValueDescriptors);
  CleanupStack::PopAndDestroy(sdpAttrValueDescriptors);
  iSdpDatabase.UpdateAttributeL(iSdpServRecordHandle,
      KSdpAttrIdBasePrimaryLanguage + KSdpAttrIdOffsetServiceName,
                                              KBTServiceName);
  iSdpDatabase.UpdateAttributeL(iSdpServRecordHandle,
                  KSdpAttrIdBasePrimaryLanguage +
  KSdpAttrIdOffsetServiceDescription, KBTServiceName);
  iSdpDatabase.UpdateAttributeL(iSdpServRecordHandle,
              KSdpAttrIdServiceAvailability, 0xFF);
  iSdpDatabase.UpdateAttributeL(iSdpServRecordHandle,
              KSdpAttrIdServiceRecordState, 1);
  }
```

First we connect to the SDP services class and open the SDP database. Next we create a service record for our application using the `TUUID` method to create a 128-bit `UUID` generated from our `KBTServiceUUID` number repeated four times, and pass a variable to store a handle to the created service record. We then need to create a descriptor to describe the service attributes (in this case, L2CAP and RFCOMM protocol support) and update the service record attributes.

The `StopAdvertisingServiceL()` method removes the service record from the SDP database and closes the `SdpDatabase` and `Sdp` connections:

```
void CBTServiceAdvertiser::StopAdvertisingL()
  {
```

```
if (iSdpServRecordHandle != NULL)
  {
  iSdpDatabase.DeleteRecordL(iSdpServRecordHandle);
  iSdpDatabase.Close();
  iSdpServRecordHandle = NULL;
  }
}
```

The `CBTServiceAdvertiser` class can now be included within the
`CBTEngine` class and the `StartAdvertisingL()` method is called
after the class is instantiated in the engine's `ConstructL()` method. A
`StopAdvertisingL()` method needs to be added to the Engine class
to call the `StopAdvertsingL()` method of the `CBTServiceAdver-
tiser` and this should be called from the `AppUi` class when the user exits
the application, i.e. the service is only advertised when the application is
running. Note that the `StopAdvertisingL()` method cannot be called
from the destructor since it may leave and so must be called before the
application is destroyed. If we do not stop advertising the service when
the program is exited then the service will continue to be advertised until
the phone is next rebooted since the service record will remain in the
SDP database.

Service Discovery

Discovering services is a little more complicated than advertising them
but we need to be able to recognize when a device is running our
application.

Firstly we need a straightforward callback function so that we can
inform the Engine class when the service-discovery process is completed:

```
class MBTServiceDiscoveryObserver
  {
  public:
    virtual void HandleBTServiceDiscoveryCompleteL(TBool aServiceFound,
                                                   TInt aPort)=0;
  };
```

The actual `BTServiceDiscovery` class is again relatively straightforward:

```
class CBTServiceDiscovery : public CBase, public MSdpAgentNotifier,
                            public MSdpAttributeValueVisitor
```

```
{
public:
  static CBTServiceDiscovery* NewL(MBTServiceDiscoveryObserver*
                                                    aObserver);
  ~CBTServiceDiscovery();
    void DiscoverIfDeviceHasServiceL(TBTDevAddr aAddress,
                                     TUUID aServiceUUID);
private:
  CBTServiceDiscovery(MBTServiceDiscoveryObserver* aObserver);
  void ConstructL();
  void NextRecordRequestComplete(TInt aError,
      TSdpServRecordHandle aHandle, TInt aTotalRecordsCount);
  void AttributeRequestResult(TSdpServRecordHandle aHandle,
      TSdpAttributeID aAttrID, CSdpAttrValue* aAttrValue);
  void AttributeRequestComplete(TSdpServRecordHandle aHandle,
                                          TInt aError);
  void VisitAttributeValueL(CSdpAttrValue &aValue,
                           TSdpElementType aType);
  void StartListL(CSdpAttrValueList &aList);
  void EndListL();
  MBTServiceDiscoveryObserver* iBTServiceDiscoveryObserver;
  CSdpSearchPattern* iSdpSearchPattern;
  CSdpAgent* iSdpAgent;
  CSdpAttrIdMatchList* iSdpAttrIdMatchList;
  TBool iRFCommFound;
  TInt iChannel;
};
```

In addition to the standard constructors and destructors, we have the following methods:

- `DiscoverIfDeviceHasServiceL()`, which begins the service-discovery process

- three methods which are inherited from the `MSdpAgentNotifier` mixin class: `NextRecordRequestComplete()`, `AttributeRequestResult()` and `AttributeRequestComplete()`

- three methods which are inherited from the `MSdpAttributeValueVisitor` mixin class: `VisitAttributeValueL()`, `StartListL()` and `EndListL()`.

Finally, we have a pointer to the `BTServiceDiscoveryObserver` and pointers to instances of the `CSdpSearchPattern`, `CSdpAgent`, and `CSdpAttrIdMatchList` classes which provide functionality for accessing the SDP. We also have a flag to identify when the RFCOMM

attribute values are found and a variable in which we can store the port
or channel number for the service. The SDP classes require the inclusion
of the `btsdp.h` file and the `TBTDevAddr`, which is used to identify the
Bluetooth device, requires the `bttypes.h` header. Additionally we need
to link against the `sdpdatabase.lib` and `sdpagent.lib` libraries.

The construction of the class is simple, requiring the creation of a new
`iSdpSearchPattern` object, as shown below:

```
CBTServiceDiscovery::CBTServiceDiscovery(MBTServiceDiscoveryObserver*
                aObserver) : iBTServiceDiscoveryObserver(aObserver)
  {
  }
...
void CBTServiceDiscovery::ConstructL()
  {
  iSdpSearchPattern = CSdpSearchPattern::NewL();
  iSdpAttrIdMatchList = CSdpAttrIdMatchList::NewL();
  iSdpAttrIdMatchList->AddL(KSdpAttrIdServiceAvailability);
  iSdpAttrIdMatchList->AddL(KSdpAttrIdProtocolDescriptorList);
  }
```

The `iSdpAttrIdMatchList` sets up a list of attributes in the service
record we wish to find: in this case the service availability and the protocol
descriptor. Note that we do not yet need to instantiate the `SdpAgent`
although we do need to destroy it if it has been created by the time we
get to the destructor:

```
CBTServiceDiscovery::~CBTServiceDiscovery()
  {
  if (iSdpSearchPattern)
    {
    iSdpSearchPattern->Reset();
    delete iSdpSearchPattern;
    iSdpSearchPattern = NULL;
    }
  if (iSdpAgent!=NULL)
    {
    iSdpAgent->Cancel();
    delete iSdpAgent;
    iSdpAgent = NULL;
    }
  if (iSdpAttrIdMatchList!=NULL)
    delete iSdpAttrIdMatchList;
  }
```

Next we need to search for our service on a particular Bluetooth device, as shown below:

```
void CBTServiceDiscovery::DiscoverIfDeviceHasServiceL(TBTDevAddr aAddress,
                                                      TUUID aServiceUUID)
  {
  iRFCommFound = EFalse;
  if (iSdpSearchPattern)
    {
    iSdpSearchPattern->Reset();
    delete iSdpSearchPattern;
    iSdpSearchPattern = NULL;
    }
  iSdpSearchPattern = CSdpSearchPattern::NewL();
  iSdpSearchPattern->AddL(aServiceUUID);
  if (iSdpAgent!=NULL)
    {
    iSdpAgent->Cancel();
    delete iSdpAgent;
    iSdpAgent = NULL;
    }
  iSdpAgent = CSdpAgent::NewL(*this, aAddress);
  iSdpAgent->SetRecordFilterL(*iSdpSearchPattern);
  iSdpAgent->NextRecordRequestL();
  }
```

If the `iSdpSearchPattern` object is not null we reset it, delete it, set the pointer to null, and then reinitialize it using the service UUID which is passed as a parameter into the method. We then repeat the process resetting the `SdpAgent` instance and setting the search filter to our service UUID before calling the `NextRecordRequestL()` method which begins the asynchronous service record search. When the search is complete the `NextRecordRequestComplete` callback function is called:

```
void CBTServiceDiscovery::NextRecordRequestComplete(TInt aError,
        TSdpServRecordHandle aHandle, TInt aTotalRecordsCount)
  {
  TInt error;
  if (KErrNone==aError && aTotalRecordsCount>0)
  {
    TRAP(error, iSdpAgent->AttributeRequestL(aHandle,
                        *iSdpAttrIdMatchList));
  }
  else
    TRAP(error, iBTServiceDiscoveryObserver->
        HandleBTServiceDiscoveryCompleteL(EFalse, 0));
  }
```

If there are no errors and more than one record is found, then we call the `AttributeRequestL()` method of the `SdpAgent` class to browse the record attributes, otherwise we use the callback function with the parameter `EFalse` to inform the engine that the service wasn't found on any device. When each attribute is retrieved the `AttributeRequestResult()` mixin callback method is called. Note that the callback is specified as a non-leaving function and so we must ensure it doesn't leave. From here we call the `AcceptVisitor()` method on the `SdpAttrValue` parameter allowing us to parse the attribute:

```
void CBTServiceDiscovery::AttributeRequestResult
          (TSdpServRecordHandle aHandle, TSdpAttributeID aAttrID,
                                       CSdpAttrValue* aAttrValue)
  {
  TRAPD(error, aAttrValue->AcceptVisitorL(*this));
  }
...
void CBTServiceDiscovery::VisitAttributeValueL(CSdpAttrValue &aValue,
                                          TSdpElementType aType)
  {
  switch (aType)
    {
    case ETypeUUID:
      {
      if (aValue.UUID() == TUUID(KRFCOMM))
        iRFCommFound = ETrue;
      break;
      }
    case ETypeUint:
      {
      if (iRFCommFound)
        {
        iRFCommFound = EFalse;
        iChannel=aValue.Uint();
        }
      break;
      }
    default:
      break;
    }
  }
```

When parsing the attribute values there are two that we are interested in: the RFCOMM attribute, defined in `bt_types.h`, and the value that immediately follows which is the port on which the service is advertised and to which we wish to connect.

If we successfully parse the attribute data then we can return the channel number via the callback function:

```
void CBTServiceDiscovery::AttributeRequestComplete
    (TSdpServRecordHandle aHandle, TInt aError)
  {
  TInt error;
  if (KErrNone!=aError)
    {
    TRAP(error, iBTServiceDiscoveryObserver->
        HandleBTServiceDiscoveryCompleteL(EFalse, 0));
    }
  else
    TRAP(error, iBTServiceDiscoveryObserver->
        HandleBTServiceDiscoveryCompleteL(ETrue, iChannel));
  }
```

The CBTServiceDiscovery class can now be incorporated into the CBTEngine class together with a new method DiscoverServicesL() and an integer variable iIndex to keep track of individual Bluetooth devices.

When the device discovery is complete we check to see if any devices have been found, using a simple method called DeviceDataList() which returns a pointer to the array of device information, and, if so, we begin the service-discovery process, otherwise we move to the EBTNoDevicesFound state:

```
void CBTEngine::HandleBTDeviceDiscoveryCompleteL()
  {
  if (iBTDeviceDiscovery->DeviceDataList()->Count() > 0)
    {
    iState = EBTDiscoveringServices;
    iBTEngineObserver->HandleBTEngineStateChange();
    DiscoverServicesL();
    }
  else
    {
    iState = EBTNoDevicesFound;
    iBTEngineObserver->HandleBTEngineStateChange();
    }
  }
```

When we begin the service-discovery process we set the iIndex counter to zero and search for the advertised service on the first of the discovered devices:

```
void CBTEngine::DiscoverServicesL()
  {
  iState = EBTDiscoveringServices;
  iBTEngineObserver->HandleBTEngineStateChange();
  iIndex = 0;
  RBTDeviceDataArray* devices =
      iBTDeviceDiscovery->DeviceDataList();
  TBTDeviceData* device = (*devices)[iIndex];
  iBTServiceDiscovery->DiscoverIfDeviceHasServiceL
      (device->iDeviceAddr, TUUID(KBTServiceUUID, KBTServiceUUID,
                              KBTServiceUUID, KBTServiceUUID));
  }
```

When the search for services is completed, we call the relevant callback function to see if the service was found and save the port number before switching to the EBTConnecting state. (In this example, we connect to the first compatible device discovered although you may wish to create a menu of devices for the user to select from.) If the service is not found then we continue searching on the next device. Once the list of available devices is exhausted we switch to the EBTServiceNotFound state:

```
void CBTEngine::HandleBTServiceDiscoveryCompleteL(TBool aServiceFound,
                                                  TInt aPort)
  {
  if (aServiceFound)
    {
    RBTDeviceDataArray* devices = iBTDeviceDiscovery->DeviceDataList();
    TBTDeviceData* device = (*devices)[iIndex];
    device->iRfCommServicePort = aPort;
    iState = EBTConnecting;
    iBTEngineObserver->HandleBTEngineStateChange();
    }
  else
    {
    iIndex++;
    if (iIndex<iBTDeviceDiscovery->DeviceDataList()->Count())
      {
      RBTDeviceDataArray* devices = iBTDeviceDiscovery->DeviceDataList();
      TBTDeviceData* device = (*devices)[iIndex];
      iBTServiceDiscovery->DiscoverIfDeviceHasServiceL
              (device->iDeviceAddr, KBTServiceUUID);
      }
    else
      {
      iState = EBTNoServicesFound;
```

```
      iBTEngineObserver->HandleBTEngineStateChange();
      }
   }
}
```

Server Class

The server class is the more complicated of the two communications classes. It must bind the application to a socket to listen for connection requests, provide a socket for handling communications, and set the security parameters for the communications channel.

The server contains its own state machine for controlling asynchronous actions and has the following states:

- `EBTServerDisconnected`: The initial state with no socket bindings

- `EBTServerConnecting`: The server is waiting for a request from a client

- `EBTServerWaiting`: The server is waiting for data from the client

- `EBTServerSending`: The server is sending data to the client

- `EBTServerConnected`: The server is connected but idle.

These are encapsulated in a new enumerated type, `TBTServerState`:

```
enum TBTServerState {EBTServerDisconnected=0, EBTServerConnecting,
        EBTServerWaiting, EBTServerSending, EBTServerConnected};
```

We also need to send messages back to the user interface, and this is handled through a mixin observer:

```
class MBTServerObserver
   {
   public:
     virtual void HandleBTServerConnected()=0;
     virtual void HandleBTServerDisconnected()=0;
     virtual void HandleBTServerMessageRecvd()=0;
     virtual void HandleBTServerMessageSent()=0;
     virtual void HandleBTServerError(TInt aError)=0;
   };
```

The callback functions inform the user interface when a client connects to the server; when the client disconnects from the server; when a message is received from the client; when a message has been sent; and when an error has occurred.

The server is a standard class derived from `CActive` with additional methods for starting the server, stopping the server, sending a message, and setting the channel security:

```
class CBTServer : public CActive
  {
  public:
    static CBTServer* NewL(MBTServerObserver& aObserver);
    ~CBTServer();
    TInt StartL(RSocketServ& aSocketServ);
    void Stop();
    void SendL(const TDesC8& aMessage);
  protected:
    void RunL();
    void DoCancel();
  private:
    CBTServer(MBTServerObserver& aObserver);
    void ConstructL();
    void SetChannelSecurityL(TBool aAuthentication, TBool aEncryption,
        TBool aAuthorisation, TInt aChannel, TBTSockAddr& aSockAddr);
    TBTServerState iBTServerState;
    RSocket iListenSocket;
    RSocket iConnectedSocket;
    TBuf8<KMaximumMessageLength> iBuffer;
    TSockXfrLength iLen;
    MBTServerObserver& iBTServerObserver;
  };
```

The server uses two sockets: one for listening for connection requests, `iListenSocket`, and one for handling connections, `iConnected-Socket`. A buffer is used for receiving data from the socket and this is declared as a constant in the header. The `TSockXfrLength` variable is used to feed back the length of the data received.

Going through the methods in more detail, the constructor simply initializes the active object's priority, sets the initial state of the server, and stores a reference to the observer instance:

```
CBTServer::CBTServer(MBTServerObserver& aObserver) :
    CActive(EPriorityNormal), iBTServerState(EBTServerDisconnected),
                              iBTServerObserver(aObserver)
  {
  CActiveScheduler::Add(this);
  }
```

The `StartL()` method opens the listening socket using the RFCOMM protocol and then calls the `GetOpt()` method to retrieve an available port number through which a communications channel can be initiated. A TBTSockAddr variable stores information about the socket port number and this is used to bind the listening socket to the communications channel through the available port. The sockAddr variable is also used to set the channel security and is passed to the SetSecurityL() method together with the channel security parameters which we will discuss shortly. We close the connection socket before opening it, to ensure that we are not reopening an open socket. We can then set the listening socket to wait asynchronously for a client request using the Accept() method, passing the connection socket as the socket to be used for actual communications. The server state is then set to EBTServerConnecting and the object is set as active so that it waits for the asynchronous request to complete:

```
TInt CBTServer::StartL(RSocketServ& aSocketServ)
  {
  TProtocolDesc pdesc;
  User::LeaveIfError(aSocketServ.FindProtocol(_L("RFCOMM"), pdesc));
  User::LeaveIfError(iListenSocket.Open(aSocketServ, pdesc.iAddrFamily,
                                        pdesc.iSockType, KRFCOMM));
  TInt port;
  User::LeaveIfError(iListenSocket.GetOpt
     (KRFCOMMGetAvailableServerChannel, KSolBtRFCOMM, port));
  TBTSockAddr sockAddr;
  sockAddr.SetPort(port);
  User::LeaveIfError(iListenSocket.Bind(sockAddr));
  User::LeaveIfError(iListenSocket.Listen(5));
  SetChannelSecurityL(EFalse, EFalse, ETrue, port, sockAddr);
  iConnectedSocket.Close();
  User::LeaveIfError(iConnectedSocket.Open(aSocketServ));
  iBTServerState = EBTServerConnecting;
  iListenSocket.Accept(iConnectedSocket, iStatus);
  SetActive();
  return port;
  }
```

The Stop() method closes the sockets canceling any outstanding requests:

```
void CBTServer::Stop()
  {
  iBTServerState = EBTServerDisconnected;
  Cancel();
  iConnectedSocket.CancelAll();
  iConnectedSocket.Close();
  iListenSocket.Close();
  }
```

The `SetChannelSecurityL()` method sets the channel security using a connection to the Bluetooth manager to set the authentication, encryption and authorization parameters for the channel. In this example, we have set the authentication to `EFalse` so that connections can be made without user authentication, the encryption to `EFalse` so that transmissions are made unencrypted and the authorization to `ETrue` so that user input is required if the device is untrusted. The security settings are made by calling the `SetSecurity()` method of the `TBTSockAddr` variable (prior to version 2 feature pack 2, the `RBTSecuritySettings::RegisterService()` method should be used):

```
void CBTServer::SetChannelSecurityL(TBool aAuthentication,
              TBool aEncryption, TBool aAuthorization,
              TInt aChannel, TBTSockAddr& aSockAddr)
  {
  RBTMan btManager;
  User::LeaveIfError(btManager.Connect());
  CleanupClosePushL(btManager);
  TBTServiceSecurity serviceSecurity;
  serviceSecurity.SetAuthentication(aAuthentication);
  serviceSecurity.SetEncryption(aEncryption);
  serviceSecurity.SetAuthorization(aAuthorization);
  aSockAddr.SetSecurity(serviceSecurity);
  CleanupStack::PopAndDestroy();
  }
```

The `SendL()` method for sending messages is quite straightforward, canceling any previous requests before using the asynchronous `Write()` method to send the message to the client:

```
void CBTServer::SendL(const TDesC8& aMessage)
  {
  iConnectedSocket.CancelAll();
  Cancel();
  HBufC8* message = aMessage.AllocL();
  iConnectedSocket.Write(*message, iStatus);
  delete message;
  iBTServerState = EBTServerSending;
  SetActive();
  }
```

The hard work is carried out in the `RunL()` method:

```
void CBTServer::RunL()
  {
```

```
if (iStatus==KErrNone)
  {
  switch(iBTServerState)
    {
    case EBTServerDisconnected:
      break;
    case EBTServerConnecting:
      iBTServerObserver.HandleBTServerConnected();
      iBTServerState = EBTServerWaiting;
      iConnectedSocket.RecvOneOrMore(iBuffer, 0, iStatus, iLen);
      SetActive();
      break;
    case EBTServerWaiting:
      iBTServerObserver.HandleBTServerMessageRecvd();
      iBTServerState = EBTServerConnected;
      break;
    case EBTServerSending:
      iBTServerObserver.HandleBTServerMessageSent();
      iBTServerState = EBTServerWaiting;
      iConnectedSocket.RecvOneOrMore(iBuffer, 0, iStatus, iLen);
      SetActive();
      break;
    case EBTServerConnected:
      break;
    }
  }
else if (iStatus==KErrDisconnected)
  {
  Cancel();
  Stop();
  iBTServerObserver.HandleBTServerDisconnected();
  }
else
  {
  iBTServerObserver.HandleBTServerError(iStatus.Int());
  }
}
```

If the `KErrDisconnected` error code is detected, then the server is stopped and the `HandleBTServerDisconnected()` callback method is invoked. Any other error is passed to the `HandleBTServerError()` callback. If there are no errors, we process the state machine:

- `EBTServerDisconnected`: no action required

- `EBTServerConnecting`: a client has connected and so we set the server to the `EBTServerWaiting` state and call `HandleBT-ServerConnected()` before using `RecvOneOrMore()` to wait for data on the connection socket

- `EBTServerWaiting`: we have received some data from the client; we call `HandleBTServerMessageRecvd()` and move into the `EBTServerConnected` state

- `EBTServerSending`: we have sent data over the channel; we move into the `EBTServerWaiting` state, call `HandleBTServerMessageSent()` and tell the object to wait for more data

- `EBTServerConnect`: no action required.

Finally, before the class compiles, we need to include the `bt_sock.h` header file for the `TBTServiceSecurity` and `TBTSockAddr` objects; `btmanclient.h` for the Bluetooth manager (we also need to link against the `btmanclient.lib` library); and the `es_sock.h` header for the socket.

Client Class

The client is a simpler version of the server, needing only a single socket and not needing to set the security for the channel:

```
class MBTClientObserver
  {
  public:
    virtual void HandleBTClientConnected()=0;
    virtual void HandleBTClientDisconnected()=0;
    virtual void HandleBTClientMessageSent()=0;
    virtual void HandleBTClientMessageRcvd()=0;
    virtual void HandleBTClientError(TInt aError)=0;
  };
class CBTClient : public CActive
  {
  public:
    static CBTClient* NewL(MBTClientObserver& aObserver);
    ~CBTClient();
    void ConnectL(RSocketServ& aSocketServ, TBTDevAddr aBTDevAddr,
                                             TInt aPort);
    void Disconnect();
    void SendL(const TDesC8& aMessage);
  protected:
    void RunL();
    void DoCancel();
  private:
    CBTClient(MBTClientObserver& aObserver);
    void ConstructL();
    MBTClientObserver& iBTClientObserver;
    RSocket iClientSocket;
    TBTClientState iBTClientState;
```

```
    TBuf8<KMaximumMessageLength> iBuffer;
    TSockXfrLength iLen;
};
```

The `ConnectL()` method connects the client to the server and the `Disconnect()` method disconnects the client from the server. A corresponding group of callback methods are used to communicate with the user interface.

The connection is made by opening a socket to the device discovered by the `ServiceDiscovery` object which is identified using the `TBTDevAddr` parameter to the `ConnectL()` method. An asynchronous request is made to the server and the object is set as active:

```
void CBTClient::ConnectL(RSocketServ& aSocketServ, TBTDevAddr aBTDevAddr,
                                                        TInt aPort)
  {
  TBTSockAddr sockAddr;
  sockAddr.SetBTAddr(aBTDevAddr);
  sockAddr.SetPort(aPort);
  User::LeaveIfError(iClientSocket.Open(aSocketServ,
                        KBTClientProtocolName));
  iBTClientState = EBTClientConnecting;
  iClientSocket.Connect(sockAddr, iStatus);
  SetActive();
  }
```

The disconnection cancels any outstanding requests and shuts down the socket connection:

```
void CBTClient::Disconnect()
  {
  iBTClientState = EBTClientDisconnected;
  Cancel();
  iClientSocket.CancelAll();
  iClientSocket.Shutdown(RSocket::ENormal, iStatus);
  SetActive();
  }
```

The `SendL()` method is virtually identical to that used in the server class:

```
void CBTClient::SendL(const TDesC8& aMessage)
  {
  if (IsActive())
    Cancel();
```

```
iClientSocket.CancelAll();
HBufC8* message = aMessage.AllocL();
iClientSocket.Write(*message, iStatus);
delete message;
iBTClientState = EBTClientSending;
SetActive();
}
```

Similarly the client's `RunL()` method mirrors the servers, except that on connection the client waits to send data rather than waiting to receive data (i.e. on connection the client can send and the server can receive). The client and server then take it in turns to send and receive data:

```
void CBTClient::RunL()
  {
  if (iStatus==KErrNone)
    {
    switch (iBTClientState)
      {
      case EBTClientDisconnected:
        break;
      case EBTClientConnecting:
        iBTClientState = EBTClientConnected;
        iBTClientObserver.HandleBTClientConnected();
        break;
      case EBTClientConnected:
        break;
      case EBTClientSending:
        iBTClientObserver.HandleBTClientMessageSent();
        iBTClientState = EBTClientWaiting;
        iClientSocket.RecvOneOrMore(iBuffer, 0, iStatus, iLen);
        SetActive();
        break;
      case EBTClientWaiting:
        iBTClientObserver.HandleBTClientMessageRcvd();
        iBTClientState = EBTClientConnected;
        break;
      }
    }
  else if (iStatus==KErrDisconnected)
    {
    Disconnect();
    iBTClientObserver.HandleBTClientDisconnected();
    }
  else
    {
    iBTClientObserver.HandleBTClientError(iStatus.Int());
    }
  }
```

Client–Server Communication

We are finally ready to link the client and server. The application is controlled from the `HandleCommandL()` method of the `AppUI`:

```
void CBTExampleAppUi::HandleCommandL( TInt aCommand )
  {
  switch( aCommand )
    {
    case EEikCmdExit:
    case EAknSoftkeyExit:
      iBTEngine->StopAdvertisingL();
      Exit();
      break;
    case EBTCmdConnect:
      {
      iBTEngine->DiscoverDevicesL();
      }
      break;
    case EBTCmdSend:
      {
      LIT8(KMessage, "Message");
      iBTEngine->SendMessageL(KMessage);
      }
      break;
    default:
      Panic(EBTExampleUi);
      break;
    }
  }
```

The application exits on the Exit command or when the Exit softkey is pressed; begins the connection process by initiating the device-discovery process when the Connect menu option is selected; and sends a message, using a new `SendMessageL()` method which has been added to the Engine class, when the Send option is selected:

```
void CBTEngine::SendMessageL(const TDesC8& aMessage)
  {
  if (iIsServer)
    iBTServer->SendL(aMessage);
  else
    iBTClient->SendL(aMessage);
  }
```

Here, a Boolean member variable is used to determine whether the application is connected as the server or the client and redirects the message to be sent accordingly.

The client and server callback methods handle the program flow according to the original state model for the application. For simplicity, in this example information notes are displayed on the screen to inform the user of client–server events. When the server is connected, the application moves into the `WaitingToReceive` state; when disconnected, the application moves into the `Error` state (note that you may decide to end the game or application here, to reinitialize the service, to enter a new menu structure, etc.). If a message is received, it starts waiting for a message; if a message is sent, it starts waiting for the user to send a message. Finally, any error takes us to the error state:

```
void CBTEngine::HandleBTServerConnected()
  {
  CAknInformationNote* note = new (ELeave) CAknInformationNote;
  TRAPD(err, note->ExecuteLD(_L("Server Connected")));
  iState = EBTWaitingToReceive;
  iBTEngineObserver.HandleBTEngineStateChange();
  }
void CBTEngine::HandleBTServerDisconnected()
  {
  CAknInformationNote* note = new (ELeave) CAknInformationNote;
  TRAPD(err, note->ExecuteLD(_L("Server Disconnected")));
  iState = EBTError;
  iBTEngineObserver.HandleBTEngineStateChange();
  }
void CBTEngine::HandleBTServerMessageRecvd()
  {
  CAknInformationNote* note = new (ELeave) CAknInformationNote;
  TRAPD(err, note->ExecuteLD(_L("Server Message Received")));
  iState = EBTWaitingToSend;
  iBTEngineObserver.HandleBTEngineStateChange();
  }
void CBTEngine::HandleBTServerMessageSent()
  {
  CAknInformationNote* note = new (ELeave) CAknInformationNote;
  TRAPD(err, note->ExecuteLD(_L("Server Message Sent")));
  iState = EBTWaitingToReceive;
  iBTEngineObserver.HandleBTEngineStateChange();
  }
void CBTEngine::HandleBTServerError(TInt aError)
  {
  CAknInformationNote* note = new (ELeave) CAknInformationNote;
  TBuf<32> msg;
  msg.Format(_L("Server Error: %d"), aError);
  TRAPD(err, note->ExecuteLD(msg));
  iState = EBTError;
  iBTEngineObserver.HandleBTEngineStateChange();
  }
```

The client callback functions are handled in a similar manner:

```
void CBTEngine::HandleBTClientConnected()
  {
  iIsServer = EFalse;
  iState = EBTWaitingToSend;
  iBTEngineObserver.HandleBTEngineStateChange();
  CAknInformationNote* note = new (ELeave) CAknInformationNote;
  TRAPD(err, note->ExecuteLD(_L("Client Connected")));
  }
void CBTEngine::HandleBTClientDisconnected()
  {
  iState = EBTError;
  iBTEngineObserver.HandleBTEngineStateChange();
  CAknInformationNote* note = new (ELeave) CAknInformationNote;
  TRAPD(err, note->ExecuteLD(_L("Client Disconnected")));
  }
void CBTEngine::HandleBTClientMessageSent()
  {
  CAknInformationNote* note = new (ELeave) CAknInformationNote;
  TRAPD(err, note->ExecuteLD(_L("Message Sent")));
  iState = EBTWaitingToReceive;
  iBTEngineObserver.HandleBTEngineStateChange();
  }
void CBTEngine::HandleBTClientMessageRcvd()
  {
  CAknInformationNote* note = new (ELeave) CAknInformationNote;
  TRAPD(err, note->ExecuteLD(_L("Message Received")));
  iState = EBTWaitingToSend;
  iBTEngineObserver.HandleBTEngineStateChange();
  }
void CBTEngine::HandleBTClientError(TInt aError)
  {
  CAknInformationNote* note = new (ELeave) CAknInformationNote;
  TBuf<32> msg;
  msg.Format(_L("Client Error: %d"), aError);
  TRAPD(err, note->ExecuteLD(msg));
  }
```

The application now implements a simple Bluetooth communications engine which allows to phones to connect and alternately send messages to each other affecting their application states. This is sufficient for many applications, including the card game you have been working on, and your final challenge is to build the Bluetooth engine into your game structure. Card games are, by their nature, turn-based so you need to build a state model for your card game and implement it in a similar manner to the methods above.

8

Routes to Market

Introduction

Having encouraged you to develop Symbian OS applications, we feel that it is only right to give some guidance about how to turn an application into one that is of sufficient quality to be distributed as a commercial product. The first step along this route is thorough testing, to ensure that your application meets the requirements of the users and does not produce any effects that are detrimental to the operation of their phones. Quality assurance is not there to ensure that your application is the 'best' in terms of containing all the 'bells and whistles' but, rather, to ensure that you are utilizing practices that ensure that your application meets the requirements of your original specification. It also ensures that all the applications you produce are developed with a consistent level of quality. In Section 8.2, we briefly discuss some practices you can use to aid you in this process. These should also ensure that your pieces of code can be utilized in more than one application.

8.1 Testing an Application

Mobile-phone applications written for Symbian OS are like any other type of software; you should aim to ensure that the application delivers its functionality and maintains usability under all operating conditions of the phone. The most important aspect of testing is that you adopt a systematic process to map the actual behavior of your software compared with the behavior you defined in your design specification. In other words, you are trying to find errors, or lack thereof, within your code with the aim of giving your customers a product that they can be confident in using.

Testing is best done iteratively from the start of the project – this can prevent major problems in the design remaining undetected until a long way into the project. Symbian C++ can be a complex language to learn and therefore we again recommend that you adopt an iterative process of testing. This includes testing each new feature as you develop it, right from the beginning of the project, with appropriate, dedicated test code. New software development methodologies, such as *extreme programming*, emphasize incremental development and testing and it is a technique that we have utilized with great success.

Section 8.3 discusses in greater detail how to test for compliance with the Symbian Signed test criteria. However, we recommend the following tools for testing purposes.

Files and Disk Space Usage

In general, the phone's file system is not intended to be visible to the end user. However, it is highly advantageous that developers can see where the application is installing or creating files. There are a number of freeware file-explorer programs available at sites such as NewLC (**www.newlc.com**) and they make the task of testing files and disk space usage much easier. They are not supported or endorsed by Symbian or the authors of this book but they can prove very useful to developers. The Symbian Signed website (**www.symbiansigned.com**) also contains some relevant links.

Memory Load

There is a low-memory tool available to registered developers at the Symbian Signed website. It allows you to test the startup of your application during low-memory situations.

Task List

The task list allows you to view the current tasks running on the mobile phone. On S60 phones, you access it by holding down the Menu or Applications key. The task list allows you to bring forward applications from the background and to close down applications. It is useful when testing the ability of your application to pause and respond to system events, etc. For UIQ phones, the Symbian Signed website contains relevant links.

Receiving Messages

A second functional phone with a working SIM card is useful if you are going to test what happens to your application when the phone receives a call, SMS or MMS.

Automated Testing

The Symbian Signed website offers a free tool called AppTest Lite. It allows you to run most of the Symbian Signed tests on your application to check its performance and verify whether it is likely to pass the process or not.

8.2 Quality Assurance

You need to ensure that your application's quality is related to the processes and checks you adopt throughout your development process, including, amongst other things, the documentation and specification of the application and the recording of changes. In this respect, developing a mobile-phone application is the same as any other software engineering exercise and we do not believe it is necessary to document these practices within this book.

However, there are certain elements in the design of your application that you should pay attention to in order to ensure that the application is of a sufficient standard to be released to the general public. Nokia and Symbian recommend that you address the following specific issues in your application design:

- the application speed does not compromise the use and purpose of the application

- the application does not consume the phone's processor power and memory excessively

- the application does not affect the use of the system features or other applications

- the application does not cause any harm to the user, other applications, or data

- only vital data is saved locally to the phone's internal memory

- communication initiated by the application is kept within reasonable limits, i.e. your application does not unnecessarily cost the user extra through excessive network usage

- occasional tasks, exceptional tasks (for example, for emergency conditions) and tasks that cope with errors (for example, caused by the interruption of a network connection during the application's use) must be considered and treated appropriately

- the application must be able to handle exceptional, illegal or erroneous actions

- the application can be uninstalled completely i.e. all files, icons, images, etc. should be removed from the phone

- the application must be capable of being installed on any drive.

Note that all of these form part of the verification process for Symbian Signed software.

8.3   Symbian Signed Software

Symbian Signed is an industry-backed program allowing Symbian OS software developers to obtain a digital signature for their applications and passive content. Symbian Signed is run by Symbian and endorsed by network operators and manufacturers. Symbian Signed applications follow industry-agreed quality-test guidelines and support network-operator and phone-manufacturer requirements. Symbian Signed complements Symbian's application security strategy.

Symbian Signed focuses on both the application and the developer. In order to obtain a digital signature, the company or individual responsible for the development of an application must be clearly identified. An application originator's identity is verified through a certificate authority, ensuring that signed applications can be tracked back to their source.

Application signing is a method of adding a tamper-proof *digital signature* to software. It is an industry-standard technique and is used in phones based on Symbian OS to ensure that, once an application has

Figure 8.1 Symbian Signed logo

been installed onto the phone, it has not been tampered with, proving that it has not been 'modified' or maliciously altered.

Achieving Symbian Signed status for your application demonstrates that it has passed targeted tests ensuring that it does not cause any unpleasant surprises. Reaching this quality level is becoming increasingly important as users have minimal tolerance for application failures. Certain network operators, phone manufacturers, distributors and aggregators accept only Symbian Signed applications in their channel.

Applications that are Symbian Signed also have the option to display the 'for Symbian OS' logo (see Figure 8.1) and may be placed in the applications catalog. The applications catalog is a reference list of applications that have been Symbian Signed and in which the developer has chosen to allow their application and organization details to be displayed. It provides a powerful route-to-market which covers key players in application sales and distribution.

The test criteria covers a number of basic operations for an application and does not delve into functionality testing. An example of a test category includes 'Phone operation'. In this category, tests for 'service interruption' ensure that interruptions are handled appropriately and the application continues to operate according to the functional specification after the interruption. The application should in no way affect the standard operation of the phone, i.e. whatever the application is doing, a user expects to be able to receive incoming communications either in the form of an SMS or a voice call.

Symbian OS v9 and Symbian Signed

Unless the channel requires it, developers of applications based on versions of Symbian OS before v9 do not need to get the application Symbian Signed. The benefits of Symbian Signed are primarily driven by market demand. Nokia, Sony Ericsson and Orange all state that applications are to be Symbian Signed if they are to be distributed through their channels. There has been broad support for the Symbian Signed program across the industry.

For developers, Symbian Signed saves them both time and money because they only need to go through one certification scheme rather than many to get their applications certified.

If an application based on Symbian OS v9 or higher uses 'capabilities' (and 40% of Symbian OS v9 APIs are categorized under certain capabilities), it must be Symbian Signed. If an application is not Symbian Signed, it will fail to install on a Symbian OS phone. If the application does not use any sensitive capabilities (that is, it uses the remaining 60% of APIs which are not classified into capabilities) then it will install on a phone. However, the phone presents the user with an installation warning dialog (e.g. 'Application is untrusted and may have problems. Install only if you trust provider.'), as it does for applications targeted at versions of Symbian OS before v9 that have not been through the Symbian Signed program.

During your development process, you must determine which capabilities, if any, your application requires:

- basic capabilities deal with APIs associated with areas such as local services (access to a local network e.g. via Bluetooth) and the user environment (access to live confidential information in the user's environment)

- extended and phone-manufacturer-approved capabilities deal with APIs that are more sensitive; applications using such capabilities must complete a declarative statement as part of the submission process. In addition, an application attempting to utilize phone-manufacturer-approved capabilities may be required to submit the application via the relevant phone manufacturer's Symbian Signed website along with a capability request form. This capability request form requires information about which APIs are used within the application. More details are provided in the submission process.

To find more information about which capabilities are associated with which APIs, consult the SDK of the target phone.

Developer Certificates

The Symbian Signed program recognizes that there must be a way by which an unsigned v9 application can be tested because it cannot otherwise be installed on the phone.

Developer certificates (devcerts) enable access to restricted APIs during the development and test phase, making it possible to test applications that use sensitive APIs (capabilities) on production phones, without the need for the application to be Symbian Signed. This reduces the cost of application development.

Standard developer certificates can be obtained through the Symbian Signed website (**www.symbiansigned.com**). In order to reduce the risk of compromising the platform security model of Symbian OS v9, standard developer certificates last only six months, allow access to a predefined set of capabilities and are granted only to a specific list of phones.

These certificates are suitable for the vast majority of developers. Where there is a need for more than one phone to be supported through the developer process, then an ACS Publisher ID (ACS) is required. Full instructions for obtaining a publisher ID can be found on the Symbian Signed website. Once a publisher ID has been purchased, the developer can obtain a certificate to provide access to 100 phones.

If a developer certificate with phone-manufacturer-approved capabilities is required, the request is passed onto the relevant phone manufacturer who will review it and generate a certificate subject to request approval. The process of requesting a phone-manufacturer-approved developer certificate has been integrated into the Symbian Signed website and follows a slightly different workflow to that of requesting a standard devcert.

Please note that Symbian Signed is still needed to distribute the application commercially.

Routes to Signing an Application

Subject to agreement, Symbian Signed offers flexible and extended signing options to cater for differing needs within the Symbian OS ecosystem. These options include:

- Test houses: this route is suitable for developers who develop a small number of applications. Applications are submitted to the Symbian Signed website and tested by an independent third-party test house (CapGemini, NSTL or Mphasis)

- Self certifier: this route is suitable for developers who wish to use their internal, recognized quality assurance processes. This enables extra flexibility and may reduce the per-application cost of signing

- Publisher certifier: this route is suitable for application publishers or public software distribution portal owners. The publisher tests and certifies the application using its quality assurance processes on behalf of the originating developer

- Freeware: the ability to Symbian Sign freeware applications is also available through a Symbian Signed publisher certifier.

Prior to getting your Symbian OS v9 application Symbian Signed, ensure you have been allocated application UIDs from the protected range. Protected application UIDs can be obtained instantly from the Symbian Signed website once you have been registered.

If you are developing an application on behalf of an organization (i.e. you are an employee) then you need an ACS Publisher ID ('Route A'). If you are developing an application as an individual with no direct route to market then you may not need an ACS Publisher ID ('Route B').

The signing process involves exporting the certificate and signing the SIS file.

Route A

An ACS Publisher ID (also known as a developer identity certificate), uniquely identifies the software provider and allows software passing through Symbian Signed to be traced to its source.

There is a per annum charge for acquiring and renewing an ACS Publisher ID and it can be used to sign an unlimited number of applications (depending on available Content IDs) through Symbian Signed.

You can get an ACS Publisher ID from the VeriSign website by following these steps:

1. Provide contact details of someone in your organization. This person will be contacted during the process of applying for an ACS Publisher ID.

2. VeriSign notifies you via email as soon as they have verified your details. Access the URL in the email. You will be asked to enter the PIN provided in the notification email and the challenge phrase you gave when registering.

3. After successful authentication, download your ACS Publisher ID. Do not change any of the default options but do ensure that the 'Check this box. . .' checkbox is cleared. If it is selected, the private key will be protected from being extracted from the certificate store, which will prevent you from signing your SIS file later.

4. Check that the certificate has been loaded into your browser correctly: go into Microsoft Internet Explorer (which is the only browser VeriSign guarantees to support), select Tools, Internet Options, Content and click Certificates. You should see a certificate issued by VeriSign; this is your ACS Publisher ID.

An ACS Publisher ID consists of two parts: a public certificate and a private key. The private key should be kept private as it allows files to be signed with your identity. The public certificate allows third parties to verify that files have been signed with your valid private key.

Your public certificate and private key must be exported from your web browser into a .pfx file. To export your ACS Publisher ID from Microsoft Internet Explorer, complete the following steps:

1. Select Tools, Internet Options.

2. Click on the Content tab.

3. Click on the Certificates button.

4. Navigate to your ACS Publisher ID certificate.

5. Select your ACS Publisher ID and click on the Export button.

6. Ensure the option to export the private key is selected.

7. Select the PKCS#12 format (we recommend the default format). We recommend that you provide a password to protect your keys.

8. Provide a file name (the extension is .pfx).

9. Export the file to a location to be used by the ACS Export tool.

Route B

Individual developers do not require an ACS Publisher ID and cannot acquire one from VeriSign, which does not cater for individuals. To ensure that you still have a viable route to market for your products, Symbian has created various Publisher Certifiers. These companies take your SIS file, test your application, sign it with their ACS Publisher ID and, if it passes the tests, put it through the Symbian Signed process. When installing an application on a phone, the Publisher Certifier's information will appear when viewing the certificate details.

Using the ACS Export tool

Before progressing further, download the ACS Export tool (`vs_pkcs.exe`) from VeriSign. This tool is required to convert your private key and public certificate into a format that MakeSIS can use.

The ACS Export tool takes the `.pfx` file that you exported from your web browser and produces a certificate file and a private key file. The certificate and key files are output in a format that MakeSIS can use.

Copy `vs_pkcs.exe` to the folder containing the `.pfx` file. Run the ACS Export Tool from a command line as follows:

```
vs_pkcs -p12 p12File [-passwd p12Password] [-key keyFile] [-cer certFile]
```

- `p12File` is the PKCS#12 file that contains the private key and certificate

- `p12Password` is the optional password for the PKCS#12 file

- `keyFile` is the private key file (if no name is specified, a `.key` file is created)

- `certFile` is the certificate file (if no name is specified, a `.cer` file is created)

```
vs_pkcs -p12 myfile.pfx -passwd mypfxpassword -key myACS.key
                                              -cer myACS.cer
```

ACS Publisher ID Signing: Symbian OS pre-v9

Copy the private key (`myACS.key`) and public certificate (`myACS.cer`) files to the same directory as the `.pkg` file. Add the following line to the `.pkg` file on the code lines above those specifying the files to be copied onto the device:

```
*"Private.key","Public.cer",KEY="****"
```

where **** is the password for the private key. If the private key is not password-protected you should add the following line:

```
*"Private.key","Public.cer"
```

See below for an example UIQ .pkg file, where the appropriate code lines have been added:

```
;Languages
&EN,FR
;Header and app name, KExample UID -  0x20000085
#{"Example-EN", "Example-FR"}, (0x20000085), 1, 2, 3, SH
;Supported Platform Definitions
(0x101F617B), 2, 0, 0, {"UIQ20ProductID","UIQ20ProductID"}
;Signing files (and password if applicable)
*"Private.key","Public.cer",KEY="*****"
;And finally, the files to install
"\epoc32\release\thumb\urel\tExample.exe"-"!:\System\tExample.exe"
"\epoc32\release\thumb\urel\tExampleData.dat"-"!:\System\tExampleData.dat"
```

Execute MakeSIS (using the −d option), as usual, to create your SIS file. The SIS file is signed and ready to be submitted for testing.

ACS Publisher ID Signing: Symbian OS v9 and higher

The process of signing a SIS file has been decoupled from the MakeSIS tool since Symbian OS v9. An additional step is required to sign a SIS file after running the MakeSIS tool:

1. Create the package file and apply changes related to Symbian OS v9. Remove the certificate/key line from the. pkg file.

2. Run MakeSIS to create the SIS file.

3. Run the signsis.exe tool to sign the SIS file with the ACS Publisher ID.

Submitting an Application for Testing

Figure 8.2 illustrates the process for submitting a file for testing.

1. Visit the Symbian Signed website at *www.symbiansigned.com*.

2. Log in using the username and password you created when you first registered.

3. Select the 'My Symbian Signed' tab at the top of the page.

4. Then select 'Applications' on the left-hand menu and 'Submit' (if the application is intended to be freeware, follow the freeware link).

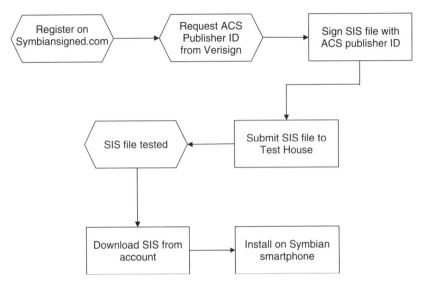

Figure 8.2   How to get your applications Symbian Signed

5.   Select the test house you require to test your application.

6.   Once you have selected a test house, you will be shown your user information. You can add or edit information for this specific submission if you wish. Note that changing any details during this step will result in a change to your main account details.

7.   You must now submit your application details including the application name, a description and which phones it runs on.

8.   Finally, you must submit the actual application itself and supporting materials.

What to Submit in the ZIP File

You must include the following files/documents in the ZIP file you submit.

•   Your SIS file (signed with your ACS Publisher ID), which will be tested by the test house and, if successful, the SIS file will be re-signed with a unique application certificate (Content ID) and returned to you for distribution

- The PKG file used to create the SIS file, which will be cross-referenced by the test house to ensure correct target platform and specification.

- A completed Readme.txt or a user guide in PDF format, which should include any release notes and quick advice on how to use the application (alternatively, you can include a separate user guide in the ZIP file in its own right).

8.4   Marketing

As with most marketing exercises, the primary aim here is branding – in other words you are creating a trade mark that means something special to your customers when they buy and use your mobile-phone application. The whole branding exercise requires careful thought when operating in the mobile phone environment.

As we have previously highlighted, mobile phones have a limited screen size and color capabilities, both of which also vary from device to device. This means that the name of your company or application may not fit on the display of all devices. For example, we developed a mobile phone football application that we initially named *m-football*. On some of the smaller devices, it appeared as *m-footb*. We decided that this did not satisfy our needs and adopted *mfooty* as the name for final release.

In certain cases, such as company names, you may just have to live with the problem, but for other cases it may be worthwhile considering choosing a name that fits within the capabilities of most devices. Alternatively, in the case of an existing product, you might want either to create a complementary mobile phone brand name or to adopt a shortened brand nickname.

The size issue also affects your logo, which is another brand identifier. If you have an existing web logo it is worthwhile ascertaining if it works equally well on the mobile phone. If your logo does not work well then you may need to consider whether you have a mobile-phone-specific logo or brand your applications in their own right. If you – like us – have formed a company specifically for the mobile-phone market, then you can develop a logo that works equally well as an icon on the phone. There are basically two sizes of icon for S60: the list icon is 42×29 pixels and the context pane icon is 44×44 pixels (see Figure 8.3). Note that we have also included an example icon with reduced color depth, suitable for use on lower capability phones.

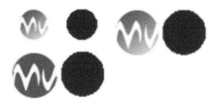

Figure 8.3   Examples of list and context pane Icons

Figure 8.4   Examples of company and product splash screens

If you have decided to create dedicated icons for your application, then you still have the opportunity of branding your application with splash screens at startup to inform the user of your company name, etc. The main thing to watch with this is that the screen should be there long enough for the user to read, but not long enough to cause irritation. The branded screen should then be followed by the splash screen that defines the individual application. For example, in our game Underwater Attack squad, the screens in Figure 8.4 (which are the standard S60 size of 176 × 208 pixels) were shown on application startup.

The final thing we need to discuss is your product fact sheet, which is a vital marketing tool whether you are presenting your game to an aggregator for inclusion on their portal or providing information directly to a portal. Generally, the most important elements you need to provide are a short and exciting game precis, along with a series of screen shots that highlight the most positive aspects of your game and a list of all the phones that will support your application. An example of a fact sheet from one of our early games is shown in Figure 8.5.

<u>mash-a-mate</u> is an addictive reaction testing boxing game with the added twist that you can add a picture of a 'friend' as the face of your opponent. The game requires a S60 phone with a camera and you take a picture following the simple menu instructions. The game is played in rounds which you win by scoring a punch before your opponent. The punches are made by hitting the key number highlighted on the screen as quickly as possible. If you're fast enough you hit your opponent but if your reactions are too slow they hit you. The game speed increases between rounds and if you reach the high-score it is preserved until your next big fight.

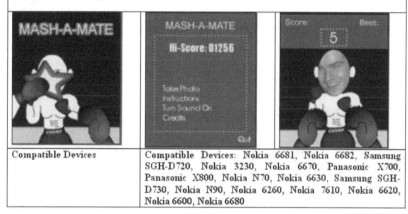

| Compatible Devices | Compatible Devices: Nokia 6681, Nokia 6682, Samsung SGH-D720, Nokia 3230, Nokia 6670, Panasonic X700, Panasonic X800, Nokia N70, Nokia 6630, Samsung SGH-D730, Nokia N90, Nokia 6260, Nokia 7610, Nokia 6620, Nokia 6600, Nokia 6680 |

Figure 8.5   An example product fact sheet

8.5   Portals

In terms of distributing your application, a portal is a digital shop window to your potential customers, through which you can sell your applications (we are considering only applications, but the same applies to other content, e.g. videos and ringtones). There appear to be three basic business models currently in operation.

In the first model (Figure 8.6), content site providers and content developers make use of the operator's subscriber base and billing capabilities to sell their content. In practice, content-site providers promote and price their content and services on their own portals and liaise with the operators, who have well-established means of delivery, charging and collection of micro-payments. The operators can charge for the use of their billing infrastructure and also receive traffic revenue from delivering the content. The onus is on the content-site provider to source and maintain a large range of content. An example of this type of operation is used very successfully by companies such as Handango (*www.handango.com*), MonsterMob (*www.monstermob.com*) and SymbianGear (*www.symbiangear.com*).

In the second model (Figure 8.7), the operators act as aggregators, effectively promoting the content of third-party developers or providers on their own portal site. In this model, the content revenue is split between the developers or providers and the operators. In this model, the operators must source and maintain a large range of content if their site is to continue to be attractive to their customers.

In the third model (Figure 8.8), the operator brands all the content as their own and must then pay the content developers either for the content itself or for licenses from them. In this case there is no revenue sharing and the operator is solely responsible for marketing, delivery, charging and billing.

The current view of the content-downloading business is based on volume rather than margin. Users are encouraged to try the content even if it is only to listen to the tune or play the game once. Thus the price at which your application is sold should not be seen to deter this practice. In effect, the portals aim for users to download content frequently and erase it when they get bored, so that they can personalize their phone with new content. As we see in Section 8.6, this climate may well change; as a developer you can prepare for this in your long-term business strategy.

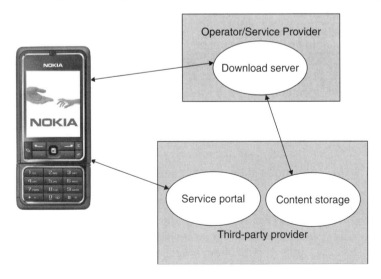

Figure 8.6   Content-site provider portal

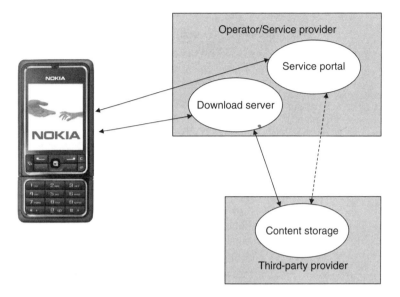

Figure 8.7 Aggregator portal

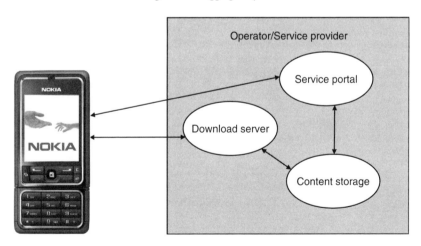

Figure 8.8 Operator as supplier

8.6 Digital Rights Management

No discussion of routes to market for mobile-phone applications would be complete without discussing Digital Rights Management (DRM). DRM is a 'catch-all' phrase that refers to a range of activities, from documenting rights holders and availability status, through to the actual management of permissions to view or use digital resources. This means that DRM is not simply a mobile-phone issue but affects all manner of digital content. As the focus of this book is mobile-phone applications, we will limit our discussion to issues related to this medium.

The downloading of content to mobile phones is already big business particularly through ringtones and wallpapers. With the increasing functionality of mobile phones and the development of new content (applications, videos, etc.) this situation can only be expected to increase. DRM is designed to increase the protection of this extended content, offering greater control for those distributing and selling mobile-phone content. Its aim is to ensure that the content owners feel secure in the knowledge that they will get paid for their content. At present, it is very difficult to confirm that content has been delivered successfully and that operators can bill fairly for the content.

Much of the work governing DRM for mobile-phone systems is organized through the Open Mobile Alliance (OMA), which has done work on standardizing download procedures to prevent illegal distribution of media. It will provide new business models such as preview, super-distribution, gifting, rights updates and more. For example, a user can download a game to his mobile phone for a day or a week and be given the option to buy refreshed rights after his original rights have expired. It is hoped that this will have a positive effect on developers in terms of producing more applications (and of a much higher quality) as they will be more confident of receiving the revenues related to their work. The anticipated benefit for the operators is that these new business models will encourage higher usage of content-download services, resulting in higher data traffic and hence higher revenues per customer.

The OMA proposals are chiefly concerned with content delivered by WAP or MMS and currently provide for three basic methods, all based around a DRM message that contains a media object and an optional rights object.

- Forward-lock delivery is most often associated with subscription-based services for news, sports, information and images intended solely for the subscriber, without any associated rights to forward the content to other users. The content itself is hidden inside the DRM message that is delivered to the phone – the message contains no rights to the media object, so it cannot be distributed further.

- Combined delivery enables the content provider to create a set of usage rules for the media object by adding the rights object into the DRM message. The rights object defines how the phone can render the content and can be limited using both time and usage count constraints. Combined delivery provides for the downloading of content previews.

- Separate delivery is the most advanced option, intended for higher value media. The media object and the rights object are delivered through separate channels, which is an inherently more secure method than combined delivery. The media object is encrypted into DRM content format using symmetric encryption, while the rights object holds the content encryption key, used by the DRM user agent on the phone to decrypt the media object. Super-distribution is an application of separate delivery: the phone can forward the media but not the rights. Users who have received content forwarded from another phone must contact the retailer to obtain rights to preview or purchase the media. This enables marketing by a 'viral distribution' effect where customers can pass the product on to their friends. Developers can maximize the number of potential customers while retaining control of the rights acquisition.

Appendix A

Web Resources

General
www.symbian.com
www.s60.com
www.uiq.com

Tools and SDKs
www.forum.nokia.com
http://developer.symbian.com/main/tools/

Developer Forums
www.newlc.com
www.allaboutsymbian.com
www.symbianone.com

Certification
www.symbiansigned.com

Accreditation
www.majinate.com

Appendix B

Specifications of Phones Based on S60 for Symbian OS

This appendix contains notes on the UI, screen size, and other attributes relevant to application developers of currently available open Symbian OS phones. Further technical information and an up-to-date list of phones can be found at: www.symbian.com/phones

The information contained within this appendix was correct at time of going to press. For full, up-to-date information refer to the manufacturer's website.

Nokia 3230

OS Version	Symbian OS v7.0s
UI	S60 2nd Edition
Built-in memory available	6 MB
Expandable memory type	RS-MMC
Screen	176 × 208 pixels
	65 536 colors
Data input methods	Keypad
Camera	1.3 megapixels resolution
	3x digital zoom
Network Protocol(s)	GSM 900/1800/1900
	HSCSD
	GPRS (Class 10)
	EGPRS
Connectivity	Bluetooth
	Infrared
	USB
Browsing	WAP 2.0
	xHTML/HTML

Nokia 3600/3650

OS Version	Symbian OS v6.1
UI	S60 1st Edition
Built-in memory available	3.4 MB
Expandable memory type	MMC
Screen	176 × 208 pixels 4096/65 536 colors
Data input methods	Keypad
Camera	0.3 megapixels resolution
Network Protocol(s)	3600: GSM 850/1900 3650: GSM 900/1800/1900 HSCSD GPRS (Class 8; B)
Connectivity	Infrared Bluetooth
Browsing	WAP 1.2.1 xHTML

Nokia 3620/3660

OS Version	Symbian OS v6.1
UI	S60 1st Edition
Built-in memory available	4 MB
Expandable memory type	MMC
Screen	176 × 208 pixels 4096/65 536 colors
Data input methods	Keypad
Camera	0.3 megapixels resolution
Network Protocol(s)	3620: GSM 850/1900 3660: GSM 900/1800/1900 HSCSD GPRS (Class 8; B)
Connectivity	Infrared Bluetooth
Browsing	WAP 1.2.1 xHTML

Nokia 6260

OS Version	Symbian OS v7.0s
UI	S60 2nd Edition
Built-in memory available	3.5 MB
Expandable memory type	MMC
Screen	176 × 208 pixels 65 536 colors
Data input methods	Keypad
Camera	0.3 megapixels resolution 4x digital zoom
Network Protocol(s)	GSM 900/1800/1900 GSM 850/1800/1900 HSCSD GPRS (Class 6, B)
Connectivity	Infrared Bluetooth USB
Browsing	HTML xHTML WAP 2.0

Nokia 6290

OS Version	Symbian OS v9.2
UI	S60 3rd Edition
Built-in memory available	50 MB
Expandable memory type	Micro SD
Screen	240 × 320 pixels 16 777 216 colors
Data input methods	Keypad
Camera	2.0 megapixels resolution 4x digital zoom
Network Protocol(s)	WCDMA 2100 GSM 850/900/1800/1900 HSCSD CSD GPRS EGPRS
Connectivity	Infrared Bluetooth 2.0 Mini USB USB 2.0
Browsing	HTML xHTML WAP 2.0

Nokia 6600

OS Version	Symbian OS v7.0s
UI	S60 2nd Edition
Built-in memory available	6 MB
Expandable memory type	MMC
Screen	176 × 208 pixels 65 536 colors
Data input methods	Keypad
Camera	0.3 megapixels resolution 2x digital zoom
Network Protocol(s)	GSM 900/1800/1900 HSCSD GPRS (Class 8; B and C)
Connectivity	Infrared Bluetooth
Browsing	WAP 2.0 xHTML

Nokia 6620

OS Version	Symbian OS v7.0s
UI	S60 2nd Edition
Built-in memory available	12 MB
Expandable memory type	MMC
Screen	176 × 220 pixels 65 536 colors
Data input methods	Keypad
Camera	0.3 megapixels resolution
Network Protocol(s)	GSM 850/1800/1900 GPRS (Class 8; B) HSCSD EGPRS
Connectivity	Infrared Bluetooth USB
Browsing	WAP 2.0 xHTML

Nokia 6630

OS Version	Symbian OS v8.0
UI	S60 2nd Edition.6
Built-in memory available	3.5 MB
Expandable memory type	MMC
Screen	176 × 208 pixels 65 536 colors
Data input methods	Keypad
Camera	1.2 megapixels resolution 6x digital zoom
Network Protocol(s)	GSM 900/1800/1900 WCDMA 2000 GPRS (Class 10, B) EGPRS 3G
Connectivity	Bluetooth USB
Browsing	WAP 2.0 HTML xHTML

Nokia 6670

OS Version	Symbian OS v7.0s
UI	S60 3rd Edition
Built-in memory available	8 MB
Expandable memory type	RS-MMC
Screen	176 × 208 pixels 65 536 colors
Data input methods	Keypad
Camera	1 megapixel resolution 4x digital zoom
Network Protocol(s)	GSM 850/900/1800/1900 GPRS (Class 6, B) HSCSD
Connectivity	Bluetooth USB
Browsing	WAP 2.0 HTML xHTML

Nokia 6680/6681/6682

OS Version	Symbian OS v8.0
UI/Category	S60 2nd Edition.6
Built-in memory available	10 MB
Expandable memory type	RS-MMC
Screen	176 × 208 pixels 262 144 colors
Data input methods	Keypad
Camera	*Front* 1.2 megapixels resolution 6x digital zoom *Back* 0.3 megapixels resolution 2x digital zoom
Network Protocol(s)	GSM 900/1800/1900 WCDMA 2100 EGPRS GPRS (Class 10, B)
Connectivity	Bluetooth USB
Browsing	WAP 2.0 xHTML/HTML

Nokia 7610

OS Version	Symbian OS v7.0s
UI/Category	S60 2nd Edition.1
Built-in memory available	8 MB
Expandable memory type	RS-MMC
Screen	176 × 208 pixels 65 536 colors
Data input methods	Keypad
Camera	1 megapixel resolution 4x digital zoom
Network Protocol(s)	GSM 850/900/1800/1900 GPRS (Class 10; B)
Connectivity	Bluetooth USB
Browsing	WAP 2.0 xHTML

Nokia N-Gage

OS Version	Symbian OS v6.1
UI	S60 1st Edition
Built-in memory available	4 MB
Expandable memory type	MMC
Screen	176 × 208 pixels 4096 colors
Data input methods	Keypad
Camera	No
Network Protocol(s)	GSM 900/1800/1900 HSCSD GPRS (Class 6, B and C)
Connectivity	Bluetooth USB
Browsing	WAP 1.2.1 xHTML

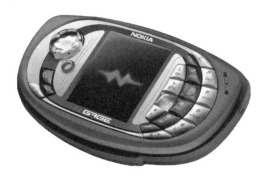

Nokia N-Gage QD

OS Version	Symbian OS v6.1
UI	S60 1st Edition
Built-in memory available	3.4 MB
Expandable memory type	MMC
Screen	176 × 208 pixels 4096 colors
Data input methods	Keypad
Camera	No
Network Protocol(s)	GSM 850/900/1800/1900 HSCSD GPRS (Class 6, B)
Connectivity	Bluetooth
Browsing	WAP 1.2.1 xHTML

Nokia N90

OS Version	Symbian OS v8.1a
UI/Category	S60 2nd Edition
Built-in memory available	30 MB
Expandable memory type	RS-MMC
Screen	352 × 416 pixels 262 144 colors *Cover* 128 × 128 pixels 65 536 colors
Data input methods	Keypad
Camera	1.9 megapixels resolution 20x digital zoom
Network Protocol(s)	GSM 900/1800/1900 WCDMA 2100 EGPRS GPRS (Class 10, B)
Connectivity	Bluetooth USB
Browsing	WAP 2.0 xHTML/HTML

Nokia 5500 Sport

OS Version	Symbian OS v9.1
UI/Category	S60 3rd Edition
Built-in memory available	10 MB
Expandable memory type	MicroSD card up to 1 GB
Screen	208 × 208 pixels 262 144 colors
Data input methods	Keypad
Camera	2.0 megapixels resolution 4x digital zoom
Network Protocol(s)	GSM 900/1800/1900 GPRS EGPRS CSD HSCSD
Connectivity	USB 2.0 via Pop-Port interface Bluetooth 2.0 Infrared
Browsing	WAP 2.0 xHTML 1.1 HTML 4.0

Nokia 3250

OS Version	Symbian OS v9.1
UI/Category	S60 3rd Edition
Built-in memory available	10 MB
Expandable memory type	MicroSD Card up to 1 GB
Screen	176 × 208 pixels 262 144 colors
Data input methods	Keypad
Camera	2 megapixels resolution 4x digital zoom
Network Protocol(s)	GSM/GPRS 900/1800/1900 GPRS EGPRS CSD HSCSD
Connectivity	Bluetooth USB
Browsing	HTML xHTML WAP 2.0

Nokia E60

OS Version	Symbian OS v9.1
UI/Category	S60 3rd Edition
Built-in memory available	Up to 72 MB
Expandable memory type	MMC
Screen	352 × 416 pixels 16 777 216 colors
Data input methods	Keypad
Camera	2 megapixels resolution 4x digital zoom
Network Protocol(s)	GSM 900/1800/1900 WCDMA 2100 (3 GPP Release 4) HSCSD CSD GPRS
Connectivity	USB via Pop-Port interface Infrared WLAN Bluetooth
Browsing	HTML 4.0 WAP 2.0 xHTML

Nokia E61

OS Version	Symbian OS v9.1
UI/Category	S60 3rd Edition
Built-in memory available	Up to 64 MB
Expandable memory type	miniSD card
Screen	320 × 240 pixels 16 777 216 colors
Data input methods	Mini keyboard
Network Protocol(s)	GSM 850/900/1800/1900 WCDMA 2100 (3GPP Release 4) HSCSD CSD GPRS EGPRS
Connectivity	USB 2.0 via Pop-Port interface Infrared Bluetooth 1.2 WLAN
Browsing	HTML 4.0 xHTML WAP 2.0

Nokia E70

OS Version	Symbian OS v9.1
UI/Category	S60 3rd Edition
Built-in memory available	72 MB
Expandable memory type	miniSD
Screen	352 × 416 pixels 262 144 colors
Data input methods	Keypad
Camera	2.0 megapixels resolution 8x digital zoom
Network Protocol(s)	GSM 900/1800/1900 WCDMA 2100 HSCSD CSD GPRS EGPRS
Connectivity	USB 2.0 via Pop-Port interface Bluetooth WLAN Infrared
Browsing	HTML 4.0 WAP 2.0 xHTML

Nokia N70

OS Version	Symbian OS v8.1
UI/Category	S60 2nd Edition
Built-in memory available	35 MB internal dynamic memory
Expandable memory type	MMC
Screen	176 × 208 pixels 262 144 colors
Data input methods	Keypad
Camera	2 megapixels resolution 20x digital zoom
	VGA camera (640 × 480 pixels) 2x digital zoom
Network Protocol(s)	GSM 900/1800/1900 WCDMA 2100
Connectivity	Bluetooth 2.0 USB 2.0 via Pop-Port interface
Browsing	XHTML HTML WAP 2.0

Nokia N71

OS Version	v9.1
UI/Category	S60 3rd Edition
Built-in memory available	35 MB
Expandable memory type	MMC
Screen	176 × 208 pixels 262 144 colors
Data input methods	Keypad
Camera	2 megapixels resolution 20x digital zoom VGA camera (640x480 pixels) 2x digital zoom
Network Protocol(s)	GSM 900/1800/1900 WCDMA 2100 GPRS EGPRS CSD HSCSD
Connectivity	Bluetooth 2.0 USB 2.0
Browsing	WAP 2.0 xHTML HTML

Nokia N72

OS Version	v8.1
UI/Category	S60 2nd Edition
Built-in memory available	Up to 20 MB
Expandable memory type	MMC
Screen	176 × 208 pixels 262 144 colors
Data input methods	Keypad
Camera	2 megapixels resolution 20x digital zoom
Network Protocol(s)	GSM 900/1800/1900 HSCSD CSD GPRS EGPRS
Connectivity	Bluetooth 2.0 Infrared USB 2.0 via Pop-Port interface
Browsing	XHTML 1.1 HTML 4.0 WAP 2.0

Nokia N73

OS Version	v9.1
UI/Category	S60 3rd Edition
Built-in memory available	42 MB
Extendable memory type	miniSD (hot swappable)
Screen	240 × 320 pixels 262 144 colors
Data input methods	Keypad
Camera	3.2 megapixels resolution 20x digital zoom
Network Protocol(s)	WCDMA 2100 GSM 850/900/1800/1900 HSCSD CSD GPRS EGPRS
Connectivity	USB 2.0 Bluetooth 2.0 Infrared
Browsing	HTML 4.0 XHTML WAP 2.0

Nokia N75

OS Version	v9.1
UI/Category	S60 3rd Edition
Built-in memory available	Up to 40 MB
Expandable memory type	*
Screen	240 × 320 pixels 16 777 216 colors
Data input methods	Keypad
Camera	2 megapixels resolution 16x digital zoom
Network Protocol(s)	WCDMA GSM 850/900/1800/1900 GPRS EGPRS
Connectivity	USB 2.0 Bluetooth 2.0 Infrared
Browsing	HTML XHTML WAP 2.0

Nokia N80

OS Version	v9.1
UI/Category	S60 3rd Edition
Built-in memory available	40 MB
Expandable memory type	miniSD card
Screen	352 × 416 pixels 262 144 colors
Data input methods	Keypad
Camera	3 megapixels resolution External display: 65K colors (96 × 68 pixels)
Network Protocol(s)	GSM 850/900/1800/1900 WCDMA 1900/2100 HSCSD CSD GPRS EGPRS
Connectivity	Bluetooth 2.0 USB 2.0 Infrared WLAN
Browsing	WAP 2.0 xHTML HTML 4.0

Nokia N91

OS Version	v9.1
UI/Category	S60 3rd Edition
Screen	176 × 208 pixels
Memory available	10 MB available for storage 4 GB of HDD
Data input methods	Keypad
Camera	2 megapixels resolution 8x digital zoom
Network Protocol(s)	WCDMA 2100 GSM 900/1800/1900 GPRS EGPRS
Connectivity	Bluetooth 2.0 USB 2.0 WLAN 802.11b/g
Browsing	XHTML HTML WAP 2.0

Nokia N93

OS Version	v9.1
UI/Category	S60 3rd Edition
Memory available	Up to 50 MB internal dynamic memory
Expandable memory type	128 MB miniSD card
Screen	Active matrix 2.4″ QVGA color display with wide 160° viewing angle: 320 × 240 pixels
Data input methods	Keypad
Camera	3.2 megapixels resolution 3x optical zoom
Network Protocol(s)	GSM 900/1800/1900 WCDMA 2100 GPRS EGPRS HSCSD CSD
Connectivity	WLAN (802.11 b/g) UPnP (Universal Plug and Play) Bluetooth 2.0 USB 2.0 via Pop-Port interface Infrared
Browsing	HTML xHTML WAP 2.0

Nokia 7650

OS Version	Symbian OS v6.1
UI	S60 1st Edition
Built-in memory available	72 MB expandable memory
Screen	Illuminated high-contrast, full-graphics color display
Data input methods	Keypad
Camera	Image capture at 640 × 480 resolution
Network Protocol(s)	GSM 900/1800 GPRS
Connectivity	Infrared Bluetooth
Browsing	WAP 1.2.1

Lenovo P930

OS Version	Symbian OS v8.0
UI	S60 2nd Edition
Built-in memory available	32M user space, expandable with SD/MMS
Screen	not known
Data input methods	Keypad
Camera	1.3 megapixels resolution
Network Protocol(s)	Dual-band GSM 900/1800
Connectivity	Bluetooth Infrared miniUSB

Panasonic X700

OS Version	Symbian OS v7.0s
UI/Category	S60 2nd Edition
Built-in memory available	4 MB
Expandable memory type	miniSD
Screen	176 × 280 pixels 65 536 colors
Data input methods	Keypad
Camera	0.3 megapixels resolution
Network Protocol(s)	GSM E900/1800/1900 GPRS (Class 10; B)
Connectivity	Infrared Bluetooth USB
Browsing	WAP 2.0 xHTML

Panasonic X800

OS Version	Symbian OS v7.0s
UI/Category	S60 2nd Edition
Built-in memory available	8 MB
Expandable memory type	miniSD
Screen	176 × 280 pixels 65 536 colors
Data input methods	Keypad
Camera	0.3 megapixels resolution
Network Protocol(s)	GSM E900/1800/1900 GPRS (Class 10)
Connectivity	Infrared Bluetooth USB
Browsing	WAP 2.0 xHTML

Samsung SGH-D730

OS Version	Symbian OS v7.0s
UI/Category	S60 2nd Edition
Built-in memory available	32 MB
Expandable memory type	MMC Micro
Screen	176 × 208 pixels 262 144 colors
Data input methods	Keypad
Camera	1.3 megapixels resolution 4x digital zoom
Network Protocol(s)	GSM 900/1800/1900 WCDMA 2100 EGPRS GPRS (Class 10, B)
Connectivity	Bluetooth USB
Browsing	WAP 2.0 xHTML/HTML

Sendo X

OS Version	Symbian OS v6.1
UI	S60 1st Edition
Built-in memory available	12 MB
Expandable memory type	MMC and SD
Screen	176 × 220 pixels 65 536 colors
Data input methods	Keypad
Camera	0.3 megapixels resolution
Network Protocol(s)	GSM 900/1800/1900 GPRS (Class 8; B)
Connectivity	Infrared Bluetooth USB Serial
Browsing	WAP 2.0 xHTML

Siemens SX1

OS Version	Symbian OS v6.1
UI	S60 1st Edition
Built-in memory available	3.5 MB
Expandable memory type	MMC
Screen	176 × 220 pixels 65 536 colors
Data input methods	Keypad
Camera	0.3 megapixels resolution
Network Protocol(s)	GSM 900/1800/1900 HSCSD GPRS (Class 10; B)
Connectivity	Infrared Bluetooth USB
Browsing	WAP 2.0 xHTML

Index